Developing Grammar in Context

intermediate

Mark Nettle and Diana Hopkins

CAMBRIDGE
UNIVERSITY PRESS

PUBLISHED BY THE PRESS SYNDICATE OF THE UNIVERSITY OF CAMBRIDGE
The Pitt Building, Trumpington Street, Cambridge, United Kingdom

CAMBRIDGE UNIVERSITY PRESS
The Edinburgh Building, Cambridge CB2 2RU, UK
40 West 20th Street, New York, NY 10011–4211, USA
477 Williamstown Road, Port Melbourne, VIC 3207, Australia
Ruiz de Alarcón 13, 28014 Madrid, Spain
Dock House, The Waterfront, Cape Town 8001, South Africa

http://www.cambridge.org

First published 2003

Printed in Italy by G. Canale & C. S.p.A

Typeface Berkeley 10/13pt. *System* QuarkXPress® [OD&I]

A catalogue record for this book is available from the British Library

ISBN 0 521 627117 (without answers)
ISBN 0 521 627125 (with answers)

Contents

Acknowledgements v
Introduction vi

1 Learning grammar, and how to use this book 1

Time and tense

2 The present simple 7
3 The present continuous 12
4 The past simple 18
5 The past continuous and the past simple 23
6 *Used to* and *would* 29
7 The present perfect simple 35
8 The present perfect continuous 41
9 The past perfect 47
10 *Going to* and *will* 53
11 Present tenses for talking about the future 58
12 The future continuous and the future perfect 63
Review Unit 1 Units 2–12 Time and tense 69

Sentences

13 Word order 73
14 The imperative and instructions 78
15 *Do* and other auxiliaries for emphasis 83
16 Features of spoken English 89
17 Question forms 1: basic questions 95
18 Question forms 2: tags and indirect questions 101
19 Reported speech 1: *say*, *tell*, *ask* 107
20 Reported speech 2: reporting verbs 113
21 Defining relative clauses 119
22 Non-defining relative clauses 125
Review Unit 2 Units 13–22 Sentences 130

Other verb forms

23 Verbs followed by the infinitive or the *-ing* form 133
24 First, second and zero conditional sentences 139
25 The third conditional, wishes and regrets 145
26 The passive 151
27 Verbs confused with the passive 157
28 *Get / have something done* 163
29 *Be / get used to* 168
Review Unit 3 Units 23–29 Other verb forms 174

Naming and describing

30 Articles 1: general introduction 177
31 Articles 2: special uses 183
32 Personal, possessive and reflexive pronouns 189
33 Possessives and demonstratives 194
34 Countable and uncountable nouns and expressions of quantity 200
35 Adjectives and adverbs 206
36 The order of adjectives 212
37 *-ed* and *-ing* adjectives 218
38 *Too*, *(not) very*, *(not) enough*, *so* and *such* 223
Review Unit 4 Units 30–38 Naming and describing 229

Functional areas

39 Requests, permission and offers 223
40 Suggestions and advice 239
41 Talking about ability 244
42 Frequency expressions and *tend to* 250
43 Ways of comparing 1 255
44 Ways of comparing 2 261
45 Describing with *look* and *like* 267
46 Similarities and differences: *so* and *neither* 273
47 Possibility in the present 278
48 Possibility in the past 284

49 Present obligation and necessity 290
50 Past and future obligation and necessity 296
Review Unit 5 Units 39–50 Functional areas 302

Appendix 1 Irregular verbs 306
Appendix 2 Phonemic symbols 308

Glossary 309

Acknowledgements

Much time has elapsed since this book was first thought of. We would like to thank first of all Bob Obee for putting us in touch with Cambridge University Press, and then Jeanne McCarten for leading us up to the commissioning of the title and beyond. Since those early days our thanks go also to Alison Sharpe, Mickey Bonin and Brigit Viney, who helped us see the project through to the final stages. Along the way we also owe thanks to Nóirín Burke, Geraldine Mark, to Jean Hudson for CANCODE data, and to all the staff at Cambridge University Press involved in the development and production of the book. Thank you too to Bell International for providing writing time for Mark.

For our children, Laura and Alex, who nearly stopped the whole thing in its tracks, and for our parents.

The authors and publishers would like to thank the following people and institutions who reviewed and pilot tested material from this book and helped to shape it.

Prof. Snezana Bilbija, Montenegro, The Federal Republic of Yugoslavia
Trevor Bryant, Language Studies International, Cambridge, UK
Henny Burke, British Language Centre, Madrid, Spain
Stephen Bush, The British Institute of Florence, Italy
Claire Embleton, London, UK
Chiara Ferdori, Casalecchio, Italy
Leigh Fergus, Executive Language Services, Paris, France
Mick Gammidge, London, UK
Rebecca Hughes, University of Nottingham, UK
Lindsay Kelly, Turkey
Key Language Services, Quito, Ecuador
Samantha Lewis, Centro de Estudios de Ingles, Madrid, Spain
Raul Mar, Universidad de Cuautitlan Izcalli, Mexico
Prof. Antonio Morales, School of Tourism, Cienfuegos, Cuba
Leticia Moreno, Universidad Juarez de Durango, Mexico
Graham Palmer, Bell School, Saffron Walden, UK
Maroussa Pavli, Athens, Greece
Mary Nava, L'Università Cattolica and IULM, Milan, Italy
Josefina Peña, Sol y Son, Habana, Cuba
Peter Strutt, British Institute, Paris, France
Wayne Trotman, The British Council, Izmir, Turkey
G.N. Woods, The Language Factory, Cuorgné, Italy

The authors and publishers are grateful to the authors, publishers and others who have given permission for the use of copyright material identified in the text. It has not been possible to identify, or trace, sources of all the materials used and in such cases the publishers would welcome information from copyright owners.

pp.2, 53, 77, 119 (bottom), 150 (Classwork), 180, 190 and 296 (left): adapted extracts from *The One Hundred Stupidest Things Ever Done*, by Ross and Kathryn Petras reprinted by permission of Michael O'Mara Books Ltd; p.7: 'Fame and Foster', by Gabrielle Donnelly from Sainsbury's *The Magazine*, December 1996; p.8: 'My kind of day: Jane Seymour', from *Radio Times*, 9–15 November 1996; p.11: 'Just nipping to the shops … for a few days', by Michael Booth from *The Independent on Sunday*, 19 January 1997; p.12: 'Trufflers dognapped', © *The Observer*, 2 February 1997; p.18: 'The trickle-down family economy', by Vivek Chaudhary © *The Guardian*, 14 August 1996; p.21: 'Wheel of fortune', by Mark Lawson © *The Guardian*, 27 December 1995; p.29: 'Father's story, daughter's story', by Val Sampson from the *Daily Mail*, 5 December 1995; p.35: 'New job/old job', by Peter Carty © *The Guardian*, 13 December 1995; p.41: 'Mystery of Yuletide cards from nowhere', by Richard Smith from *The Independent*, 21 December 1996; p.47: 'The plane that flew solo', by Martin Kettle © *The Guardian*, 25 November 1997; p.63: 'Doctors' orders in a brave new world', by Sarah Boseley © *The Guardian*, 3 December 1998; pp.70 (top), 75 and 197: adapted extracts from *Tall Stories*, by Russell Ash and Mike Gordon, reproduced by permission of Russell Ash, Aurum Press 1994; p.70 (bottom): 'Zoo waits for its 297 lb baby to take her bow', by Nicholas Schoon from *The Independent*, 19 January 1996; p.73: 'Golden goal makes it 425 1', by Richard Smith from *The Independent*, 9 November 1998; pp.78, 79 and 82: extracts from *The Exploratory's Adventures in Science*, used by permission of The Exploratory, Bristol; p.83: 'Hardlife – The parapsychologist forever sceptic', by Johnny Beardsall © Telegraph Group Limited, 21 October 1995; p.95: 'The questionnaire – Pat Cash', compiled by Rosanna Greenstreet, as seen in *The Guardian*, 4 July 1998; p.107: 'Gunman flees with £650,000 Picasso', by Dan Glaister © *The Guardian*, 7 March 1997; p.113: 'Branson's crew ditched $2,000', by Paul Marston © Telegraph Group Limited, 10 January 1997; p.119 (top): extract from *The Guardian* © *The Guardian*, 5 April 1997; p.119 (centre): 'Monkey business fills Punjab jail', by Rahul Bedi © Telegraph Group Limited, 19 August 1997; p.121: 'Taking the Mickey II', the *Daily Express*, 9 February 1996; p.125: 'The new deal', by Douglas Kennedy from *The Independent*, 9 December 1995; p.127: 'A model come-back – after 28 years and 10 children', by Richard Smith from *The Independent*, 3 March 1997; p.128: 'Honour for hero in river rescue', the *Bath Chronicle*, 25 March 1998; p.133: extracts from the cover of *Harry Potter and the Philosopher's Stone*, by J.K. Rowling, and the cover illustration by Thomas Taylor, with the permission of Bloomsbury Publishing Plc; p.136: 'Shy 10-year-old piano prodigy', by David Ward

© *The Guardian*, 23 September 1997; pp.137 (texts 1 and 2) and 296 (right): *Bizarre Tales from New Scientist*. Reproduced with permission from *New Scientist* magazine, the global authority on science and technology news © RBI www.NewScientist.com; pp.137 (text 3), 278 and 279: adapted extracts from *Fortean Times Weird Year, 1996*; p.139: 'Jupiter, saviour of the world', by Adrian Berry © Telegraph Group Limited, 27 January 1996; p.145 (top): 'Alive after four days in a watery tomb', by Luke Harding & Christopher Zinn © *The Guardian*, 10 January 1997; p.145 (bottom): 'Talking parrot saves trapped van driver', by Sean O'Neill © Telegraph Group Limited, 19 February 1998; p.147: Cartoon copyright © 1996 Steven Appleby, first published in the *Weekend Guardian*, 23 November 1996; p.151: 'Police? I want to report a burglary', by Stuart Miller © *The Guardian*, 19 November 1997; p.154: 'Number crunching: Coca Cola', *Time Out*, 27 September–4 October 1995; p.155 (top): 'A prize reprised', by Tristan Davies © Telegraph Group Limited, 11 October 1997; p.155: 'Teenage couple' © *The Observer*, 19 October 1997; pp.157 and 288: adapted extracts from *The Giant Book of the Unexplained*, by Damon Wilson, with the permission of Constable and Robinson Publishing Limited; p.163: '50p brooch sells for £13,000' © *The Guardian*, 25 February 1998; p.168: 'It's a power thing', by Rosalyn Clark © *The Guardian*, 14 November 1996; p.177: 'Inmate copied cell keys from memory', from *The Independent*, 3 March 1998; p.183: Prospect Music and Art Tours; p.189: 'March of the machines', by Kevin Warwick from the *Daily Mail*, 5 March 1997; p.194: 'Twin troubles', reproduced by permission of *Family Circle*, December 1996; p.200: adapted extracts from *Malaysia, Singapore & Brunei, ed. 4*, Lonely Planet, 1991, reproduced by permission of Lonely Planet Publications; p.203: adapted extract from *Round the World in Recipes*, by Michael Bateman. Reproduced by permission of Hodder and Stoughton Educational Limited; p.218: 'Lost girl takes a tough trek via field and forest', by Richard Alleyne from the *Daily Mail*, 10 December 1997; p.233: The Bash Street Kids are ™ and © D.C. Thomson & Co. Ltd.; pp.224 and 225: adapted extracts from 'From music to maths' by Jamie Wilson from *The Guardian*, 23 September 1997 © Jamie Wilson; p.228: 'Beetle maniacs who make power lifters look puny', the *Daily Express*, 9 February 1996; p.229: 'The more the merrier', by Joanna Moorhead © *The Guardian*, 29 January 1997; p.239: Augusta, by Angus McGill and Dominic Poelsma from the *Mail on Sunday*, 25 February 1997; p.244 (text 1): 'Squeeze star', from the *Cambridge Evening News*, 7 February 1997; p.244 (text 2): 'Animal magic' © *The Guardian*, 23 October 1998; p.244 (text 3): the Department of Work and Pensions; p.249: 'How Rosencrantz and Macduff passed a screen test to prove that monkeys can add up', by Tim Radford © *The Guardian*, 23 October 1998; pp.255 and 257: 'Flying in the face of modern travel', by Kevin Rafferty © *The Guardian*, 28 February 1996; p.259 (text 1): 'Pain relief', *Marie-Claire*, May 1997; p.259 (text 2): 'Mind and body; big ears', by Rita Carter from *She* magazine, September 1996; p.260 (text 1): 'How to avoid getting a cold this winter', *Red*, December 1999; p.261 'At £5,000 a pair, the jeans worth inheriting', by Natalie Clarke from the *Daily Mail*, 27 January 1997; p.284 (top): 'Killer comet's deadly strike', by Steve Farrar from the *Cambridge Evening News*, 29 January 1997; p.284 (bottom:): 'Our ancestors were such an upright lot', by Charles Arthur from *The Independent*, 11 September 1996; p.285 (left): 'Stop, thief! You've dropped your cash', from the *Daily Mail*, 27 January 1997; p.285 (right): '£30,000 pedigree chum is grabbed by dog nappers', by John Hampshire from the *Daily Mail*, 15 January 1996; p.290: 'Anna Blundy calls Denise Lewis', by Anna Blundy, © Times Newspapers Limited, 14 February 1998; p.292 'Odd jobs for young Bonds', from the *Daily Mail*, 5 December 1995.

p.40: the Classwork activity is based on an activity in *Grammar Games*, Mario Rinvolucri, Cambridge University Press, 1984; p.199: the Classwork activity is based on an idea (Values Topics) in *Keep Talking*, F. Klippel, Cambridge University Press, 1984.

The authors and publishers are grateful to the following for permission to reproduce copyright photographs:

p.7: Rex Features Ltd/Stewart Cook; p.23: Advertising Archives; p.29: Rex Features/Mike Lawn; p.49: Corbis/Joseph Sohm, ChromoSohm; p.58: Eye Ubiquitous/David Lansfied; p.63: Corbis; p. 70: Chester Zoo; p.73: Corbis JFPI Studios, Inc.; p.95: Action Images Ltd; p.101: NHPA/Henry Ausloos; p.107: 'Tête de Femme – Dora Maar', 1939 by Pablo Picasso. Colour transparency © The Solomon R. Guggenheim Foundation, New York; © Succession Picasso/DACS 2003; p.113: Popperfoto; pp.125, 218 and 229: News Team International Ltd; p.137: NHPA/Eric Soder; p.145: South West News Service; p.156: Life File Photographic Agency/Andrew Ward; p.168: Guardian Newspapers Ltd/Sean Smith; p.183: Corbis/Charles & Josette Lenars; p.189: Science Photo Library/Sam Ogden; pp. 94 and 281 (centre): PowerStock/Superstock Ltd; p. 200: NHPA/Mark Bowler; p.206: Corbis/Stephen McDonough; p.212 (top and centre): Bonhams Picture Library; p.228: NHPA/James Carmichael Jr; p.250: The Bath Chronicle; p. 261: VinMag Archive; p. 266: Corbis/Adam Woolfitt; p.267 (left): Capital Pictures/Phil Loftus; p.267 (right): The Lookalikes Agency; p.281 (top): Arcaid/Ian Lambot; p.281 (bottom): Jacqui Hurst; p.290: Action Plus.

Commissioned photography by Nigel Luckhurst: pp.1 and 89.

Freelance picture research by Mandy Twells

Cover design by Mark Diaper

Concept design by Dave Seabourne

Design, illustration and page makeup by Oxford Designers & Illustrators

Introduction

Developing Grammar in Context (intermediate) is a grammar reference and practice book which can be used by learners for self-study, or can be used in class. A basic premise of the book is that learners need to meet examples of a grammatical structure in an authentic context, and think about its use, before they try to use it for themselves.

To the learner

You do not have to start *Developing Grammar in Context* at the beginning and work through to the end. You can use the Contents pages to help you find the particular areas that you want to understand and practise. We do suggest, however, that you start with Unit 1, which is different from the other units. It is a guide to using this book, and it also helps you to think about learning grammar.

To the teacher

Each unit has four sections. These are:

- *Getting started*: This section presents the grammatical structure in context in a written or spoken text. It is a good idea to do some scene-setting work before your learners read the text. For example, in Unit 4, the text is about children's spending money, and you could discuss with your class how much money children have in their country or countries. Teach any difficult words in the text before they read. Let learners do the short exercises in pairs, or let them compare their answers with one another.
- *Looking at language*: This is the language reference section of each unit. You can just read through it with your learners, stopping to do the short exercises which test learners' understanding of the explanations. You could also ask learners to make their own notes from this section. If you prefer to clarify language points in your own way, learners could read this section at home.
- *Getting it right*: Exercise 1 (accompanied by the symbol ▶) is the core exercise here. It is designed to raise awareness of a grammatical structure rather than ask learners to produce it. For this reason, always do this exercise with your learners, and do it first. Exercises 2–4 (which have the symbol ▷) provide practice of the structure, and you or your learners can choose which exercises are most useful for your learners and / or the order in which to do them. In all exercises, it is a good idea to allow learners to work in pairs or groups to discuss and compare their answers. You may be able to exploit some exercises for speaking practice.
- *Classwork*: This is a speaking activity designed to provide fluency practice. Make sure that learners are able to do the work in the pairs or groups suggested, and take notes while they are doing an activity so that you can provide feedback (both positive and negative) on their use of the language points practised, as well as their performance of the activity. Think about

how best to use your classroom for these activities; you may want to rearrange seating patterns or furniture.

Review units practise and test mixed structures, so they are best used after all the units in a particular section have been studied. Again, encourage learners to work in pairs and compare answers.

Unit 1 Learning grammar, and how to use this book

Getting started

1 **Read the text below, *How to use this book*, and answer the questions.**

a) How many sections does each unit of the book have?

....

b) Why is Exercise 1 in *Getting it right* important?

....

c) Where can you find different grammar points in the same exercise? ....

How to use this book

Each unit of the book begins with a section called *Getting started.* In this, you read a short text and answer some questions about it. The text has examples of the new grammar in the unit. Then the *Looking at language* section explains the new grammar and has some short exercises. The *Getting it right* section provides four exercises. You should always start with Exercise 1 which has a ▶ sign. This exercise checks you understand the grammar points in the unit. Then Exercises 2–4 of *Getting it right* give you practice in using the grammar. These exercises have a ▷ sign to show that you can choose which ones to do. You can use the last section, *Classwork*, in class. Here you can practise the grammar by speaking to other students.

There are 50 units in the book and five Review units. The Review units revise the grammar points in the previous group of units and let you practise different grammar points in the same exercise.

2 **Look at this sentence from the text:**

You read a short text and answer some questions about it.

Find an example of the following in the sentence:

a) a plural noun ....
b) a verb ....
c) an article ....
d) a pronoun ....
e) an adjective ....

Looking at language

Here is a list of some of the grammatical terms used in the book. How many do you know?

Nouns and related words

Noun	This is usually the name of a thing, place or person: *table, furniture, London, Sue*. Nouns can be **countable** with a **singular** and a **plural** *(table, tables)* or **uncountable** *(furniture)*.
Article	*the, a, an*
Possessive	A word which shows possession: *my, your, his, her, its, their, our* (house, car etc.)
Pronoun	A word which can replace a noun: *I, you, he, she, it, they, we, him, us, which, that, mine, ours.*
Adjective	A word which describes a noun: *lovely, bad, big, exciting.*

Verbs and related words

Main verb	A verb which usually shows actions and situations: *She **went** to bed early last night. I **live** in London.*
Auxiliary verb	*(be, do, have)* A verb which is used with a main verb to give short answers and to express negatives, questions, the passive and some tenses: *This song **was** written ten years ago. We**'re** having breakfast at the moment. **Do** you like sport? Yes, I **do**. Jamie **doesn't** eat meat. They**'ve** travelled all over the world.*
Modal verb	*(will, would, can, could, may, might, must, should* etc.) A verb which is used with a main verb to add extra meaning. Modal verbs express, for example, ability, possibility and obligation: *I **can** speak English. They **might** have some tickets. You **should** buy your mother a birthday present.*
Active verb	This is used when we want to focus on the person or thing doing the action: *Susie **opened** the parcel. Three cars **blocked** the road.*
Passive verb	This is used when we want to focus on the person or the thing affected by the action: *The parcel **was sent** three days ago. The road **was blocked**.*
Infinitive	A form of the verb: *(to) go, (to) eat, (to) write, (to) like.*
Imperative	A verb form that looks like the infinitive without *to* and is used to give orders and instructions: ***Come** here. **Take** the top off the bottle.*
Adverb	A word which describes verbs, adjectives or other adverbs. Adverbs often end with *-ly*: *easily, nicely.*
Tag question	A phrase added at the end of a sentence to make a question: *It's good, **isn't it**?*

1 Write the grammatical term for each underlined word in the story below.

Edgar Lunden was easily caught and arrested after he stole six pounds of potatoes from a supermarket. One reason for his quick arrest was that Edgar Lunden had his full name tattooed across his forehead.

1 was .... 3 he .... 5 supermarket .... 7 his ....

2 easily .... 4 a .... 6 quick ....

Words about sentence structure

Subject	A noun (or pronoun) which normally comes before the main verb: ***Sue** is busy at the moment. **Tigers** live in the jungle.*
Object	A noun (or pronoun) affected by the action of a verb: *He watched **a film**.*
Clause	A group of words which contains a subject and main verb. Sentences can have one or more clauses: *The plane took off* (clause 1) *and we were on our way* (clause 2).
Phrase	A group of words together: *very quickly, at the moment, with long hair.*

Other words about grammar

Comparative	A word used to compare two things: *bigger, easier, more comfortable.*
Conjunction	A word which joins two phrases or clauses together: *and, but, when* etc.
Contraction	This happens when a verb is shortened and joined with the previous word: ***I'll, I'd, I'm, we're, you're, it's.***
Preposition	A word usually placed before a noun to express a relationship such as time or place: *I'll see you **at** eight o'clock. It's **in** the house.*
Reported speech	This is used to report what someone said: *He said that he would like to be president. He invited me to his house.*
Superlative	Words used to compare one thing with a group of other things: *the biggest, the most comfortable.*

2 Draw lines to match each word and phrase to a grammatical term.

1 the easiest 2 on 3 they're 4 faster 5 She told me to go. 6 He's nice, *isn't he*?

reported speech contraction preposition tag question superlative comparative

Getting it right

Exercise 1 How we learn grammar

A How do you think you learn grammar? Put sentences a)–d) in the right order, 1–4.

a) You try to use the new grammar, but make some mistakes. .....
b) You notice some new grammar that you haven't seen before. ..1..
c) You read about the grammar again to understand it better, and then you can use it correctly! .....
d) You try to understand the meaning of the new grammar. .....

B Now match the underlined words in sentences a)–d) to the grammatical terms below.

Example: adjective ....*new*........

1 adverb ....
2 article ....
3 comparative ....
4 contraction ....
5 infinitive ....
6 modal verb ....
7 plural noun ....

Exercise 2 What is grammar?

A Look at the pairs of sentences and put a cross (✘) next to those which are not correct.

Example: a) Give Sally the flowers. She love flowers. ..✘...
b) Give Sally the flowers. She loves flowers. ....

1 a) I've been to New York in 1999. ....
b) I went to New York in 1999. ....

2 a) She used to live in a big old house in the country. ....
b) She would live in a big old house in the country. ....

3 a) He told me he couldn't come with us. ....
b) He said me he couldn't come with us. ....

4 a) There were too many people in the room and it got very hot. ....
b) There were too much people in the room and it got very hot. ....

5 a) While I was thinking, I walked into a garden. ....
b) While I was thinking, I walked into the garden. ....

6 a) I love Italian food. This is wonderful. ....
b) I do love Italian food. This is wonderful. ....

7 a) Do you think you could pass me that pen? ....
b) Can you pass me that pen? ....

8 a) If I can, I'll get that book for you. ....
b) If I could, I'd get that book for you. ....

B Look at these two statements about learning grammar:

a) Learning grammar is learning what is right and wrong.
b) Learning grammar is choosing the best form for a particular situation.

Look back at sentences 1–4 and 5–8 and answer the questions.

1 Which group, 1–4 or 5–8, shows us that statement a) is true? ....
2 Which group shows us that statement b) is true? ....

From your answers you can see that learning grammar is learning the correct form and choosing the best form for a particular situation.

Exercise 3 Learning from learners

Look at the corrected mistakes in these examples from learners' writing. Suggest a unit of this book that will help them avoid this mistake again.

Example: At the moment I ~~take~~ am taking a short course at a language school near my home.
Unit 3 The present continuous

1 In my spare time I enjoy ~~listen~~ listening to music and ~~read~~ reading storybooks.

....

2 When I was a child I ~~live~~ lived in Bucharest. ....

3 You ~~putting~~ put the card in the machine and the money comes out here.

....

4 People need a stadium for sport. It can also ~~use~~ be used for entertainment.

....

5 I was born in Singapore, but I ~~live~~ have lived in Kuala Lumpur since I started work.

....

6 I have not been to a single-sex school, but I feel that it is ~~more easier~~ easier for a teacher to teach in a single-sex school. ....

7 The party was really ~~excited~~ exciting. ....

8 My teacher ~~said~~ told me I needed to work harder. ....

Exercise 4 Choosing what to do

You should always do Exercise 1 in *Getting it right*. After that try to choose the most useful exercises for you.

Look at Exercises 2, 3, 4 and Classwork from Unit 2, and choose the most useful exercise(s) for learners 1–5.

Example: I have problems making questions. Exercise 2 and Classwork

Learner 1 I learn best when I can talk to other students and practise my spoken English.

....

Learner 2 I think I can improve my grammar by writing in English.

....

Learner 3 I'm sure I learn best from seeing mistakes and trying to work out how to correct them. ....

Learner 4 I like to do all kinds of grammar exercises as well as practising my writing and speaking. ....

Learner 5 I'm not sure about question forms and I also need to try more writing in English.

....

Classwork

1 **Look at the questions in the chart about learning a language. Write *yes* or *no* in the *You* column.**

2 **Interview your partner and write his / her answers in the *Your partner* column. Compare your answers. Which questions suggest good ways of learning a language?**

Question	*You*	*Your partner*
1 When you speak English, do you stop yourself when you notice you have made a mistake?		
2 Do you often guess the meaning of new words?		
3 Do you always speak to your classmates in your own language?		
4 When you are speaking, do you stop the conversation and look up words you don't know in a dictionary?		
5 Do you try to remember new words by using English explanations or pictures?		
6 If someone doesn't understand you, do you try to say the sentence again in a different way?		
7 Can you often guess the meaning of what somebody says from their facial expression or gestures?		
8 Do you try to find people to practise your English with?		

Unit 2

The present simple

Getting started

1 **The text below is from an interview with Jodie Foster, a Hollywood actress and director. Read the text and answer the questions.**

a) In what ways is Jodie Foster's life **not** like a star's life? ....

b) Why does Jodie want to have an ordinary life? ....

Jodie enjoys living a life around Los Angeles that is as un-starlike as she can make it. She refuses to have a personal assistant, does her own food shopping and takes her own letters to the post office. 'I have always lived like that,' she says, 'and I always will. I don't want to become someone who doesn't know how to do things. If I'm in Calcutta and I need to get to Bombay and a flight gets cancelled so I need to take the train, I want to know how to do that.' She lives in a rented apartment in Hollywood and says that, when she is not working, her favourite thing is to do absolutely nothing!

2 **Look at these present simple sentences from the text:**

She refuses to have a personal assistant, does her own food shopping and takes her own letters to the post office.
I don't want to become someone who doesn't know how to do things.
She lives in a rented apartment in Hollywood …

How much do you know about the present simple? Underline the correct choice, i) or ii), below:

a) The present simple is used to talk about things that are:
 i) generally true ii) happening now

b) It is used to say how often something happens, with words like:
 i) *for* and *since* ii) *always*, *sometimes* and *never*

c) It is made like this:
 i) *I / you / we / they take*
she / he / it takes ii) *I / you / we / they takes*
she / he / it take

d) Negatives and questions are made with:
 i) *do* and *does* ii) *did*

Looking at language

The present simple

Use

We use the present simple to talk about things and situations that are generally true:

*Digital cameras **cost** a lot of money. They **have** very complex parts and they **use** a lot of battery power.*

*She's 27 years old and she **has** a small flat.*

The general truth can be:

- a repeated action: *She **takes** the train to work, but I usually **drive**.*
- a permanent situation: *She **lives** in a small flat in London.*

The present simple can also be used in informal stories. For example, describing a film scene or telling a joke:

*She **walks** into the room, and **sees** the bottle and two glasses on the table, so she **knows** …*

*This man **goes** into a bar, and **orders** an orange juice and a packet of crisps …*

1 Fill in the gaps in this text by another Hollywood actress with verbs in the present simple.

Life is pretty busy at the moment. I 1 .... a 14-hour day, but I'm lucky because we're filming in the Santa Monica mountains, 15 minutes from home. I'm usually up at 4 a.m. My husband 2 .... up then, too – he 3 .... to work before the phone starts ringing – and, after a coffee, I 4 .... to Agoure to arrive at exactly 5.42. It's a wonderful drive – I see mountain lions, coyotes and sometimes snakes. My day 5 .... with hair and make-up. Then it's straight into filming.

(from *Radio Times*, 9–15 November 1996)

Form

Positive statements	*Negative statements*	*Wh- questions*
I / you / we / they **play** she / he / it **plays**	I **do not (don't) play** she **does not (doesn't) play**	Where **do** you **play**? Where **does** she **play**?
Yes / No questions	*Positive short answers*	*Negative short answers*
Do you **play**? **Does** she **play**?	Yes, I **do**. Yes, she **does**.	No, I **don't**. No, she **doesn't**.

Spelling

Other spellings of the third person singular are:

- in verbs which end in *sh*, *ch*, *ss*, *x*, an *es* is added: *washes*, *watches*, *kisses*, *fixes*. This is pronounced /ɪz/.
- in verbs which end in a consonant +*y*, the *y* is changed to an *i* and *es* is added: *try – tries*, *carry – carries*.

Other points

- We can say **how often** something happens with adverbs of frequency like (*nearly*) *always*, *usually*, (*quite*) *often*, *sometimes*, (*almost*) *never*:
  *She **nearly always** takes the train to work.*
  *I don't **often** go shopping.*
- Note the present simple form of *to be*: *I **am**, you / we / they **are**, she / he / it **is**.*
- Note the third person singular forms: *have* – ***has***, *do* – ***does***, *go* – ***goes***.
- We often use ***you*** **+ present simple** to mean 'everyone':
  You need two photos to get a passport.
- We use the present simple question *What do you do?* to mean 'What's your job?'

See Unit 3 for a comparison of the present simple and the present continuous.

Getting it right

Exercise 1 Subjects and verbs

In the advertisements below, fill in the gaps with the correct pronoun from the box. The form of the present simple verb (e.g. *doesn't have* or *don't have*) will help you.

he	it	you	I	she	they

Microwave-heated body/bed warmer

This special warmer gives you all the same warmth as a traditional hot-water bottle but .....*it*.... doesn't have the problem of dangerous hot water. **1** .... just put it in the microwave to heat up, and **2** .... stays hot for hours.

'**3** .... always use mine on cold nights. It's so easy to use!'

This electronic dictionary contains over 100,000 words.

4 .... just needs two small batteries to run for hours and hours. Ordinary dictionaries are large, and for many people **5** .... are inconvenient to carry around, but this electronic dictionary fits easily into your pocket or bag, so **6** .... can take it wherever you go.

'**7** .... never go anywhere without my electronic dictionary. My colleagues often want to borrow it, and my daughter uses it too – **8** .... checks her homework with it.'

DIETING SUCCESS

Does your weight depress you?
Do you hate dieting?

Dr Dawes's video course can help. On this new video Dr Dawes explains how to eat healthily. In six easy steps, **9** .... shows you how to change your eating habits. 'I'm much slimmer now, and **10** .... thank Dr Dawes for that.'

Extension

Write a similar advertisement for something you have bought recently.

Exercise 2 Asking questions

Linda Magee, a television news reporter, was interviewed about her day. Use the underlined sections of the article to write the interviewer's questions.

I get up around 7.00, some time before my husband, Alan. **1** He's a photographer, so he can often choose the time of day that he wants to work. I don't have breakfast, **2** because I eat a lot of snacks in the studio, but I get breakfast for the kids before I leave the house. **3** They usually have fruit and cereal or toast. **4** I generally walk or cycle to work unless the weather's bad, and **5** it takes about half an hour on foot and about ten minutes by bike. When I arrive, **6** I discuss the day's main stories with the news editor over a cup of coffee. We usually prepare the midday news after that, but sometimes new stories come in and we have to start again. At 11.00 Sandy, **7** the hair and make-up assistant, gets me ready for the camera. **8** Just before the broadcast I often feel nervous, even after all these years! **9** The programme starts at exactly 12.00 and **10** lasts 20 minutes. Then it's back to the news editor to do the whole thing again in time for the 4.00 broadcast.

Example: *What time do you get up?*

1 .... 6 ....

2 .... 7 ....

3 .... 8 ....

4 .... 9 ....

5 .... 10 ....

Exercise 3 Learning from learners

Look at this extract from a learner's letter to a penfriend. There are 11 mistakes in it. Find them and correct them. The first one has been done for you.

Dear Akram,

Thank you for your very interesting letter. I ^am very pleased to be your penfriend. Are you really have a swimming pool in the garden? It sound wonderful. As you know from my advertisement, I have 17 years old and came from Cartagena in Chile. I've got two sisters, Maria and Fernanda, and they is both older than me. My father own a small paper factory, but my mother don't work. We living in a house just outside the city. I enjoying playing football and I am like science-fiction films.

Exercise 4 Written practice

Write a description of the world's largest shopping centre using the information below and the verbs in the box in the order given.

West Edmonton Mall, Alberta, Canada
5.2 million square feet.
800 shops, 110 restaurants (25,000 meals a day).
20,000 staff.
20 million visitors per year.
Visitors' spending: $16 million per day.
A 30-minute drive from the city centre.
26 cinemas but no theatre.
Open 08.00–24.00.

(adapted from an article by Michael Booth, *The Independent on Sunday*, 19 January 1997)

~~cover~~ ~~have~~ serve employ attract spend be have not have open close

West Edmonton Mall covers 5.2 million square feet and has 800 different shops. Its 110 restaurants
....

....

....

....

....

Classwork

1 **Work in groups of three or four. Learner 1 thinks of a job.**

2 **Learners 2, 3 and 4 ask him / her questions in the present simple to find out what the job is. They can only ask ten questions. Learner 1 can only answer *Yes*, *No* or *Sometimes*.**

Example:

Do you get up early?	*Yes, I do.*
Do you wear a uniform?	*Yes, I do.*
Does this job need a lot of qualifications?	*No, it doesn't.*
Do you work inside?	*No, I don't.*
Is the job very well-paid?	*No, it isn't.*
Are you a postman?	*Yes, I am.*

Unit

3 The present continuous

Getting started

1 **A truffle is a fungus found under the ground which is very good to eat. Read the newspaper article about truffle-hunting dogs and answer the questions.**

a truffle

a) How are truffles found?

....

b) What is the problem for truffle farmers in the year of the article? ....

TRUFFLERS DOGNAPPED

Police in southern France are trying to find ten truffle-hunting dogs, stolen from their owners in the middle of the season for the fungi. Police in Carpentras believe the dogs, trained to dig up truffles growing five centimetres below the ground, have been kidnapped.

Farmers are getting around £150 a kilo for truffles this year. Hervé de Chiré, mayor of the village of Pernes-les-Fontaines, said: 'Training the dogs takes years and the truffle season is very short. Some of the farmers are offering up to £650 for the return of their dogs.'

2 **Underline three examples of the present continuous (*am / is / are + -ing*) in the article.**

3 **Tick (✓) the correct choices:**

a) The underlined verbs in the article refer to:

i) every year .....

ii) the year of the article .....

b) The present continuous is used to talk about actions and situations which are:

i) true at the moment .....

ii) always true .....

Looking at language

The present continuous

Use

The present continuous is used to talk about:

1 **Actions** that are going on **around or at the time of speaking:**
Jane's having a bath at the moment.

2 **Temporary situations.** Compare:
*He's **working** in Oxford just now.* (but next year he will do something else)
present continuous – a temporary situation
*He **works** for a company in Oxford.* (he works there all the time)
present simple – a permanent situation

3 **Changing situations**, especially with verbs like *get* and *become* and with comparative adjectives like *more, worse, better*:
*He's **getting** fat, isn't he?*
*This city **is becoming** more and more dangerous.*

4 **Behaviour that happens more often than expected**, with *always, forever* and *constantly*:
*Why **are** you always **shouting**?*
*She's forever **buying** me presents.*
Note that the auxiliary *be* comes **before** words like *always* and *forever*.

5 **Future plans**. See Unit 11.

1 Are these sentences examples of 1, 2, 3 or 4 above?

a) I'm sure the air quality *is getting worse* round here. .....

b) I hope he's OK. He's *constantly getting* headaches. .....

c) I'*m staying* with friends in New York at the moment, but I live in Washington. .....

d) You can't see her I'm afraid. She's *trying* to get some rest. .....

Stative verbs

Some verbs are not usually used in the continuous. They are called **stative verbs**, and are:

- verbs which describe thoughts, feelings and senses: *think, know, believe, agree, remember, forget, understand, like, love, hate, mind, prefer, want, see, hear, smell, taste.* So we do not say: ~~*I'm knowing the answer.*~~ or ~~*She isn't understanding anything*~~. We say: *I know the answer. She doesn't understand anything.*
  We use *can* with sense verbs. We do not say: ~~*I'm not hearing you*~~. or ~~*I don't hear you*~~.
  We say: *I can't hear you.*
- some other verbs which describe what things (and people) are, what they are like, and what they possess: *be, have, need, own, involve, depend on, seem, look, sound, smell, taste, weigh.* So we do not say: ~~*I am being hungry.*~~ or ~~*This soup is tasting nice*~~. We say: *I am hungry. This soup tastes nice.*

But some of these stative verbs **can** be used in the continuous sense. Compare *She's tasting the soup* (her action) and *The soup tastes good* (what the soup is like), and *What are you thinking about?* (what are your thoughts?) and *What do you think?* (what is your opinion?).

Form

The present continuous is formed with the present tense of *be* and the *-ing* form of the verb.

Positive statements	*Negative statements*	*Wh- questions*
I **am** (I'm) **playing** you **are** (you're) **playing** we **are** (we're) **playing** they **are** (they're) **playing** she / he / it **is** (she's / he's / it's) **playing**	**I'm not playing** **you're not playing / you aren't playing** **we're not playing / we aren't playing** **they're not playing / they aren't playing** **he's not playing / he isn't playing**	Where **are** you **playing?** Where **is** she **playing?**
Yes / No questions	*Positive short answers*	*Negative short answers*
Are they **playing?** **Is** he **playing?**	Yes, they **are.** Yes, he **is.**	No, they **aren't.** / No, they**'re not.** No, he **isn't.** / No, he**'s not** .

Spelling

- In one-syllable verbs which end in a vowel and a consonant (e.g. *stop*, *run*), the consonant is doubled in the *-ing* form: *stopping*, *running*.
- In verbs which end in *e* (e.g. *take*, *lose*), the *e* is lost in the *-ing* form: *taking*, *losing*. But verbs which end in double *e* (e.g. *see*, *agree*), keep both *es*: *seeing*, *agreeing*.

Other points

- We use *at the moment* with the present continuous to show that something is going on at the time of speaking and is temporary:
  *He's doing his homework **at the moment**.*
- We use *still* to show that something is continuing and is temporary:
  ***I'm still living** with my parents, but I want to get my own flat.*

Getting it right

▷ Exercise 1 Learning from learners

Look at this learner's text. Match the teacher's ticks (✓) and corrections 1–10 to rules a)–f) below.

My name is Kim and I'm Korean. My family is living in	lives .b).
an apartment near the centre of Seoul, and they all	1 ✓.....
1 *love the city except me. They* 2 *are thinking that*	2 think .....
cities are exciting, but 3 *I'm not agreeing with them; I*	3 don't agree .....
4 *am preferring quieter towns or villages. Anyway,*	4 prefer .....
just this month I 5 *work for a small travel agency; I*	5 'm working .....
6 *want to go travelling in Europe next month but* 7 *I'm*	6 ✓ .....
needing to earn some money first. 8 *I'm thinking of doing*	7 need .....
a course when I come back from Europe – my English	8 ✓.....
9 *gets better so maybe I can study abroad next time.*	9 is getting .....
That's very expensive, of course. Perhaps that 10 *is*	10 depends .....
depending on how much I can earn – and my parents!	

a) Use the present continuous to talk about changing situations.

b) ~~Use the present simple to talk about a permanent situation.~~

c) Use the present simple with a 'thought' or 'feeling' verb.

d) Use the present simple with verbs describing what things are, what they are like and what they possess.

e) Use the present continuous for a temporary situation.

f) Use the present continuous for a temporary thought.

Exercise 2 Choosing the correct tense

In the conversation between two friends below, put the verbs in brackets ( ) into the present simple or present continuous.

A: I hear you are working (*work*) in a pub at the moment. What's it like?

B: It is (*be*) fine, although it's very hard work. I'm always tired, but I 1 .... (*not mind*).

A: Is the money good?

B: No, not really, but I 2 .... (*like*) the hours. You know I don't like working early in the morning.

A: Oh yes, I 3 .... (*remember*) now. You never used to get up before 11.00.

B: Well, I'm not like that now, but I certainly don't like getting up before 9.00. Anyway, tell me about you. What 4 .... you .... (*do*) now?

A: I 5 .... (*be*) still a student. I 6 .... (*study*) German at university. Actually, I 7 .... (*work*) quite hard at the moment because my exams are next week. I 8 .... (*want*) to be a teacher when I finish at university.

B: Oh well, good luck in your exams. I must go – I 9 .... (*start*) work at 12.00 on Mondays, and I 10 ....(*not want*) to be late. I 11 .... (*not have*) my car any more, so I 12 .... (*cycle*) everywhere at the moment.

Exercise 3 Writing about developments

Change the text below so that it is true about developments in your country. Use verbs in the present continuous and underline the word in *italics* that you want. Use the verbs in the box if you want to. You can use the verbs more than once.

~~change~~ earn fall get go up / down increase leave rise

In my country, many things are changing . The population 1 .... , and the number of unemployed people 2 .... Young people 3 .... home *earlier / later*, and 4 .... married *earlier / later* than before. People 5 .... *more / less* money these days, while the cost of living 6 .... Our capital city 7 .... *bigger / smaller*, the number of people with cars 8 .... and traffic problems 9 .... *better / worse*. Overall, I think life in my country 10 .... *better / worse* for most people.

Exercise 4 Extending headlines

Headlines for newspaper articles often use the present simple, but the articles sometimes use the present continuous to describe activities that are still going on. Rewrite these headlines as full sentences to start the articles.

Example: **CHESTER POLICE LOOK FOR STOLEN DINOSAUR EGG**

Museum offers big reward for return of egg

Police in Chester are looking for a stolen dinosaur egg. The Museum is offering a big reward for the return of the egg.

1 **US scientists examine Mars rocks and try to find signs of life**

....

2 **GRANDMOTHER STILL WORKS IN SUPERMARKET AT 75 BUT THINKS OF RETIRING**

....

3 ***Man who lives in tree house tries to set new one-year record***

....

4 **New York man builds own rocket and plans to reach moon**

....

5 Tokyo woman celebrates 120th birthday and looks forward to 121st

....

Classwork

1 **Write three sentences about yourself 'at the moment', using the present continuous. One sentence should be untrue.**

Example:
I'm preparing for an exam at the moment.

2 **Ask questions to find out what your partner wrote, and answer your partner's questions.**

Example:
A: *What are you doing at the moment?*
B: *I'm preparing for an exam.*

3 **Which of your partner's answers is untrue, do you think?**

Unit

4 The past simple

Getting started

1 **In the texts below two children, a five-year-old boy and a ten-year-old girl, talk about how they spent their money one day. Read the texts and answer the questions.**

a) Who is speaking in each text, do you think? ....

b) Who do you think spent more money? ....

Text 1

First of all I went to a fashion shop and bought a necklace with a heart. That cost me £1.50. Then I went to the Body Shop[1] and bought shower gel and bubble bath. Then I went to the book shop and bought a Babysitters[2] book, which cost me £2.99. Then I went to the music shop and bought a CD holder which included five photos of East 17[3]. After the music shop, I went to the sweet shop and bought some sweets.

[1]a shop selling beauty products
[2]a series of books for children
[3]a former British pop group

Text 2

I spended my money on a toy car set. It cost me £6.49. It's got street lights and roads and you put it together and play with your cars on it. I didn't want to buy any sweets. Then I went to the cinema with my dad to watch my favourite film, *James and the Giant Peach*. I ate some popcorn. I wish my Mum would give me popcorn every week.

2 **a) Find these verbs in the texts:**

Text 1: went bought cost included

Text 2: spended cost put play didn't want went ate wish

Which three are not in the past simple? ....

b) There is a mistake in one of the past verbs; can you find it? ....

3 **Are the statements below true or false?**

a) The past simple is used to talk about past, completed actions and events. ....

b) You do not need to put a verb in the past simple if you use a time expression, for example, *last year*. ....

c) You need to learn the past form of many verbs as they are irregular. ....

Looking at language

The past simple

Use

We use the past simple to talk about:

- single past actions and events: *I **went** to a fashion shop and **bought** a necklace.*
- repeated past actions and events: *I always **went** shopping on Saturdays.*
- past states (long-lasting situations or feelings): *My father **knew** the Prime Minister.*

We often use a time expression with the past simple:

*I went to the supermarket **last Thursday / at lunchtime / in the evening.***

Often the time is understood but **not** mentioned:

*Oh yes, we **had** a great time!* (we had a great time *at the party last night)*

1 In the text below a boy talks about how he spent his money one day. Put the phrases a)–h) back in the right order by numbering them 1–8.

a) I've got about £250 in it. ...... b) what I'm going to do with the money. ...... c) and then I went to Burger King ...... d) The rest of the money I put into my bank account ...... e) and had a burger with chips. ...... f) I don't know ...... g) which my grandmother opened for me. ...... h) I bought a leather football for £3.99 ......

The past simple is often used in stories and descriptions of past actions and events with the past continuous (see Unit 5) and the past perfect (see Unit 9).

Form

Positive statements	*Negative statements*	*Wh- questions*
Regular verbs I / you / he / she / it / we / they **watched**	**I did not (didn't) watch**	What **did** you **watch**?
Irregular verbs I / you etc. **went / ate / had** (See Appendix 1.)	**I did not (didn't) go**	Where **did** you **go**?
Yes / No questions	*Positive short answers*	*Negative short answers*
Did you **watch** it? **Did** you **go** home then?	Yes, I **did**.	No, I **didn't**.

Spelling

- In verbs which end in *e*, a *d* is added: *liked, hated, danced.*
- In verbs which end in a consonant +y, the *y* is changed to *i* and *ed* is added: *try – tried, carry – carried.*
- In one-syllable verbs which end in a vowel and a consonant, the consonant is doubled and *ed* is added: *stop – stopped, plan – planned, jog – jogged.*

Pronunciation

The *-ed* ending has three pronunciations:

- after /t/ and /d/ we say /ɪd/: *wanted* /wɒntɪd/, *needed* /niːdɪd/
- after unvoiced consonants we say /t/: *missed* /mɪst/, *kicked* /kɪkt/
- after voiced consonants we say /d/: *turned* /tɜːnd/, *loved* /lʌvd/

  See Appendix 2 for a list of unvoiced and voiced consonants.

2 How do you pronounce the *-ed* in these past forms: /t/, /d/ or /ɪd/?

seem*ed* kiss*ed* comb*ed* repeat*ed* depend*ed* brush*ed*

Other points

- The past simple of *to be* is: *I / she / he / it was; you / we / they were. Did* is not used in negatives and questions:

  She wasn't happy.

  Were you at home this morning?
- The past of *can* is *could*:

  I couldn't understand.
- We can talk about the order of actions and events using the past simple and linking words and phrases:

  ***First of all** I went to a fashion shop **and** bought a necklace with a heart. That cost me £1.50. **Then** I went to the Body Shop **and** bought shower gel and bubble bath.*

Getting it right

Exercise 1 Thinking about use

Are the past simple verbs in these sentences single actions (sa), repeated actions (ra), or past states (ps)?

Example: I *took* the new CD player out of the box, *plugged* it in, and *switched* it on. *sa*

1 We *lived* in a small house on the coast which *didn't have* any heating, but we *had* a wonderful, exciting childhood. .....

2 As children, we *went* to the town centre on Saturday afternoons, and *spent* our pocket money on sweets and CDs. .....

3 They *left* at six in the evening and *drove* all the way home without stopping. .....

4 My friend Sally *came* to my house, and we *talked* about the new baby. .....

5 In those days I *got up* really early and nearly always *got* to work before 8.00. .....

6 I *knew* her when she *was* a shop assistant. .....

Exercise 2 Learning from learners

Some learners keep a diary about their progress in English. In this diary, write *right* if a verb form is right, or correct it if it is wrong.

We had an English lesson this morning on the past simple. It didn't was too difficult; we 1 read about some children and how they spent their pocket money, and then 2 studyied the grammar. My problem was the irregular verbs – I 3 didn't knew that there were so many of them, and I just 4 couldn't remember all the past forms. I 5 fell silly once or twice when I 6 was wrong. I also 7 didn't realise that you need to put a verb in the past even when you say the time something happens, like 'yesterday'. After the lesson I went shopping, and 8 bought some clothes, which 9 costed more than I meant to spend! I didn't even have enough money left to catch the train home, so I walked, and it 10 taked me nearly an hour.

..*right*......
..*wasn't*.....
1 ....
2 ....
3 ....
4 ....
5 ....
6 ....
7 ....
8 bought
9 cost
10 took

Read the learner's diary again. Do you feel the same as the writer about the past simple?

Exercise 3 Text completion

The article below describes an unsuccessful driving test. Fill in each gap with a verb from the box in the past simple.

be	not brake	feel	move	pay	push	~~run~~	say	say	stop	try

On my first test, I *ran* out of petrol. Shortly after the restart from the emergency stop*, the car 1 .... again, although I 2 .... I 3 .... five times to restart it.

'No,' I 4 .... to the examiner. 'It won't start.'

The examiner 5 .... into the driving seat, and I 6 .... the car to the nearest service station, where I 7 .... for the petrol.

'This is not your fault and will not affect whether you pass the test,' he 8 .... , but I 9 .... terrified and 10 .... not surprised to fail for lack of observation.

*the emergency stop is the part of the test that shows that you can stop quickly in an emergency

Exercise 4 Question formation

Complete the past simple questions in the extracts from conversations. Which extracts come from a conversation about a holiday, and which from a conversation about a job interview?

Example: Did you have a good time? (Holiday)

Yes, we did thanks. The weather was good and the hotel was lovely.

1 Where ....

In a small hotel just next to the beach.

2 Did ....

Yes, very nervous. My hands were shaking!

3 What ....

Lots of things – my education, interests, and career.

4 Why ....

Because a friend told us that it was a nice place, and he was right.

5 How much ....

Don't ask! It was very expensive, but we enjoyed ourselves so it didn't matter!

6 How long ....

About 45 minutes, and then they spent a few minutes showing me round the office.

7 What ....

I bought a new suit specially.

8 Did ....

Yes, wonderful. We ate fantastic seafood every night.

9 How many ....

Three, but one of them never said anything.

10 How long ....

Just a week. It wasn't really long enough.

Classwork

Work as a whole class, sitting in a circle if you can. Together, tell a story about something that happened yesterday. Each person must use a different verb.

Example:

A: *Yesterday I went shopping.*

B: *Yesterday I went shopping and bought a CD.*

C: *Yesterday I went shopping and bought a CD. Then I took the CD home.*

D: *Yesterday I went shopping and bought a CD. Then I took the CD home and tried to play it, but ...*

Unit

5 The past continuous and the past simple

Getting started

1 **In the extract below from a radio chat show, Barbara Noakes describes how she changed from being a secretary to making advertisements. Barbara is famous for her Levi's '501' jeans advertisement. Read the extract and answer the question.**

Why did she write an advertisement ('ad') when she was still a secretary?

....

WELL, I was reading a book and a very worried-looking man rushed in and said, 'Where's everybody? What's happening?' And I explained that everyone was away sick with flu, which is why I was reading the book. I had nothing to do. And he explained that there was this terrible problem. They needed an ad urgently, and I said, 'Oh, if you want an ad, I'll try and do one.' So I wrote an ad and I went downstairs and found an art director, and that was my first advertisement!

2 **Underline examples of the past continuous (*was / were + -ing*) in the extract.**

3 **Find examples of the past simple (e.g. regular: *liked*; irregular: *met*) in the extract, and circle them.**

4 **Fill in the gaps with *past simple* or *past continuous*.**

a) The .... is used to give an idea of the background situation (what was happening at the time).

b) The .... is used to describe the events of the story.

Looking at language

The past continuous and the past simple

Use

1 We use the past continuous to '**set the scene**' (give an idea of the **background situation**) for a story. The **events** of the story are described using the past simple. Sometimes the events **interrupt** the background situation:

*I **was reading** a book* (background situation) and *a man **rushed** in* (event).

Sometimes the events happen **at the same time as** the background situation:

*While I **was sleeping**, my mother **made** me a meal.*

Compare the past continuous with the past simple:

I read a book and a man rushed in.

Event 1 → Event 2

The past simple (*read*) here suggests that she read the book **before** the man rushed in, and that the reading was an event.

1 In the chat show, Barbara also described how she got the idea for her Levi's '501' jeans advertisement. In this advertisement a man takes off his 501s in a launderette (a shop where you can wash your clothes) and puts them in the washing machine. <u>Underline</u> the verb which sets the scene, and circle the events.

I was sitting in a launderette when a man came in and took his clothes off, and I got very frightened, but he just put them in the washing machine and washed them, sat down, put them in the dryer, put them back on and went.

2 We use the past continuous when we are interested in activities going on around a particular time, **not** their starting and finishing times or the order in which they happened:

*This time last year I **was working** for two different companies, I **was studying** for a diploma and I **was trying** to buy a house. It was a pretty busy time!*

Compare this with:

*I **worked** for three months, I **did** a diploma and I **bought** a house.*

The past simple here suggests a **sequence** (one thing after another) and **completion** (each event was finished).

Other points

The past continuous is often used with *as, when* and *while* to set the scene:
As / when / while I was waiting for the train, the man next to me started chatting.
Notice that *when* can also be used to introduce the event:
I was waiting for the train ***when*** *the man next to me started chatting.*

Form

The past continuous is formed with the past tense of *be* and the *-ing* form of the verb.

Positive statements	*Negative statements*	*Wh- questions*
I / she / he / it: **was working** you / we / they **were working**	I **was not** (**wasn't**) **working** you **were not** (**weren't**) **working**	Where **was** he **working**? Why **were** they **working**?
Yes / No questions	*Positive short answers*	*Negative short answers*
Was she **working**? **Were** you **working**?	Yes, she **was**. Yes, we **were**.	No, she **wasn't**. No, we **weren't**.

See Unit 3 for verbs that do not usually have a continuous form.
See Unit 19 for the past continuous in reported speech.

Getting it right

Exercise 1 Choosing the best form

Read what each speaker is thinking about. Tick (✓) the best sentence for the speaker to use.

Example: I want to know about your action **after** the President's death.

a) What did you do when the President died? ..✓..

b) What were you doing when the President died? .....

1 I want to describe the situation at the party when I arrived.

a) Everyone danced. .....

b) Everyone was dancing. ..✓..

2 I'm thinking of the **whole** car journey.

a) The driver drove too fast. .....

b) The driver was driving too fast. ..✓..

3 I want to tell you what sort of person he was.

a) He talked too much. ..✓..

b) He was talking too much. .....

4 I want to show that I finished my dream.

a) I dreamt about a wonderful holiday. .....

b) I was dreaming about a wonderful holiday. .....

5 I want to show that I was interrupted.

a) I talked about her when she came into the room. .....

b) I was talking about her when she came into the room. .....

6 I want to show that different things happened at the same time.

a) He made a phone call, cooked supper, and drank a coffee. .....

b) He was making a phone call, cooking supper and drinking a coffee. .....

7 I want to show that different things happened one after another.

a) She was buying a new house, writing a novel and arranging the wedding. .....

b) She bought a new house, wrote a novel and arranged the wedding. .....

8 I want to describe the situation at the time I broke my arm.

a) I was carrying a big bag up some steps. .....

b) I carried a big bag up some steps. .....

Exercise 2 Learning from learners

Look at these extracts from pieces of writing by learners of English. Tick (✓) the past simple or past continuous verbs if they are right, or put a cross (✗) if they are wrong.

Example:

The bell rang (..✓..) at one o'clock in the afternoon and the children were running (..✗..) out of their classes.

It was like the bell had released a sea of students. Children 1 were running (.....) everywhere.

While we 2 were chatting (.....) two monkeys appeared and 3 were moving (.....) towards us.

When I 4 was working (.....) as an Executive Secretary to the Managing Director I 5 was living (.....) with my parents.

When the police 6 were arriving (.....) Mr Jones was arrested.

One day, while Mr Pippett 7 took (.....) Solom out for a walk, the pair 8 met (.....) Solom's previous owner.

Exercise 3 Written practice

Read the police statement from a cyclist who was in an accident. Complete it with verbs from the box in either the past simple or the past continuous tense.

call	cycle	fall	go	~~happen~~	have	hit	hurt	lie	say	stop	take	turn

The accident *happened*... at 5.55 p.m. on 15 August. I **1** .... home from work along Manning Road. Suddenly a car **2** .... past me and **3** .... left. I **4** .... not .... time to stop, and I **5** .... the side of the car. I **6** .... off my bicycle, and I **7** .... on the ground when the car **8** .... and the driver got out. He asked if I was OK. I **9** .... 'No', because my left leg **10** .... a lot. He **11** .... an ambulance and it **12** .... me to hospital.

Look at this picture of the accident. What is wrong?

Exercise 4 Story writing

Below are the beginnings of three short stories. In each story, choose your own verb in the past continuous to set the scene in the first gap, and then continue by describing the first two or three events. Use the verbs in the boxes if you want to. We have started the first story for you.

Story 1

arrive	~~get on~~	~~leave~~	pull out	see	shout

It was a cold, dark morning, and a tall man in a grey coat ..*was standing*.... on the station platform. *Then the train arrived, and the man quickly got on. He left a small bag on the platform, and the train...*...

....

....

Story 2

score	try	win	feel

With the score at 2–0, it was nearly the end of the match and United ....
well. Suddenly everything began to change. ....
....
....

Story 3

walk	look around	take	leave

The festival was nearly over. There was still loud music, and people .... still ....
.... Then a strange man ....
....
....

Extension

Complete one of the stories above.

Classwork

The speaker at the beginning of this unit was talking about something interesting that happened to her in her past. We call short, usually true, stories like this 'anecdotes'. We often use the past continuous to set the scene at the beginning of an anecdote (*I was walking by the river …*), and use the past simple to say what happened (*… when I saw someone fall in*).

1 **Work in groups of three. Have you ever done anything dangerous, naughty, exciting or funny? Tell your anecdote to your group. Decide together which of the three anecdotes is the most interesting.**

2 **Choose a speaker – anyone in the group, not necessarily the person who it happened to – to present the anecdote to the whole class, using *I*, not *she* or *he*. The other groups decide which person in your group the anecdote is about.**

3 **Which anecdote was the most unusual?**

Unit 6

Used to *and* would

Getting started

1 **In the extracts below a famous British writer, John Mortimer, and his daughter, Emily, talk about each other. Read the extracts and answer the questions.**

a) Who is talking in each extract, the father or the daughter? ....

b) Who do you like more, the father or the daughter? ....

1 I used to love gardening, and, much to her embarrassment, I would go to collect her from some club at 2 a.m. wearing my gardening cap.

2 When I was little he used to get up every morning, dress me, cook my breakfast, and drive me to school. And I treated him very badly in return. At the age of four I used to send my eggs back unless they were perfectly cooked.

3 I was embarrassed by the fact that Dad was older and used to wish that I had a father who played cricket and built tree houses. In fact, I used to make him park around the corner from school because he was so old.

4 Emily used to do very well in public-speaking competitions. I used to write her speeches with her.

5 I used to be very embarrassed when, as a teenager, I went out to clubs and Dad would come and collect me wearing his gardening cap.

2 **Find examples of *used to* + verb in the extracts and <u>underline</u> them.**

3 **Find examples of *would* + verb in the extracts and circle them.**

4 **Are the statements below true or false?**

a) The father and daughter are talking about their lives now. ....

b) He collected her from a club many times. ....

c) She made him park around the corner once. ....

d) They still do the things they talk about using *used to* and *would*. ....

Looking at language

Used to and *would*

Use

To talk about something that was true in the past, but is not true any more, we can use ***used to* + verb**, ***would* + verb**, or the **past simple**.

1 ***Used to* + verb** is used to talk about:

a) a repeated past action that no longer happens:

*I **used to help** her with her homework.* (many times in the past, but not now)

*We **used to collect** her from school.*

b) a past state (a situation or feeling) that lasted a long time but which is no longer true:

*We **used to live** in London.* (now we live in the country)

*I **used to be** very thin.* (now I am not very thin)

2 ***Would* + verb** is only used for repeated past actions (as in 1a above):

*She **would** often **go** to noisy London nightclubs.* (many times in the past, but not now)

***Would* + verb** is **not** used for past states. We don't say: ~~*I would love gardening*~~.

We say: *I **loved** gardening* or *I **used to love** gardening.*

So *used to* and *would* are used when we are remembering the past, and trying to show that our lives are not the same now:

past present

*I **used to play** football* (but I don't now)

Would is more likely than *used to* when you describe more than one past action, like the four here:

*I'**d** come home late, and my mother **would** worry about me, and she'**d** get upset, and we'**d** start arguing.*

3 The **past simple** can also describe repeated past actions and states, but alone it does not tell us that something happened repeatedly or is no longer true. To do this you need to add extra information:

*I **often** came home late **when I was young**.* (See Unit 4.)

We use the past simple if something only happened once, or when we say how many times the action was repeated. We say: *I went to Singapore twice last year.* We don't say: ~~*I used to go to Singapore twice last year.*~~

1 Cross out the incorrect verbs in this text.

The earliest memory I have of my mother is when we **1** *lived / would live / used to live* in a beautiful house in Stratford. She **2** *played / would play / used to play* games with me in the garden, frightening me and making me laugh. She **3** *loved / would love / used to love* flowers, and we **4** *took / would take / used to take* a basket to collect them down by the river.

Form

Used to and *would* are both followed by the infinitive without *to*.

Positive statements	*Negative statements*	*Wh- questions*
I / you / she / he / it / we / they **used to** cycle. I / you / she / he / it / we / they **would** (**I'd** etc.) cycle.	**I did not (didn't) use to** cycle. I **used not to** cycle. **Used not to** is less common.	Where **did** they **use to** cycle?
Yes / No questions	*Positive short answers*	*Negative answers*
Did you **use to** cycle?	**Yes**, I **did**.	No, I **didn't**.

Negative and question forms of *would* with this meaning are not very common.

Pronunciation

- Compare the pronunciation of *used to* in these two sentences:
  *Antibiotics are **used to** treat infections.* (present passive form of main verb *use*)
  /juːzd tə/
  *We always **used to** have lunch at 1.00 p.m.*
  /juːstə/
- In the negative there is a spelling change (*used to* → *didn't use to*) but the pronunciation stays the same:
  I didn't use to like olives.
  /juːstə/
- See Unit 29 for the difference between ***I'm used to cycling** to work* and ***I used to cycle** to work*.

Getting it right

Exercise 1 Thinking about meaning

Complete each sentence, 1–6, with a suitable ending a)–n). There are more endings than you need.

Example: She used to play ..b)

1 I'd watch TV for hours .....
2 I used to have .....
3 I used to feel .....
4 We used to live .....
5 I cycled a lot yesterday .....
6 They would go .....

a) a cat. It's very unfriendly!
b) ~~tennis every morning before breakfast.~~
c) so I was quite fit.
d) lonely until I met James.
e) last night until my eyes hurt.
f) in Rome, but we're thinking of moving.
g) for a long walk in the countryside last Saturday.
h) so I felt tired. ✓
i) but I never watch it now. ✓
j) in Rome, but we moved to Naples last year. ✓
k) in the 1994 tennis final.
l) for long walks in the countryside. ✓
m) a cat, but it died last year. ✓
n) lonely because I live alone and my neighbours aren't very friendly. ✓

Exercise 2 Learning from learners

The two compositions here were written by learners of English. Correct any mistakes with *would* and *used to*.

A

Changes in my country

There have been many changes in my country in the past 20 years. The biggest change is probably in the area of technology. Twenty years ago no one had a telephone. They used ^to communicate by letter. Nowadays many people have mobile phones. People didn't used to have any electrical things in their houses, so they would to wash all the clothes by hand and keep food fresh by hanging it outside. Most people have fridges and washing machines now. Many people still travel by bicycle in my country but there use to be many more bicycles on the roads. Twenty years ago people didn't own cars, but now it's common. There is a real change in the clothes people wear too. People didn't use to wearing Western-style clothes, but now most young people wear the same things as people in the US or Europe.

B

> My life ten years ago
>
> My family used to lived in a big house in the countryside. I used to have many friends who lived near the house, and we would often playing together in the summer. My school was in the village and I wasn't use to go to the city very much. One thing I remember clearly is the peace - we'd heard animal noises but no cars. My family didn't have a car as they were too expensive, so I'd cycling everywhere. I have good memories of life in the countryside, but sometimes I'm used to get bored, and I'm happy to be in the city these days.

Exercise 3 *Used to* and *would* in spoken extracts

In the extracts below four parents talk about their children, William, Justin, Tessa and Lizzie, who are now grown up. Fill in the gaps with *used to* or *would* and an appropriate form of a verb from the box. You will have to use the past simple for one.

ask	~~dress up~~	help	love	play	play	sing	smell	tell

We had a box of old clothes and William *used to dress up* all the time as a cowboy, pirate or king. He 1 .... games, too, where he imagined he was the king of a magical country, and he 2 .... us stories for hours at a time.

Justin 3 .... in the bath all the time, and in the garden. I remember the neighbours complained quite often about the noise. And when he wasn't singing he 4 .... an old guitar, which sounded even worse.

Tessa 5 .... school, and always talked to the family about the things she had learnt. She 6 .... her sisters and friends with their homework – she was very good at explaining things.

Lizzie 7 .... for a chemistry set for her tenth birthday. We were all surprised, but when she got it she never stopped doing experiments. Often, I remember, the whole house 8 .... of strange chemicals!

Which jobs do you think the children might have now? Draw a line from the child to the job.

William   Justin   Tessa   Lizzie

actor   scientist   singer   teacher

Extension

Write a paragraph about what you used to do as a child. If you are working in class, collect the paragraphs together and guess who wrote each one.

Exercise 4 Written practice: the world's greatest learner

Jorge was a very successful language learner. In two years he became a fluent user of English and a famous TV presenter. Use the notes from a journalist's interview below to write a paragraph for a newspaper about Jorge's successful learning.

Notes

- Bought a grammar book
- Collected examples of grammatical structures from newspapers, books, radio, films
- Kept grammar and vocabulary notebooks
- Didn't worry about understanding every word
- Had special 'speak English' times with friends and family
- Learnt about English-speaking countries
- Asked teachers and friends lots of questions
- Took exams to motivate himself

Jorge had a number of techniques. He bought a grammar book, but he would also collect examples of new grammatical structures from newspapers, books, radio programmes and films. He used to ....

....

....

....

....

....

Classwork

1 Think about when you were younger and complete the sentences below.

I used to wear ....

I'd often go to ....

My hair used to be ....

I'd play ....

My favourite food used to be ....

I used to listen to ....

I didn't use to like ....

2 Go round the class asking questions.

Example:
What did you use to wear?

Who in the class had the most similar lifestyle to yours?

Unit 7 The present perfect simple

Getting started

1 Read the newspaper interview with Andrew and Esther and answer the questions.

a) What animals have Andrew and Esther worked with? ....

b) Would they like to change jobs with each other? ....

Andrew Hayton, 26, has worked at Longleat Safari Park* for more than eight years. He is currently an elephant keeper and has also looked after rhinos.

Why did you choose this job?
I had been doing various jobs here. I heard about the rhino vacancy and I thought, 'This is the job for me' – I've always liked animals.

Have you ever thought of working in a zoo?
Zoos are very good and have a place, but not for larger animals.

Esther Wenman, 30, has worked at London Zoo for nearly seven years. She is head keeper of reptiles, and before that was a bird keeper.

What made you choose this job?
I've always been interested in conservation and ecology.

Have you ever thought of working in a safari park?
You don't get such good collections of birds and reptiles in safari parks.

*a safari park is a park where wild animals are kept and in which they can move freely

a rhino

a reptile

2 Underline seven examples of the present perfect simple in the text (*have / has* + past participle).

3 Look at these sentences:
Esther has worked at London Zoo for seven years.

Elaine worked at London Zoo for seven years.

Who still works at London Zoo now: Esther or Elaine? ....

Looking at language

The present perfect simple

Use

We use the present perfect simple when we want to link the past with the present in some way. Compare it with the past simple:

The past simple:	*The present perfect simple:*
talks about the past only: *I **knew** her **when I was a child**.*	links the past with the present: *I've **known** her **for ten years**.* (I met her ten years ago, and I still know her **now**)
is concerned with a specific past time, either mentioned or understood. *I **went** to London.*	does not generally refer to a specific past time. *I've **been** to London.*
is used with time expressions to talk about finished periods of time: *I **saw** Jeremy **yesterday**.*	is used with time expressions to talk about periods of time that are not finished: *Clare's been a teacher **for five years**.*

The chart below shows three ways in which the present perfect links the past and present. Note the time expressions that often occur with these three uses.

Use	*Time expressions*	*Examples*
1 We use the present perfect simple to talk about **something that started in the past and is still continuing now.**	*for* + period of time *since* + a moment in time *always*	*Andrew **has worked** here **for eight years / since 2001.*** (he still works here) *I've **always liked** animals.* (I still like animals)
2 We use the present perfect simple to talk about **something that happened in the past and is part of our experience.**	*before* *ever* in questions = at any time before now *never* to form negatives	***He has looked after rhinos before.*** ***Have you ever thought** of working in a zoo?* *I've **never thought** of working in a zoo.*
3 We use the present perfect simple to talk about **something that happened in the past but the result is important now.** It is often used to give **news**.	*recently* = not long ago *just* = a short time before now *already* = before now *yet* = not before now but going to happen	***I've hurt** my arm.* (and it's painful now) *A rhino **has escaped** from the zoo.* (it's not in the zoo now) *I've **seen** her **recently**.* *He's **just returned** from abroad.* *I've **already** seen that film.* ***Have** you **finished yet?***

Note that the meaning of the present perfect simple changes if there is no time expression. Compare:

She's lived in Mexico City for six years. (she still lives there now – Use 1)
She's lived in Mexico City. (at some time before now, but she doesn't live there now – Use 2)

1 Fill in the gaps in the phrases with *for* or *since*.

1 .... a long time
2 .... my last birthday
3 .... ages
4 .... I last saw her
5 .... New Year's Eve
6 .... half an hour
7 .... Wednesday
8 .... 5 March 1999
9 .... a few hours
10 .... yesterday
11 .... we were children
12 .... six weeks
13 .... years
14 .... December
15 .... a fortnight
16 .... two o'clock

Form

The present perfect is formed with *have / has* and the the past participle. There are many irregular past participles: *go – gone, see – seen, become – become.* See Appendix 1 for a list.

Positive statements	*Negative statements*	*Wh- questions*
I / you / we / they **have eaten** she / he / it **has eaten**	I / you / we / they **have not (haven't) eaten** she **hasn't eaten**	Where **have** you **eaten?** Where **has** she **eaten?**
Yes / No questions	*Positive short answers*	*Negative short answers*
Have you **eaten?** **Has** she **eaten?**	Yes, we **have.** Yes, she **has.**	No, we **haven't.** No, she **hasn't.**

Other points

- *He's **been to** Mozambique* means 'he isn't there now'; it's past experience (Use 2). *He's **gone** to Mozambique* means 'he's there now'; it's news (Use 3).
- Changes are often described using the present perfect (Use 3).
  *Inflation **has risen** again in the past few months.*
- News often starts with the present perfect (Use 3) but changes to the past simple for details:
  *Have you heard about Sally? She's **lost** her job. She **found** out two days ago.*
  This tense change is also true for talking about past experience (Use 2):
  A: ***Have** you ever **been** to Japan?*
  B: *Yes, twice actually. I first **went** in 1996, and then I **returned** last year.*

2 Match each present perfect sentence to a use (1–3) from the boxes on page 36.

a) Quick! Get a cloth! I*'ve spilt* my coffee. .....

b) I love this watch. I*'ve had* it for years. .....

c) I*'ve been* in a helicopter, but I*'ve never been* in a balloon. .....

Getting it right

Exercise 1 Thinking about meaning

In situations 1–10 below, tick (✓) the best sentence, a) or b), for the speaker to use.

Example: The baby's a day old and is doing well.
a) My sister's had a baby. ..✓..
b) My sister had a baby. .....

1 It's 7.30 a.m. The postman usually comes between 7.15 a.m. and 7.45 a.m.
a) The postman hasn't come yet. ✓.....
b) The postman didn't come this morning. .....

2 I'm talking about my trip around Eastern Europe last year.
a) I haven't been to Prague. .....
b) I didn't go to Prague. .....

3 Alice is a good friend of mine.
a) She's known me since we were children. .....
b) She knew me when we were children.

4 I'm telling you this just after I heard the news.
a) A large shark has attacked a swimmer on Australia's western coast. .....
b) A large shark attacked a swimmer on Australia's western coast. .....

5 He is back with his family now.
a) No one has seen him for ten days .....
b) No one saw him for ten days. .....

6 My knee is much better now.
a) I've hurt my knee. .....
b) I hurt my knee. .....

7 I'm giving a friend recent news about Alexander.
a) Alexander has given up smoking. .....
b) Alexander gave up smoking. .....

8 Mike didn't get the job.
a) Mike's applied for a new job. .....
b) Mike applied for a new job. .....

9 I'm still studying maths with the same teacher.
a) I've learnt a lot from my maths teacher. .....
b) I learnt a lot from my maths teacher. .....

10 The drug was never used because it was dangerous.
a) Scientists have found a new drug. .....
b) Scientists found a new drug. .....

Exercise 2 Learning from learners

A learner completed a present perfect / past simple gap-fill exercise which is a conversation between two old friends. Check the answers, and write *right* or correct them.

A: Have you seen (*see*) William recently? He grew (*grow*) a beard! — right
has grown
B: Yes, actually. I 1 've seen (*see*) him last week in the supermarket. I think the beard suits him. — 1 ....
A: Yes, it's OK. He 2 's lost (*lose*) a lot of hair in the past few years though. — 2 ....
B: Oh, poor William! All of us 3 changed (*change*) quite a lot. Look at Marsha. She 4 lost (*lose*) so much weight since she was a teenager. — 3 .... 4 ....

A: Yes. I 5 have never been able to (*be able to*) lose weight. Anyway, the reason I 6 've asked (*ask*) you about William was that he 7 's decided (*decide*) to have a college reunion next month and we're all invited. He's only inviting people he 8 's met (*meet*) at college.

B: That sounds fun. I 9 met (*meet*) William on my first day of college. We were only 17 and he seemed really shy. He 10 changed (*change*) a lot since then, that's for sure.

A: Look, I'd better go. I'm going to a friend's house, but I 11 haven't been (*not be*) there before and I don't want to get lost and be late. She 12 just moved (*just move*) house and is having a party to celebrate.

5 ....
6 ....
7 ....
8 ....
9 ....
10 ....
11 ....
12 ....

Exercise 3 Getting the form right

Read the letter to a newspaper travel advice column and fill in the gaps with a verb from the box in the present perfect tense.

be be give go up ~~have~~ have hear like read return visit

Dear Susie

I have not had a holiday for a very long time, but this summer my company **1** .... me four weeks' holiday, so I want to go somewhere really exciting. I 2 .... always .... travelling and 3 .... lots of exciting trips in the past. This year I'm not sure where I want to go. I 4 .... already .... to Africa and Asia but I 5 .... never .... South America so maybe that's where I should go. A friend of mine 6 .... recently .... from Brazil and she has some wonderful photographs of the carnival in Rio. However, I 7 .... that a trip to Brazil is quite expensive and the cost of airfares 8 .... just ....

Can you give me any advice about a good place to go? I 9 .... your travel page every week for the past year, and really respect your advice. **10** .... you ever .... to Brazil yourself?

Exercise 4 Writing a text from notes

Complete the profile of Sarah Murray, international chef, using the notes in *italics* and the present perfect. What is the one factual mistake?

Sarah Murray was born in 1962 in Canada and got her first job as a hotel chef in 1989. Her career has been successful ever since (*Career very successful 1989 to the present*).

She 1 .... (*has the experience of specialising in many different kinds of cuisine*), but she always says her favourite dishes are Indian and Italian. She 2 .... (*has the experience of travelling all over the world*), but she is unusual amongst top chefs because she doesn't like staying in big hotels. She 3 .... (*has the experience of staying in small hotels*) in places such as Calcutta because she likes trying the local food.

She 4 .... (*married to Michael Whiteley 1992 to the present*), and they have two sons. They 5 .... (*moved to Florida in 1993 and still live there now*), but they also have a home in Toronto.

6 .... (*In the past she talked about stopping cooking and she still talks about it now*) when she stopped finding food interesting but it hasn't happened yet. Recently she 7 .... (*an offer from Bull Hotels to become their food director*). 8 .... (*She has the experience of working in Bull Hotels in the past*) and she always stays at a Bull Hotel whenever she travels, so she is expected to accept. This is good news for food lovers worldwide.

Classwork

1 **Work in pairs to complete one of the unfinished questions below.**

Example: Have you *been abroad* recently?

Have you .... recently? Have you already .... ?

Have you just ....? Have you .... yet?

Have you ever ....?

2 **Write your question on the board. Copy all the questions.**

3 **Go around the class and ask people the questions. Find someone who answers *Yes* to each question. Write their name next to the question. The person who gets a name for all the questions first is the winner.**

Example:

Have you been abroad recently? *Yes, I have.*

Where did you go? *The States.*

Unit 8 The present perfect continuous

Getting started

1 Read the article about some unusual Christmas cards. Why are they unusual?

....

Catherine Wild has been receiving Christmas cards from the same family for the past 17 years. This year the usual card dropped through her letter box from 'Pat and Roger and family' with an extra card they want passed on to Auntie Muriel. Mrs Wild, aged 67, has no idea who is sending the cards. She started receiving the cards after she bought her home in Worcester from a woman called Dawn. She spent years trying to solve the Christmas card puzzle, but now she has given up and puts the card up on the wall every Christmas. 'If only I knew who it was from!' said Mrs Wild.

(adapted from an article by Richard Smith in *The Independent*, 21 December 1996)

2 Look at examples a), b) and c) of different tenses from the text:

a) *Catherine Wild* <u>*has been receiving*</u> *Christmas cards from the same family for the past 17 years.*
b) *She* <u>*started*</u> *receiving the cards after she bought her home in Worcester from a woman called Dawn.*
c) *She spent years trying to solve the Christmas card puzzle, but now she* <u>*has given up*</u> *and puts the card up on the wall every Christmas.*

Match sentences a), b) and c) to the following tenses:
the past simple ..... the present perfect simple ..... the present perfect continuous .....

3 Match the tenses in Exercise 2 to the following uses:

a) an action in the past which has a result in the present ....
b) repeated actions which began in the past and are still continuing ....
c) a single past action ....

Looking at language

The present perfect continuous

Use

The present perfect continuous describes activities happening in the period **up to now**. It can be used:

1 to say how long an activity or situation has been in progress (usually with *for* and *since*). The activity (or situation) began in the past and is still going on or it has just stopped:
Catherine Wild ***has been receiving*** *Christmas cards from the same family* ***for*** *the past 17 years.*
She ***has been living*** *in Worcester* ***since*** *she bought the house.*

2 to focus on an activity itself. The result of the activity is **not** important. It is either still going on or it has just stopped:
A: *What* ***have*** *you* ***been doing****?* B: *I've* ***been cooking****.*
(the **cooking** is important; **what** you cooked is not)

Sometimes the past activity may have a present result:
A: *You look tired.* B: *Yes, I've* ***been sleeping*** *badly.*

Simple or continuous?

Compare the uses of the present perfect simple and the present perfect continuous.

We use the present perfect simple:	*We use the present perfect continuous:*
to show that an action was repeated: *I've* ***had*** *interviews* ***all year*** *but I still don't have a job.* or to say **how many times** it happened: *I've* ***had six interviews*** *but I still don't have a job.*	to show that an action was repeated: *I've* ***been having*** *interviews* ***all year*** *but I still don't have a job.* Note that we **cannot** say how many times it happened using the continuous: ~~*I've been having six interviews.*~~
to focus on the **result** or **completion** of an activity: A: *What* ***have*** *you* ***done*** *this afternoon?* B: *I've* ***watched*** *some athletics and* ***written*** *a letter.* (completed activities this afternoon)	to talk about the activity itself: A: *What* ***have*** *you* ***been doing*** *this afternoon?* B: *I've* ***been watching*** *the athletics.* (my activity this afternoon, which is not necessarily completed)
(See Unit 7 for more uses.)	We don't use adverbs like *before* and *already* with the present perfect continuous. We don't say: ~~*I've been seeing her before*~~. We say: *I've seen her before.*

Some verbs (see Stative verbs in Unit 3) are not often used in a continuous form. We use the present perfect simple for these verbs:

We don't say: ~~*I've been knowing her since I was at school.*~~
~~*They've been having that house for years.*~~

We say: *I've **known** her since I was at school.*
*They've **had** that house for years.*

See Unit 7 for the difference between *for* and *since*.

1 Are the sentences below right or wrong? Write *right* or *wrong*.

1 Oh dear. I've been breaking the window. ....
2 They've scored three goals already and it's only half time. ....
3 We've been having holidays in Spain for years. ....
4 How many exercises have you been doing? ....
5 I haven't understood these questions. ....

Form

The present perfect continuous is formed with *have / has + been + -ing.*

Positive statements	*Negative statements*	*Wh- questions*
I / you / we / they **have been working** she / he / it **has been working**	I **have not (haven't) been working** she **has not (hasn't) been working**	Where **have** they **been working?** Where **has** he **been working?**
Yes / No questions	*Positive short answers*	*Negative short answers*
Have they **been working?** **Has** he **been working?**	Yes, they **have**. Yes, he **has**.	No, they **haven't**. No, he **hasn't**.

Getting it right

Exercise 1 Understanding meaning

Tick (✓) the best statement for each response.

Statements	**Responses**
Example: I've been thinking about changing my job.	Oh really? What did you decide?
I've thought about changing my job. ..✓	
1 a) I've been writing a letter.	Oh. Have you posted it yet?
b) I've written a letter.	
2 a) I think he's been working in a restaurant.	Yes, I think he was a waiter.
b) I think he's worked in a restaurant.	
3 a) I've been thinking.	Have you? What about?
b) I've thought of something.	
4 a) They've been paying me too much.	Lucky you! For how long?
b) They've paid me too much.	
5 a) She's taken painkillers.	I know. I think she should stop.
b) She's been taking painkillers.	
6 a) I've had a problem with the computer.	What's the matter with it?
b) I've been having problems with the computer.	
7 a) He's climbed Mont Blanc, you know.	Really? When did he do that?
b) He's been climbing Mont Blanc, you know.	
8 a) I've been mending the roof.	I know. Have you nearly finished?
b) I've mended the roof.	

Extension

Write a response for each statement you didn't tick.

Example: I've been thinking about changing my job. Response: *Oh really? Why's that?*

Exercise 2 Matching

Complete each sentence, 1–11, with a suitable ending, a)–l). If two endings are possible, write both letters. You can use endings more than once.

Example: I've cut g), c)

1 I've been cutting ....
2 We've talked ....
3 We've been talking ....
4 The foreign minister has been visiting ....
5 The foreign minister has visited ....
6 He's been having ....
7 He's had ....
8 The kids have played ....
9 The kids have been playing ....
10 My mother's made ....
11 My mother's been making ....

a) another accident.
b) Brunei twice in the last year.
c) some pictures out of magazines.
d) football in the park since lunchtime.
e) a lot of arguments recently.
f) about you.
g) my finger, and it hurts!
h) my wedding dress. It's going to look wonderful when it's finished.
i) two games of cards already.
j) about getting a dog before, and the answer is 'No'!
k) my wedding dress. It's wonderful.
l) Malaysia, Brunei and the Philippines.

Exercise 3 Choosing the right tense

In this conversation, fill in the gaps using the verb in brackets in the past simple or the present perfect simple or continuous.

A: I'm exhausted. I 've been shopping (*shop*) all afternoon and I don't seem to have found anything.

B: What 1 .... (*you / look*) for?

A: Oh, 2 I .... (*try*) to find Suzie a birthday present.

B: Well, what does she like?

A: She loves clothes, so I've been to about ten clothes shops but I 3 .... (*not find*) anything suitable yet. I 4 .... (*go*) to about five others yesterday too!

B: She 5 .... (*read*) a lot recently, hasn't she? 6 .... (*you / think*) of a book? I 7 .... (*just / look*) at some really good new novels at that bookshop in the shopping centre.

A: Good idea – I'll have a look. What about you? Have you had a good day?

B: Well, I 8 .... (*look*) for weeks for a bag to match this jacket, and at last I 9 .... (*find*) one. Here it is!

▶ Exercise 4 Learning from learners

A student has asked her teacher to check an e-mail to a friend. The teacher has underlined the mistakes. Rewrite the mistakes using the past simple, present perfect simple or present perfect continuous.

> Hi Kyoko
> I'm sorry I didn't write for such a long time. How are you? **1** What you do since **2** I have last seen you in Tokyo last Christmas? I remember you weren't feeling too good. **3** Did you meet the man of your dreams yet? As for me, for the last two months **4** I am trying to do two things at once – preparing for my final exams in June, and looking for a job. **5** I've been having three interviews with different magazine companies, but **6** I don't have any luck yet. Did you know that **7** I wrote short weekly articles for the local newspaper since April? **8** I've been writing ten or twelve already. E-mail me soon and tell me your news.
> Bye!

Example: I haven't written ....

1 .... 5 ....

2 .... 6 ....

3 .... 7 ....

4 .... 8 ....

Classwork

1 **Sometimes we can tell what people have been doing by the way they look or how they say they feel. For example, working on the computer can give you sore eyes. Think of an activity and its effect. Then get into groups of three or four.**

2 **Imagine you have been doing this activity. Don't tell your group the activity but tell them, or show them, the effect.**

Example:
You could rub your eyes to show that you've got sore eyes.

3 **The group asks you questions, using the present perfect continuous, to find out what the activity was.**

Example:

Have you been chopping onions?	*No, I haven't.*
Have you been watching television?	*No, I haven't.*
Have you been using a computer?	*Yes, I have. Now it's your turn.*

4 **Continue until everyone in the group has had a turn.**

Unit 9

The past perfect

Getting started

1 **Read the unusual story and number the events in the box in the order they happened, 1–6.**

a) The plane took off without the pilot. .....
b) The plane had mechanical trouble. .....
c) The pilot got out to restart the plane. .....
d) The pilot took off. .....
e) The plane started to move along. .....
f) The pilot landed. .....

The plane that flew solo

Carol Hall looked out of her office window and wondered what was going on. A yellow, single-engine plane was moving along the runway, apparently ready for take-off, except that it just missed another aircraft that was coming in to land.

'We couldn't understand what the pilot was trying to do,' said Ms Hall.

A moment later, she found the answer, as the pilot rushed into her office and called the emergency services. His plane had left without him. If that was unusual, what followed was almost unbelievable, as the plane got faster, lifted off into the air, and climbed to 2,000 feet.

The pilot, Paul Sirks, had taken off early in the morning to meet friends for breakfast in Illinois.

But his plane began having mechanical trouble and as he landed at Grimes Field, the engine stopped – so he got out to restart it by turning the propeller. As he did so, the engine started. And before he could get back in, the plane began to move across the airfield.

'It just got away from him and took off,' Ms Hall explained.

2 **Put these events from the story in the correct points on the timeline below:**

a) The pilot called the emergency services.
b) The plane left without its pilot.

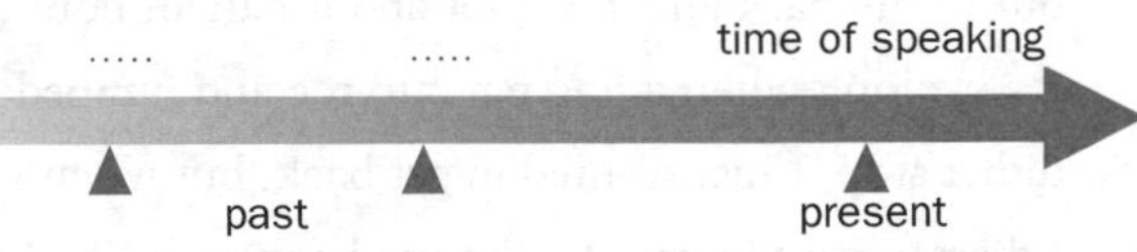

3 **Why is the past simple used for one event in the text (*the pilot ... called the emergency services*) and the past perfect used for another (*His plane had left without him.*)?**

....

Looking at language

The past perfect

Use

1 The past perfect is used when we are talking or writing about the past, and want to go back to an earlier time. This is usually for:

- giving information about what happened **before** the events of the story.
  *He remembered their previous meeting. She'd **told** him her life story.*
- explaining or commenting on something in the story (often following *because*). We often use words like *always, often, never*.

Event in a story	*Comment / explanation*
He took a second helping.	*He'd **always liked** ice cream.*
*I felt uneasy about him **because***	***I'd seen** his face somewhere before.*
They met at the café on the corner.	*They'**d been meeting** there for years.*

2 We choose the past perfect continuous when we talk about activities that continued for a time:

*It **had been snowing** heavily and the ground was white when John arrived.*
*After the match I had a sore throat because **I'd been shouting** so much.*

3 If the order of events is clear because of words like *after, before,* and *as soon as*, we do not always have to use the past perfect. Instead we can use the past simple:

*After he **had** his lunch he went out.* or *After he **had had** his lunch he went out.*

4 The past perfect is also common:

- in reported speech. Compare:
  *'We've already **seen** the film.'* (direct speech, with the present perfect)
  *They told me they **had** already **seen** the film.* (reported speech, with the past perfect)
  (See Units 19 and 20.)
- with *wish* to express regrets: *I wish **I'd worked** harder at school.* (See Unit 25.)
- in some conditional constructions: *If **I'd gone** to Thailand instead of Turkey I wouldn't have met you.* (See Unit 25.)

1 Read about a boy who was bitten by a dog. Put phrases a)–d) in the correct gaps.

a) bit me   b) I'd been running   c) had bitten me   d) I was running

That day we did a long run. I think it was five or six miles round the park. Anyway, I'd come out of the park and **1** ..... for about half an hour and I was going back towards school, and **2** ..... along when a dog ran into me and jumped up and **3** ..... on the leg. It didn't hurt so I didn't stop, I just wanted to get back, but when I got back to school, it was hurting a lot. I discovered the dog **4** ..... quite badly and I had to go to hospital.

Form

The past perfect simple is formed with *had* + past participle, and the past perfect continuous is *had been* + *-ing*.

Positive statements	*Negative statements*	*Wh- questions*
I / you etc. **had worked** I / you etc. **had been working**	they **had not (hadn't) worked** she **had not (hadn't) been working**	Where **had** they **worked**? How long **had** she **been working**?
Yes / No questions	*Positive short answers*	*Negative short answers*
Had they **worked**? **Had** she **been working**?	Yes, they **had**. Yes, she **had**.	No, they **hadn't**. No, she **hadn't**.

Getting it right

Exercise 1 Thinking about time

A The text opposite is about the mysterious disappearance of Jim Thompson in Malaysia in 1967.

Read it and underline any examples of the past perfect.

When they got back at about 4.00, the news was not good. They had searched the main paths from the house and with help from local people they had also searched a large area of the jungle, but had found nothing. Martin had gone down to the town and asked at the taxi and bus stands, but again had found out nothing. No one had seen a tall man in his sixties. Martin and Jones had a rest and then went out again to make further enquiries.

This time they went to the golf club in Tanah Rata to ask people there if anyone had seen Jim. When they got there they found that the police had just been and interviewed everyone. One man claimed he had seen a man that looked like Jim at about 3.00 the afternoon before, walking down the hill from the golf club. When Martin and Jones asked him more questions, however, they discovered that the description did not really match. The man he had seen was wearing blue trousers and a white jacket, but Jim was wearing a pair of grey trousers and had left his jacket behind.

B In the columns below, write four events that happened before 4.00, four events that happened after 4.00, and one event on that day for which we do not know the time.

Before 4.00	*After 4.00*	*Don't know*
Example: *they searched the main paths*	....	....
....	....	....
....	....	....
....	....	....
....	....	....
....	....	....

This is a true story. Unfortunately, no one knows what happened to Jim Thompson. He has never been seen since his mysterious disappearance.

Exercise 2 Comments and explanations

Add a comment or explanation to the sentences below using the words in brackets and the past perfect simple or continuous.

Example: That year he bought a large and expensive Mercedes. *He'd always wanted one.*
(*always / want*)

1 She refused the shellfish when it was offered at her table. ....
(*never / like*)

2 He looked exhausted and was breathing heavily. .... (*run*)

3 They finally let him have a better computer. ....
(*ask for / for weeks*)

4 I was surprised when she ordered a dessert because ....
(*already have / three courses*)

5 His health wasn't too good. ....
(*have / several operations*)

6 She was delighted to be offered the work. .... (*just / lose her job*)

7 I wasn't able to drive them to the airport. ....
(*car / break down*)

8 I was relieved when the bus came. .... (*wait / since 7.00*)

9 When Jim Thompson's friends woke up after their lunchtime sleep he wasn't there. They didn't expect him to be out long because ....
(*not take / jacket*)

10 Their performance was wonderful. ....
(*practise / for months*)

Exercise 3 Learning from learners

Read the extracts from three learners' essays. Underline any mistakes with tenses and correct them. If there are no mistakes, tick (✓) the extract.

Example: My mother packed the picnic lunch and we all collected together our things. At last everything had been ready for us to go. was

1 Mimi's family moved into the house next to mine. She became my best friend and we did everything together. ....

2 We were lucky that a group of scouts left a rope which helped us reach the bottom safely. ....

3 It has been almost six years since I last saw her. I miss everything we had done together. ....

4 This was his second marriage. He had been married before, but he had become bored. ....

5 He told his ex-wife that he has decided to marry again. ....

6 After lunch my brother and I went exploring. We had climbed a small hill behind the wood. ....

7 He met her at a disco. She had been dancing with one of his colleagues. ....

8 When I first had met her she was very quiet. ....

9 We couldn't find the way home because we have lost the path. ....

Which extracts are from an essay about: a) a friend's marriage breakdown? b) the learner's best friend c) a picnic?

a) .... b) .... c) example...............

Exercise 4 Text completion

In this story about an argument between neighbours, fill in the gaps using the verb in brackets in the past perfect simple or continuous. You can use any other language you need.

The arguments started quite suddenly one Sunday. Everything had been perfectly friendly between the neighbours up to that point.

Graham had just got home (*get home*) when his neighbour, Sally, stopped him on the path they shared. She was holding up her muddy hands – she **1** .... (*garden*) and she looked very angry.

'I was just going to cut back my rose bushes but someone **2** .... (*do*) it. Was it you?'

Graham denied it, but secretly he felt quite pleased because the bushes **3** .... (*grow*) over the path. A few days later Graham received a note through his door asking him to cut down one of the trees in his garden because it was blocking Sally's view. He wrote her a note refusing. When he got home from work the next day, he discovered that someone **4** .... (*cut down*). He was furious.

A few weeks later, Sally decided to pick some vegetables from her garden. She had seen them the day before and she 5 .... (*decide*) they were ready to eat. But they 6 .... (*go*)!

She was very angry with Graham, but then she and Graham read about someone who 7 .... (*cut down*) bushes and trees. The police 8 .... (*catch*) him while he was cutting down a small tree!

Classwork

1 Work alone. Choose one of the sentences below, and think of a way of ending it using the past perfect.

a) She was wearing one red sock and one white, because ...

b) She was fired from her job because ...

c) She looked exhausted because ...

d) She was furious with Holly because ...

e) She spent much more than usual because ...

f) She got home more than three hours late because ...

g) The house was a complete mess because ...

h) She couldn't afford a taxi because ...

2 Tell the class your ending only. Can they guess the correct beginning?

Example:

A: *Here's my ending: 'she'd forgotten to post her letters.'*

B: *Is it d)?*

A: *That's right.*

Unit

10 Going to *and* will

Getting started

1 **Read Stories 1 and 2 about unusual sea crossings and answer the questions.**

a) Which types of boat are mentioned?

....

....

b) Which type was unsuccessful?

....

Story 1

In the late 1960s, Kenneth Blyton successfully crossed the English Channel in a metal bottle with a small motor. It was his third crossing, but his first time by bottle. When he landed in France, he described his next plan. 'I have already crossed by bed and by barrel,' he said. 'Next year I'm going to cross by giant banana.'

Story 2

A man from Kentucky tried to row across the icy Bering Strait, between Alaska and Russia, in a bath. Unfortunately, things went a bit wrong for him. According to the explorer, 'By late afternoon on the fourth day, although the sun was still high, the sea went rather thick. Next morning I was frozen in.'

No problem. He left the bath in the ice and walked to land, where he told reporters, 'I'll try again in the summer.'

2 **Look at these sentences from Stories 1 and 2 and answer the questions.**

i) *Next year I'm going to cross by giant banana.*

ii) *I'll try again in the summer.*

a) Which sentence suggests that the man decided something **before** speaking? .....

b) Which suggests he decided at **the same time as** speaking? .....

Looking at language

Going to and *will*

Use

Be going to and *will* can be used to talk about the future. Sometimes the difference between them is small, but note these points:

We usually choose *be going to* when:

1 we've already made a decision:
*Next year I'm **going to** cross by giant banana.*
*I'm **going to** study Arabic next term.* (I've already decided)

2 the present situation tells us something about the future:
*She's **going to** win.* (she's only got to win one more point)

We usually choose *will* when:

3 we haven't decided about the future yet, or we make a prediction. We often use words such as *think*, *probably*, *sure*, *suppose*, *definitely*, *doubt*:
*We think we'**ll** buy them some glasses as a wedding present.* (haven't decided yet)
*I'**ll** probably go home in a few minutes.* (haven't decided yet)
*She'**ll** definitely feel homesick in the States.* (prediction)
*The shops **will** be really busy tomorrow.* (prediction)
*I doubt that you'**ll** see him tonight.* (prediction)

4 we decide at the time of speaking to do something (this can be an offer or promise or a response to an offer):
A: *Have you bought Sally a birthday present?* B: *No! I'**ll** buy her some flowers at lunchtime.* (decision at the time of speaking)
A: *Oh, I've forgotten to turn off the iron!* B: *Don't worry. I'**ll** do it.* (an offer)
*I'm sorry. I'm busy, but I promise I'**ll** help you later.*
(See Units 39 and 40 for *shall* in offers and suggestions.)

The choice of *be going to* or *will* depends on the speaker's emphasis. Compare:
*What's he **going to** do when he gets here?* (I think he's thought about it)
*What **will** he do when he gets here?* (I don't think he's decided)

1 Are these sentences right or wrong? Write *right* or *wrong* and correct the wrong sentences.

1 A: So, have you thought about your holiday yet? B: Yeah, we'll go to Austria.

....

2 A: Oh dear. I've left my keys in the car. B: Don't worry. I'll go back and get them.

....

3 A: Would you like me to help you? B: Oh, no thanks. I'm going to be OK.

....

4 A: Have you heard from Miyoko? B: Yes, she'll have a baby in April.

....

Form

	Will	Be going to
Positive statements	I / you etc. **will** (I'll / you'll) stay	I **am** (I'm) / you **are** (you're) etc. **going to** stay
Negative statements	I **will not (won't)** stay	I **am** (I'm) **not going to** stay
Questions	**Will** you stay? Where **will** you stay?	**Are** you **going to** stay? Where **are** you **going to** stay?
Short answers	Yes, I **will**. No, I **won't**.	Yes, I **am**. No, I'**m not**.

Pronunciation and spelling

- In informal and spoken English *will* is contracted: ***I'll*** (/aɪl/), ***you'll*** (/juːl/), ***we'll*** (/wiːl/), ***she'll*** (/ʃiːl/), ***he'll*** (/hiːl/), ***it'll*** (/ɪtəl/), ***they'll*** (/ðeiəl/) *be here in a minute.*
- We often pronounce *be going to* /gənə/, and spell it *gonna* in very informal English:
  *I'm **gonna** see her tonight.*

Other points

- *Shall* (*shan't*) can be used in place of *will* (*won't*) for Use 4 to emphasise our decision. It is usually only used with *I* and *we*:
  *I **shall** phone the doctor immediately.*
- *Won't* can be used to talk about annoying problems:
  *The coffee machine **won't** turn off.*
- Future-in-the-past: *was / were going to* can be used if you planned something but didn't do it:
  I was going to make something to eat, but in the end I went out.

Getting it right

Exercise 1 Thinking about use

In this conversation about a wedding, match each example of *be going to* or *will* to Uses 1–4 in *Looking at language*. You can use each rule more than once.

A: What *are you going to wear* to the wedding? ..1..
B: I don't know. I thought about wearing my suit, but **1** *I'll have to buy* new shoes if I do that. What about you? 1 .....
A: I have no idea. I don't know what **2** *I'm going to do*. I suppose **3** *I'll buy* something new, but I don't know what. Have you bought them a present yet? 2 ..... 3 .....
B: No, but I know what **4** *I'm going to get* them. 4 .....
A: Oh, what?
B: A painting of their village. A friend of mine is painting it.

A: That sounds great. I'm sure 5 *they'll love* it. 5 .....

B: Hope so. Have you got anything yet?

A: No, I haven't. Judy loves cooking, so I've ordered a new cookbook for them. I just haven't had time to pick it up.

B: Oh, 6 *I'll get* it for you if you like – I'm going into town now. Which shop is it? 6 .....

A: That's really sweet of you, but it's OK, thanks. I need to go into town and look for something to wear, so 7 *I'll do* it then. 7 .....

B: Well, why don't you come into town with me now? 8 *I'm going to do* a bit of shopping. 8 .....

A: OK. 9 *I'll just get* my purse, and we'd better take umbrellas. I think 9 .....
10 *it's going to rain*, don't you? 10 .....

Exercise 2 Learning from learners

In this conversation between two learners, underline the best form: *will* or *be going to*.

A: I get very confused when I think about *be going to* and *will*. Can you help at all?

B: *I'll / I will / I'm going to* try. When you make a decision at the time of speaking you're more likely to use 1 *will / be going to*. 2 *Will / Be going to* is used if you have already made your decision.

A: OK. Anything else?

B: Another use of 3 *will / be going to* is for making predictions. 4 *Will / Be going to* is more likely when the present situation tells us about the future, so for example when you go into an expensive restaurant you might say 5 '*It'll / It's going to* be expensive' because you can see the expensive surroundings.

A: You make it sound easy! 6 I think *I'll / I will / I'm going to* buy a new grammar book. I saw a good one yesterday.

B: Good idea. Perhaps 7 *I'll / I will / I'm going to* do that too.

Exercise 3 Choosing the right future form

Complete each sentence using the verb or phrase in brackets and *will* or *be going to*. You may need to make some verbs negative.

Example: I've had a cold for ages. It just won't go (*go*) away.

1 Perhaps I .... (*stay*) at home tonight and watch a film.

2 I .... (*ask*) Sally to walk the dog, but then my son offered.

3 We .... (*have*) a barbecue but it started to rain.

4 I feel awful. I think I .... (*be*) sick.

5 A: Careful with my camera! B: I .... (*not break*) it, promise!

6 The two men .... probably .... (*reach*) the Amazon sometime in early November.

7 That new video I bought doesn't work. It .... (*not record*).

8 It's raining, so she .... probably .... (*come*) by car.

9 Don't try to stop me. I .... (*go*) and see her.

Exercise 4 Writing about the future

Write sentences, thinking carefully about which forms of *will* or *be going to* you need to use.

Examples: Write something you have already decided about the future.

I'm going to study business next year.

Make a prediction about daily life in the future.

I think people will work from home much more in future.

1 Write something you have already decided about the future.

....

2 Make a prediction about daily life in the future.

....

3 Write something your country's government has decided to do in the future.

....

4 Write about a past change of plan in your life.

....

5 Write about something you have decided to do in the future.

....

6 Write about the weather later today or tomorrow.

....

7 Write a promise about your future behaviour.

....

8 Write a question about somebody's future intention.

....

Classwork

Some people believe that dreams can predict the future. In small groups, discuss what you think the following dream images might predict.

Example:
Combing your hair
A: *I think it means you're going to try to change something in your life.*
B: *Good idea, or maybe it means you're going to solve a problem.*

a) Going up an escalator
b) Going down an escalator
c) Green grass
d) A journey
e) A hand
f) A wolf
g) A dove
h) A parcel or package

Unit

11 Present tenses for talking about the future

Getting started

1 **Read part of a conversation between two teachers about their next school holiday and answer the questions.**

a) What are their holiday plans?

....

....

b) What, do you think, are the relationships between:

Doug and Robin ....

....

Doug and Christine ....

....

Debbie and Mark? ....

....

Debbie: What are you doing in your holidays?
Doug: Robin hasn't got school that week, and Christine's working. I'll be in charge of Robin for the week. He wants to go to the swimming pool, but I'm hoping to do as little as possible.
Debbie: You haven't asked me what I'm doing. I'm going on holiday with Mark.
Doug: You're going on holiday? Where are you going?
Debbie: We're going to Scotland.
Doug: Scotland? Whereabouts?
Debbie: Well, we're going to St Andrews where I went to university.
Doug: Is that where you and Mark met?
Debbie: No, Mark's never been to St Andrews.

2 **Look at these extracts from the conversation. Decide if statements a)–c) are true or false.**

... Christine's working.
You haven't asked me what I'm doing. I'm going on holiday ...
... we're going to St Andrews ...

The underlined verb forms:

a) are in the present continuous tense. ....

b) refer to something happening at the time of speaking. ....

c) describe future activities which have already been planned. ....

Looking at language

Present tenses for talking about the future

The names of tenses in English are not always very helpful. The **present continuous** and **present simple** can both be used to talk about **future** events.

The present continuous with future meaning

We can use the present continuous to talk about **planned** or **arranged** future events. The time of the future event is either given or understood:

Robin hasn't got school that week, and Christine's ***working****.* (it's already arranged)

I spoke to Simon yesterday. We're ***having*** *lunch tomorrow.* (we arranged it when we spoke)

The present continuous or *be going to*?

The difference between *be going to* and the present continuous for future plans is often small:

I'm going to see / I'm seeing *him tomorrow.*

Note, however:

The **present continuous** is more likely when an arrangement is made:

Sue and I ***are having*** *lunch together tomorrow.* (she knows and I know)

For personal intentions, we use ***be going to:***

I'm going to *visit my cousins in Australia next summer, if I have enough money.* (not yet fixed with the cousins)

See Unit 10 for more details of *be going to*.

The present simple with future meaning

The present simple is used for future events which are part of a timetable:

My plane ***leaves*** *at 4.30, so I need to be at the airport by 3.00.* (it's on a timetable)

His new job ***starts*** *on Monday. He's really looking forward to it.* (the contract start date is Monday)

We ***leave*** *the beach at 12.00 and* ***climb*** *into the mountains.* (an extract from a travel itinerary)

Be as a main verb in the present simple is common in spoken English to refer to the future:

Don't worry. ***I'm*** *here tomorrow so I'll let you in.*

She's 50 next week, so I think we should plan a surprise.

1 **Underline the verb which refers to future time in the conversation.**

A: I'm looking for a book about modern Greek. Have you got any?

B: I don't think we have any here, but our other shop keeps a lot of language titles. Is it urgent?

A: Well, my course starts at the end of September.

Other points

We use **present** forms after *when*, *if* and *as soon as* to refer to the future:

If I see her, I'll tell her.

As soon as he gets back, we'll start the meeting.

When you're talking to her later today, ask her about her weekend.

See Units 2 and 3 for details of the form and other uses of the present simple and present continuous tenses.

Getting it right

Exercise 1 Thinking about meaning

Decide if the verbs in *italics* in the sentences refer to present time (p) or future time (f).

Example: I'*m spending* a few weeks with an uncle in the States this summer. ..f..

1 I can't find Barbara. Maybe she's *meeting* the others for lunch. .....
2 When you *see* her, could you tell her to give me a call? .....
3 The show *starts* at 8.30 every day except Monday. .....
4 I hope everyone's ready. We *leave* first thing in the morning. .....
5 I can't talk to you then. I'*m meeting* Joe for coffee. .....
6 Sorry about the noise. My neighbour's *having* a party. .....
7 I'*m going to make* something for supper. Are you hungry? .....
8 After 12 weeks in London, the show *opens* on Broadway at the end of the month. .....
9 We'*re* at home next weekend, aren't we? We've been invited to a party. .....

Exercise 2 Choosing the best way to talk about the future

Fill in the gaps with a suitable form of the verb in brackets.

Example: A: You're looking pleased with yourself. What's happened?

B: I've won some tickets for Disneyland. I ..'m taking.. (*take*) the children next month.

1 My exams .... (*start*) in two weeks so I've got to work hard. As soon as I .... (*get*) my degree, I'll try and find work abroad.

2 My sister .... (*get married*) next month. I .... (*go*) to the wedding but my boyfriend can't come. He's got to work then.

3 A: What's the director's programme for tomorrow?

B: He's got a really busy day. He .... (*arrive*) at 9.00 and .... (*have*) three meetings before lunch. They're about the conference which .... (*open*) on 3 March.

4 Don't forget to phone Dad when you .... (*get*) to Paris. He won't be very pleased if you .... (*forget*).

5 This season's gone really quickly. We've only got one more match! Who .... we .... (*play*)?

Exercise 3 Learning from learners

In the conversation below, two students overuse *will* to talk about the future. If a present form is more suitable, <u>underline</u> the verb phrase and write a correction. Not all examples of *will* need replacing.

A: What <u>will you do</u> at the weekend? — *are you doing*

B: I haven't decided yet. Maybe I'll go shopping. I'll meet my friend Noriko on Saturday and we'll decide together. What about you? Will you do anything interesting?

A: Oh, I will go to the country. My friend's got a house there.

B: That sounds nice. Will you drive? You've got a car, haven't you?

A: No, actually I haven't any more. It broke down and was too expensive to fix. I'll get the train to Ipoh, which is the nearest town and my friend will meet me.

B: When will you go? Tonight?

A: No, I'll get the early train tomorrow which will get in at 10.00 in the morning, so it still gives me plenty of time there.

B: Well, have a good time.

A: Thanks, and you.

1 ....

2 ....

3 ....

4 ....

5 ....

6 ....

7 ....

8 ....

9 ....

Exercise 4 Completing conversations

Complete the conversations using a present tense you have studied in this unit.

Example: A: What are you doing at the weekend?

B: Nothing much but *I'm going shopping on Saturday.*

A: Are you looking for anything in particular or just going for fun?

1 A: I really like camping. I think it's the best kind of holiday.

B: So do I. In fact ....

A: Oh, I've been there. I'll give you my maps if you like.

2 A: We're going to Singapore for our honeymoon. Did I tell you?

B: No! That's wonderful. .... ?

A: We're having the first two nights in the Raffles Hotel and then we're moving to a cheaper place.

3 A: I haven't seen Maisie for months. Have you seen her at all?

B: No, but ....

A: Oh, well, can you give her my love?

4 A: Don't forget you're coming to the cinema tonight.

B: No, of course not. .... ?

A: Seven thirty, but let's meet outside at 7.15, shall we?

5 A: Hello, 874372.

B: Hello, this is Sophie. I'm just ringing to see how you are.

A: Oh, I'm much better thanks. The doctor says I can go out in a couple of days.

B: Oh good. .... Can I get anything for you?

A: That's very kind. Yes, actually. Could you get me some milk?

6 A: Laura's growing really fast. I can't believe she's one next week!

B: .... ?

A: No, we're not. We haven't got room for a big party and she's too young anyway.

Classwork

1 What is your perfect holiday? Plan a holiday by choosing one option from each column in the chart.

Example:
A skiing holiday in a large hotel in Japan in winter.

Type of holiday	*Accommodation*	*Country*	*Time of year*
beach	large hotel	France	spring
skiing	camping	Japan	summer
sightseeing	small hotel	Argentina	autumn
cruise	apartment	Egypt	winter

2 Ask questions using the present continuous with future meaning and try to find someone in the class who is planning the same holiday as you.

Example:
A: *Where are you staying on holiday?*
B: *In a hotel.*
A: *Me too. What … ?*

3 If you find someone, plan a programme for someone going on this holiday. Tell the class about it, using the present simple.

Example:
On Monday you visit the Great Pyramid and on Tuesday you fly to Aswan …

4 If you can't find anyone, join other students who have not found a match and plan a different holiday together.

Unit 12

The future continuous and the future perfect

Getting started

1 **What do you think will be different about medicine and the treatment of diseases in 20 or 30 years' time?**

....

2 **Read the text about scientists' predictions. How many different ways of diagnosing problems does it discuss?**

....

Will we be using doctors in the future?

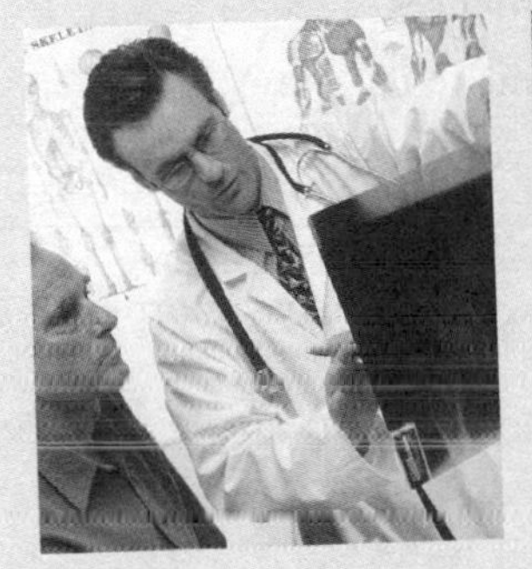

In the future doctors will be diagnosing illnesses differently, but we may not need to use doctors at all. We will be able to decide for ourselves what the problem is. We will look up symptoms on the Internet and order a testing kit to check our blood for diseases we think we have. We may not even have to do this. Science will have advanced so much that we will have microchips in our bodies to monitor our blood pressure, temperature and heartbeat on a daily basis.

3 **Match the underlined verb forms from the text with the correct tense names, i)–iii).**

a) *... doctors will be diagnosing illnesses differently* .....
b) *We will look up symptoms on the Internet* .....
c) *Science will have advanced so much* .....

i) the future with *will*
ii) the future continuous
iii) the future perfect

4 **Fill in the gaps in the descriptions with the correct tense names from Exercise 3.**

To make predictions about the future in general we often use a) ....

To predict an action in progress at a particular time in the future we use b) ....

c) .... locates an action that will happen **before** a particular time in the future.

Looking at language

The future continuous and the future perfect

The future continuous: use

We use the future continuous:

1 To describe or predict an activity in progress at a particular time in the future:
*This time next week **I'll be flying** to Mexico.*

2 To describe a future action or event that is already organised, decided or known. Compare:
*Don't worry, **I'll be picking** Karen up at 8.00.* (already decided)
*OK, **I'll pick** Karen up at 8.00.* (decision at the time of speaking)
This use sounds more formal than the present continuous for future plans. (See Unit 11.)

3 To describe something we know is happening now somewhere else:
*I mustn't phone my father now. **He'll be watching** the football.*

1 Which use of the future continuous, 1, 2 or 3, are these sentences?

a) *I'll be seeing* Terry tomorrow. Is there anything you want me to tell him? ....
b) On Monday at this time *you'll be taking* your exam, poor you. ....
c) Is it 5.00 already? That means Grace *will be leaving* work. ....
d) I'm sorry I can't go for a coffee with you but *I'll be working* on Thursday morning. ....

The future perfect: use

We use the future perfect:

1 To describe or predict an event that will be completed before a particular time in the future:
*Phil **will have completed** his course by this time next month.*

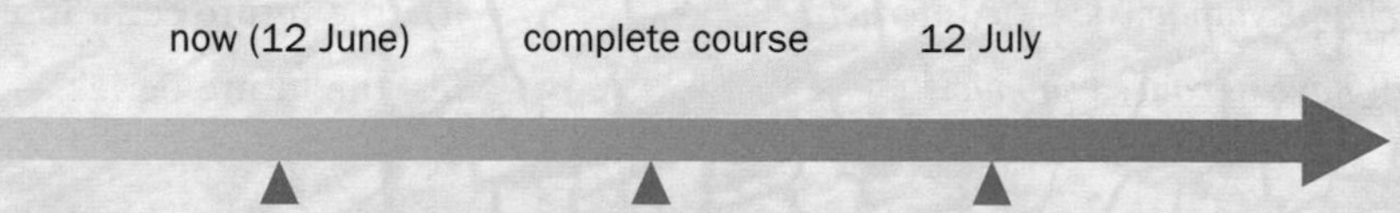

2 When you're sure, because of your knowledge of events, that something has happened somewhere else:
*Maddie **will have met** Peter at the airport by now.* (I know the plane arrived at 4.00 and it is now 4.30)

The future perfect with *in* and *by*
We use *by* + fixed points of time with the future perfect:
by the 4th of December, by my birthday, by the summer, by this time next week.
We use *in* + period of time + *time* with the future perfect:
in a couple of hours' time, in a week's time, in two days' time.

2 Label the timeline to show the meaning of this sentence:
Pierre will have sold his house by the time we all next meet.

Form

The future continuous is formed with *will* + *be* + *-ing* form. The future perfect is formed with *will* + *have* + past participle.

	The future continuous	*The future perfect*
Positive statements	I / you etc. **will (I'll) be flying**	I / you etc. **will (I'll) have flown**
Negative statements	I / you etc. **will not (won't) be flying**	I / you etc. **will not (won't) have flown**
Questions	**Will** he **be flying?** Where **will** he **be flying?**	**Will** he **have flown?** Where **will** he **have flown** to?
Positive short answers	Yes, he **will.**	Yes, he **will.**
Negative short answers	No, he **won't.**	No, he **won't.**

Other points

- *Could, might* and *may* make predictions less certain:
  *Doctors **could be diagnosing** illnesses differently in the future.*
  ***I might have finished** this project by next week. You never know.*
- We don't use *could* in negative sentences. We say: *Doctors **might not be using** traditional ways of diagnosing illnesses in the future.* We don't say: ~~*Doctors couldn't be using traditional ways of diagnosing illnesses in the future.*~~
- Texts that talk about the future often contain **a mixture** of the future with *will*, the future perfect and the future continuous:
  *I got a really cheap package holiday deal to Malaysia at the last moment. **I'll be touring** round the country, staying in some really nice hotels. **I'll probably be able to** meet up with Helen while I'm there too – she'**ll have finished** her contract in Singapore a few days before I arrive.*

Getting it right

Exercise 1 Thinking about tenses

Match the grammar rules, a)–e), to the example sentences, 1–5.

Rules

a) Use the **future continuous** to predict something in progress at a particular time in the future.

b) Use the **future continuous** to describe something that is already organised for a particular time in the future.

c) Use the **future continuous** to describe something we know is happening now somewhere else.

d) Use the **future perfect** with time expressions to show that an event will happen **before** a particular time.

e) Use the **future perfect** when you're sure that something has already happened somewhere else.

Example: By four o'clock tomorrow *I'll have taken* my driving test. ..d)

1 Don't worry. *I'll have tidied* my room by the time your friends arrive. .....

2 Moira *will be coming round* for a meal this evening. .....

3 It's nearly lunchtime. My friend in the USA *will be getting up* now. .....

4 Lucky you! This time next week *you'll be lying* on a beach in Thailand. .....

5 It's half past five. Kate *will have finished* her interview by now. .....

Exercise 2 Choosing the best tense

Underline the correct tenses in the text below about future changes in the medical world. Sometimes you will be able to underline both alternatives.

Scientists predict many advances in medicine over the next 50 years. The role of the doctor *will change* / *will be changing* dramatically in the future. We 1 *will no longer have* / *will no longer have had* our own doctor but we 2 *will contact* / *will be contacting* a doctor on the Internet. In a few minutes the doctor 3 *will diagnose* / *will have diagnosed* your problem and told you what medicine is needed.

Other areas that 4 *will change* / *will have changed* include old age. Scientists predict that in 50 years' time people 5 *will be dying* / *will have died* at a much older age than now. By the year 2050 we 6 *will all be living* / *will all have lived* until we are at least 100. By 2050 scientists 7 *will have found* / *will find* cures for illnesses such as Parkinson's, and other illnesses 8 *will be becoming* / *will have become* easier to avoid because of genetic knowledge. People 9 *will be having* / *will have had* children later in life because the 'biological clock' will no longer be a problem.

Exercise 3 Future perfect or continuous?

Put the verbs in brackets into the future perfect or future continuous.

Example: My holidays start tomorrow. I wonder what I *'ll be doing* (*do*) at six o'clock tomorrow evening?

A: I think I **1** .... probably .... (*work*) this time next year.

B: Really? Have you got something planned?

A: Yes. I **2** .... (*join*) the family company when I've got my degree.

B: Lucky you.

A: I wonder what we **3** .... (*do*) in two years' time.

B: Who knows!

A: I expect we **4** .... still .... (*study*) English here.

B: Not me. I **5** .... (*take*) my exams by then.

A: Lucky Ruth. Her flight left this morning so she **6** .... (*arrive*) in Jamaica by now.

B: Yes. I wish I was with her, don't you?

A: Yes.

A: Shall we call Lorenzo and ask him for his advice?

B: Not now. He **7** .... (*watch*) that stupid programme that he never misses and he won't answer the phone.

A: Well, we **8** .... (*finish*) this by the time he's ready to answer the phone, so that's no good.

A: I can't believe that I **9** .... (*work*) here for ten years next week.

B: No. It seems like only yesterday that you began. The question is, **10** .... you .... (*work*) here in another ten years' time?

A: Who knows?

Exercise 4 Thinking about your future

For each of the following times, write what you think you will (or won't) be doing at that time, or something that you will (or won't) have done by then.

Example: the end of this month *I will have sent more than 150 e-mails to friends by the end of this month.*

1 midnight tonight ....

2 this time next week ....

3 the end of this year ....

4 the middle of next summer ....

5 ten years from now ....

Classwork

1 **To play the board game below you will need a dice and coins.**

2 **Work in groups of three or four. On pieces of paper write 20 time expressions for the future using *at*, *in* or *by*.**

Examples: by this time next week | at 6.00 tonight | in two years' time

3 **Put the pieces of paper upside down in a pile. Take turns to throw the dice, and turn over a piece of paper. Make a sentence using the future perfect or continuous, the word in the square and the time expression on your piece of paper. If the sentence is correct, move forward two places. If not, stay where you are. If the sentence is correct and you land on a tunnel (●), you can go down to the tunnel on the next row. The first player to reach the end is the winner.**

Example: Dice 3, word: *shopping*, at 6.00 tonight *At 6.00 tonight, I'll be doing the shopping.*

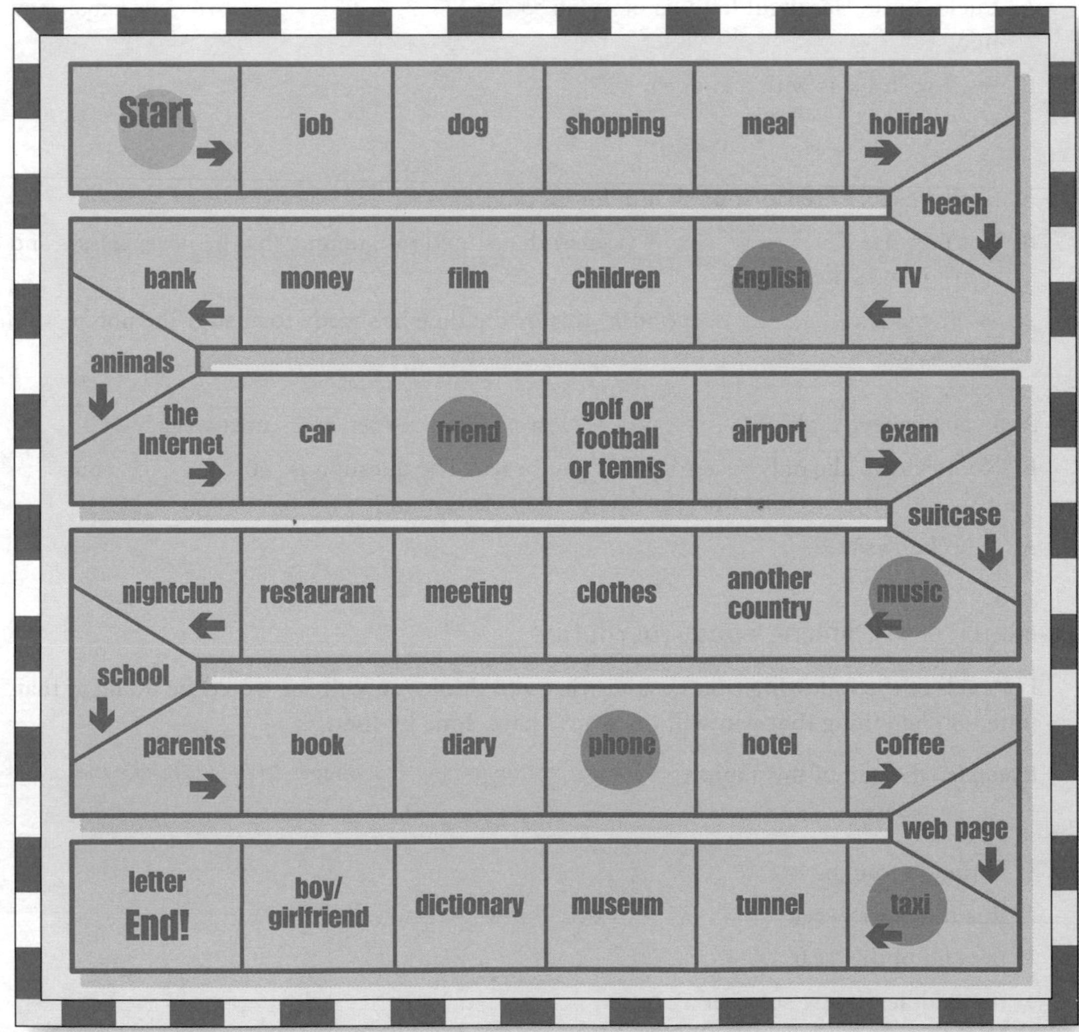

Review unit

1 Units 2–12 Time and tense

Exercise 1 Mixed tenses Units 2–12

Match the sentences, 1–10, to the tenses, a)–h), and the uses, i)–xi). You can use tenses a)–h) more than once.

Example: I've met a few famous singers.

1 I often work evenings and weekends.

2 I'm working for a local radio station just now.

3 I don't want to change my job at the moment.

4 I'd always wanted to work in the music industry.

5 I bought my first CD when I was ten.

6 I was running a disco when I got this job.

7 I've been with this radio station for two years.

8 I'm tired – I've been preparing tonight's programme.

9 I'm spending some time in America next year.

10 I'll play your favourite song tonight.

Tenses	*Uses*
a) Present simple	i) A temporary present activity
b) Present continuous	ii) A promise about the future
c) Past simple	iii) A repeated action or situation
d) Past continuous and past simple	~~iv) A past experience~~
~~e) Present perfect simple~~	v) A background situation and past event
f) Present simple and present perfect continuous	vi) An event at a particular time in the past
g) Past perfect simple	vii) A present result of a past activity
h) Future with *will*	viii) A planned future activity
	ix) A past before the past we're interested in
	x) A temporary situation (verb doesn't take the continuous)
	xi) Started in the past and not finished

Example: e) iv)

1 .... 2 .... 3 .... 4 .... 5 .... 6 .... 7 .... 8 .... 9 .... 10 ....

Exercise 2 Past tenses Units 4, 5, 9

In the story below, put the verbs in brackets into a suitable tense.

California Highway Patrol officer Dave Guild ..*stopped*.. (*stop*) a moving car because its bonnet 1 .... (*be*) open and a man 2 .... (*be*) under it. He 3 .... (*be*) a mechanic and 4 .... (*work*) on the engine. The driver and the mechanic 5 .... (*have*) trouble with the car and the man under the bonnet 6 .... (*keep*) the engine running. They 7 .... (*not understand*) why the police 8 .... (*stop*) them.

Exercise 3 Mixed tenses Units 2, 3, 4, 7, 8, 10

Underline the best tenses in the text. Sometimes you will be able to underline both alternatives.

New baby elephant

Workers at Chester Zoo *are celebrating* / *celebrate* a new arrival. The zoo **1** *will show* / *is showing* its new baby elephant to the public tomorrow. She **2** *was* / *had been* born just before Christmas. She **3** *drinks* / *has drunk* 12 litres of milk a day, **4** *is putting on* / *has put on* 30 kg in just four weeks and now **5** *is weighing* / *weighs* 135 kg.

Viewers of a children's television programme **6** *chose* / *have chosen* the baby elephant's name. Her mother **7** *isn't looking after* / *hasn't been looking after* her, but she **8** *is being* / *is* lively and well. There **9** *are being* / *are* between 34,000 and 51,000 of these elephants in the wild and the population **10** *is falling* / *falls* fast.

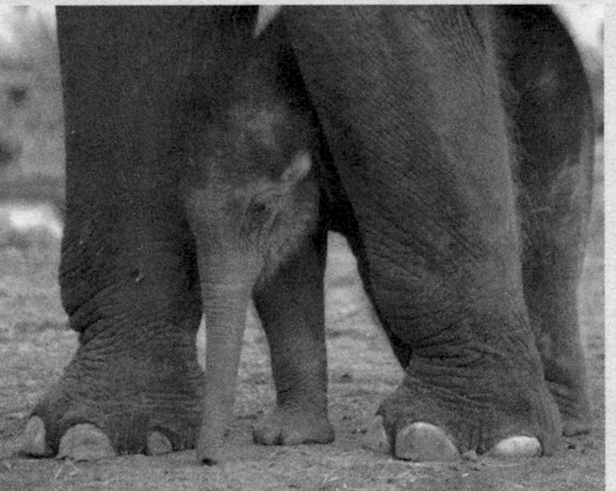

(adapted from an article by Nicholas Schoon in *The Independent*, 19 January 1996)

Exercise 4 Mixed tenses Units 2–12

Match the sentence beginnings, 1–12, to the endings, a)–m).

Example: I haven't got many smart clothes because ..d)

1 I usually wear a dress to work but .....
2 Olivia arrived late and .....
3 The film started while .....
4 We always went to a farm for our holidays and .....
5 We always went to a farm for our holidays because .....
6 She doesn't want to go to the south of Spain because .....
7 Joe's got dirt on his hands because .....
8 I have to go to the station now because .....
9 I haven't decided for certain but .....
10 I don't feel too good and .....
11 Marty's been working really hard on his book and .....
12 Marianne's house is nearly finished and .....

a) our friends used to live there.
b) she's been there several times before.
c) he thinks he'll have finished it by next month.
~~d) I wear a uniform to work.~~
e) we'd already started the meeting.
f) I'd help to feed the animals.
g) today I'm wearing trousers.
h) I think I'll apply for that job I told you about.
i) this time next week she'll be moving in.
j) my train leaves at 4.00.
k) he's been digging in the garden.
l) I think I'm going to be sick.
m) I was talking to my brother on the phone.

Exercise 5 The future Units 10–12

Fill in the gaps using the verbs in brackets in an appropriate future form. There is one example of the future in the past.

A: I need to get back to Oxford by 6.00 this evening.

B: Right. I ...'ll check (*check*) the timetable. OK, there's a train that 1 .... (*leave*) at 4.10 and 2 .... (*get in*) at 5.45. That 3 .... (*be*) the one for you.

A: Yes, great.

A: Rosie 4 .... (*come*) to stay on Wednesday, and she 5 .... (*bring*) her new man with her.

B: Oh. What's he like?

A: Well, I don't know. I haven't met him yet. I 6 .... (*tell*) you next week.

A: Have you finished the work you were doing on your house?

B: Not quite, no.

A: Oh, I 7 ....(*ask*) if I could come round next week to see it.

B: Oh, that 8 .... (*be*) fine. I 9 .... definitely .... (*finish*) it by then. I've got the rest of the week off work so I 10 .... (*work*) on the house every day and should finish by Saturday.

Exercise 6 Past tenses **Units 4–6 and 9**

A Read the story and underline the best ending: a), b) or c).

Today nearly ended in disaster. I had been away from my flat in Edinburgh which I share with two friends, but when I returned to the flat I couldn't find my key. I had left it on the table when I'd left the flat a week earlier. We used to leave a spare key in the plant pot outside the front door, but it wasn't there. We always used to remove it if all three of us were going to be away for a while. I'd seen lots of TV programmes where people opened a lock with a credit card. It didn't work for me, however. So I tried suddenly pushing the door with my shoulder – I'd seen that on TV too. That didn't work either.

In the end I had to call the police. A policeman opened the door easily with his shoulder, but it broke the lock. He didn't let me in until I described where the key was, though. The stupid thing was that I'd done all this because I wasn't expecting my flatmates back for another three days, but

a) … in fact, I had got my dates wrong and they didn't come back for five days.
b) … while I was fixing the lock, my flatmate turned up. She'd decided to come back early.
c) … I found a spare key in my pocket.

B Now try to rewrite the story by filling in the gaps without looking back at the original. Each gap is one word.

Today nearly ended in *disaster*. I had been away from my flat in Edinburgh which I share with two friends, but when I **1** .... to the flat I **2** .... my key. I **3** .... it on the table when I'd left the flat a week earlier. We **4** .... a spare key in the plant pot outside the front door, but it wasn't there. We always **5** .... remove it if all three of us were going to be away for a while. I **6** .... lots of TV programmes where people opened a lock with a **7** .... It **8** .... for me, however. So I tried suddenly pushing the door with my shoulder – I **9** .... that on TV too. That didn't work either.

In the end I had to call the police. A policeman **10** .... the door easily with his **11** .... , but it broke the lock. He didn't let me in until I described where the **12** .... was, though. The stupid thing was that I **13** .... all this because I **14** .... my flatmates back for another three days, but **15** .... I **16** .... the lock, my flatmate **17** .... up. She'd decided to come back early.

Unit

13 Word order

Getting started

1 **Read the article about the Sutton St Nicholas football team. Fill in the missing statistics about the team.**

a) goals scored against Sutton ....

b) goals scored by Sutton ....

c) age of the goal scorer ....

d) number of games lost by Sutton this term ....

e) number of hours of play without scoring ....

f) the score in Sutton's most successful match ....

Golden goal makes it 425–1

A village football team have finally scored their first goal after letting in 425.

The Sutton St Nicholas boys' team, formed a year ago, failed to score at all last season. This term the team lost 32 successive matches.

Worse still, 12-year-old Daniel Durkin became Sutton's second goalkeeper to decide to leave. But he agreed to carry on playing for the team in a different position after his mum offered him £2 per match.

And during his first full game in midfield Daniel delighted Sutton's frustrated fans when he scored with a close range shot to end almost 33 games without a goal. Sutton's fans didn't mind at all that visitors Bromyard Town won the game 12–1.

(adapted from an article by Richard Smith in *The Independent*, 9 November 1998)

2 **Here are some terms we use to describe parts of a sentence. Match them to the correct parts of the sentence from the text below:**

a) object ....

b) subject ....

c) other information ....

d) verb group ....

A village football team have finally scored their first goal after letting in 425.

3 **Here are some other ways of organising the sentence. Are they acceptable or not? Write a ✓ or a ✗.**

a) After letting in 425, a village football team have finally scored their first goal. .....

b) Their first goal have a village football team finally scored after letting in 425. .....

c) Scored have a village football team finally their first goal after letting in 425. .....

Looking at language

Word order

This unit looks at word order – how to organise what you want to say or write.

The most common word order

The most common word order in statements is SVO: **subject, verb, object**. '**Other information**' often follows the object:

subject | verb group | object | other information

A village football team have finally scored their first goal after letting in 425.

We don't usually put 'other information' between the subject and verb, or between the verb and object. We don't say:

~~*A village football team after letting in 425 have finally scored their first goal.*~~
~~*A village football team have finally scored after letting in 425 their first goal.*~~

1 Are the verbs and objects together in these sentences? Which sentence sounds strange?

1 He kicked the ball straight into the back of the net. ....

2 At the end of the match they received from the President the trophy. ....

Other word orders

There are other ways of starting a sentence or clause:

- You can start with '**other information**':
  After letting in 425, *a village football team have finally scored their first goal.*
  This term, *the team had 32 successive defeats.*
  In Sutton *most children prefer other sports.*
  As he kicked the ball *he felt a sharp pain in his back.*
- You can start with the **object** to show contrast or strong emphasis:
  S V O O S V
  *Sutton scored their first goal in November. **Their second** they didn't score until February.*
  S V O O S V
  *The head teacher punished the whole class. **This** we thought was wrong.*
- You can start with words and phrases that tell us about your **attitude**: *in my opinion, as far as I'm concerned, in my view, luckily, unfortunately*:
  Unfortunately, Sutton still lost 12–1.

Although SVO is the most common word order, a longer text written using **only** this word order can sound very uninteresting:

*The team played very poorly. They didn't score any goals in their first season, **and they** scored only one in their second season.*

Compare this with:

*The team played very poorly. **In their first season** they didn't score any goals, **and in their second** they scored only one.*

See Unit 26 for other ways of organising a text.

2 **Do these sentences start with 'other information', an object, or an 'attitude' word or phrase?**

1 My first girlfriend I met while I was still at school. ....

2 As far as I'm concerned, you're much too young. ....

3 While I was talking, she came back into the room. ....

Getting it right

Exercise 1 Identifying starting points

In the true stories below, match the sentence beginnings, 1–8, to the starting points, a)–d). You can use a)–d) more than once.

1 *A six-foot-three man* tried to rob the same bank in Arlington, Virginia twice in a four-hour period. 2 *This* was not a very good idea, as each time the cashier put the money in a bag, she also put in a tiny bomb that exploded and changed the colour of the money. 3 *Unfortunately* the bomb exploded each time just outside the bank and the robber ran away empty-handed.

4 *As she left an ice-cream parlour*, a 52-year-old woman in Albany, New York met a man who wanted to steal her bag. 5 *The woman* did not give it to him, but hit him repeatedly with her ice cream! 6 *After two or three minutes*, the man ran away with nothing.

7 *As a joke*, Dallas disc jockey Ron Chapman invited listeners to send him $20, promising 'absolutely nothing' in return, but telling them to 'beat the deadline'. 8 *This* his listeners did, sending him $240,000 without getting a single thing in return!

a) Subject starting point .1..............

b) 'Other information' starting point ....

c) Object starting point ....

d) Attitude starting point ....

Exercise 2 Choosing word order

Read the article about an unusual job, and underline the most suitable word order when you have a choice.

WINDOW CLEANER TO THE SHARKS

The advertisement was interesting / Interesting the advertisement was: WANTED: WINDOW CLEANER. WATER PROVIDED. MUST WORK WELL UNDER PRESSURE AND LIKE FISH. 1 *It sounded good / Good it sounded* but how could I guess that 'pressure' referred to the air in a scuba tank? Because this was a job cleaning the shark tank at a Sea Life centre.

2 *Luckily, I have always sharks liked, / Luckily, I have always liked sharks*, but when the moment came to get into the tank I was a little nervous.

3 *I dived finally in. / Finally, I dived in.* 4 *It was cold / Cold it was.* 5 *It was time to start now the job. / Now it was time to start the job.*

6 *Fortunately, the sharks showed no interest in me. / Fortunately, the sharks showed in me no interest.* They just swam around looking bored as I cleaned the glass walls of the tank.

7 *It took about 15 minutes to clean the windows, / About 15 minutes it took to clean the windows,* but at £6 per hour there are probably better ways to earn money.

Exercise 3 Learning from learners

Rewrite the underlined sections from a learner's essay to make the style more interesting.

I will never forget that match. I hadn't been playing for my college team for very long, and I'd been injured for some of the time. I was ready to take on anyone fortunately that Saturday. Our opponents were the best team in the area. 1 They at the start of the match played well. Their first two goals came within ten minutes 2 and a third half an hour later they scored. But suddenly we started to play better. In the five minutes before half time, our goalkeeper saved two shots 3 and their leading players several times of the ball lost control. 4 A quick change made the coach at half time. He told me to move up and attack and he told the defenders to come forward.

We weren't sure about all this, but with nothing to lose at 0-3 we wanted to try it. 5 It within minutes succeeded. 6 The score was after half an hour 3-3. The closing minutes were difficult. Our opponents got their energy back. 7 There was left one minute, and it was then that 8 I sent into the back of the net the ball.

Example: *Fortunately, I was ready to take on anyone that Saturday.*

1 ....

2 ....

3 ....

4 ....

5 ....

6 ....

7 ....

8 ....

Exercise 4 Rebuilding a story

Complete the story with starting points from the boxes.

As they tried to enter the bank,	Everyone	In desperation,	~~In 1975~~	The staff

In the end,	The other two	They	They	They	Unfortunately for them,

In 1975 three men decided to rob a large bank in Scotland. 1 .... they were not successful. 2 .... they got stuck in the revolving doors of the bank entrance. 3 .... helped to free them and they left the building.

4 .... came back a few minutes later and announced they were robbing the bank. 5 .... started to laugh, thinking it was a good joke. 6 .... tried again. 7 .... asked for £5,000 but the cashier was laughing so much that he didn't give it to them. The robbers lowered their demand to £500, then to £50. 8 .... they asked for any money at all, but got nothing.

9 .... one of the robbers jumped over the counter to get the money himself. Unfortunately he fell over instead and hurt his ankle badly. 10 .... decided to try to escape, but they got stuck in the revolving door again!

Classwork

Work in groups of three or four. Take it in turns to continue the story that starts with the sentences below. When it is your turn, choose a starting point for your sentence from the boxes. You cannot use a starting point more than once.

Story:

It was a warm lunchtime in September. Harry crossed the road and had the strange sensation that someone was following him …

Suddenly,	He	There	At the end of the road,
Without a sound,	Harry	At that moment	When
And	The stranger	Luckily,	He

Unit 14 The imperative and instructions

Getting started

1 **Read the text about illusions. (An illusion is something that looks or feels different from what it really is.) Then answer the question.**

How many illusions does the text discuss? ....

LOOK AT THE PICTURE. Is it a young or old woman that you see? Most people see one or the other but not both. You have to make an effort to see the two different images. Illusions happen because sometimes our brains become confused by information from our senses. To experience an illusion that depends on touch, fill three bowls with cold, nearly warm, and hot water. Put one hand in the hot water and the other in the cold water for a few seconds. Then put both hands into the nearly warm water. The nearly warm water will feel cold to the hand that was in the hot water, but hot to the hand that was in the cold water.

2 **Underline all the imperative verbs (verbs which tell you to do something).**

Example: Look.

3 **What do the underlined verbs do? Tick (✓) the right answer.**

a) They ask questions. .....
b) They give instructions. .....
c) They tell a story. .....
d) They answer questions. .....

4 **Which statement about the imperative is correct? Tick (✓) one.**

a) The imperative looks like the infinitive without *to*. .....

b) The imperative looks like the past simple of the verb. .....

Looking at language

The imperative and instructions

Use

The imperative is used in a variety of ways. For example, to give:

- instructions: ***Fill** three bowls with water.*
- orders that you expect to be obeyed, or requests: ***Stand up. Open** the window.*
- warnings: ***Watch out! Don't walk** on the ice – it's dangerous.*
- advice and reminders: ***Don't listen** to her. **Remember** to phone your mother.*

Form

The imperative is formed exactly like the infinitive without *to*. Usually there is no subject:

*(You) **Take** two cans of beans.*

We form negative imperatives by using ***don't* + infinitive without *to***:

***Don't forget** your appointment this afternoon.*

We can add *you* when **describing** how to do something in spoken English.

A: *Tell me how to cook spaghetti.*

B: *Well, **you boil** some water and then **you add** your spaghetti with a little olive oil.*

In these kinds of instructions we often use *need (to)* and *have to*:

*First you **need to buy** some real Italian olive oil.* (See Unit 49.)

Need to and *have to* cannot be used without *you* when giving instructions.

1 The illusion described below is from a spoken extract. Add *you* in two of the gaps where it is necessary, and in one other place to make the text sound more natural.

For this illusion 1 ..... need two cans of tomatoes, one large and one small. 2 ..... open the large can and remove some of the tomatoes so that it is the same weight as the small can. 3 ..... can use your kitchen scales to check this. When you have done that, 4 ..... cover the top of each can and 5 ..... ask people to lift the two cans, one in each hand and say which they think is heavier. Most people say that the smaller can is heavier. We expect big things to be heavier and are surprised when they aren't, so that we think they are actually lighter!

Tag questions can be used with imperatives. They are similar to saying *please* in requests, and add emphasis in reminders, advice and warnings:

Positive imperative + tag question for requests:

*Open the door for me, **will ↗you**?*

*Open the door for me, **won't ↗you**?*

Negative imperative + tag question for reminders:

*Don't forget your appointment, **will ↗you**?*

(See Unit 18 for more on tag questions.)

Getting it right

Exercise 1 Thinking about function

Decide if the imperative is used in the extracts below to give instructions (i), advice / reminders (a / r), orders / requests (o / r) or warnings (w).

Example: Don't touch this wire. It's dangerous. ..*w*..

1 Find a shiny spoon. Each side is a different type of mirror. Look at the reflection of your face in both sides. What are the differences? .....
2 Jake, switch on the television for me, will you? .....
3 It's very easy to make. You heat the sugar and butter in a pan, then add the milk. .....
4 Remember to wear comfortable shoes. And take some warm clothes too. .....
5 Look out, there's a car coming. .....
6 Take care, won't you? It's quite icy on the road. .....
7 Don't forget you're meeting your bank manager at 2.00 today. .....
8 Look at the pie, will you, and tell me if it's ready. .....
9 First put your money in the machine and then press the button. .....
10 Do Exercise 10 for homework. .....

Exercise 2 Learning from learners

In the following recipe written by a learner, there are nine mistakes. We have corrected the first one. Can you correct the other eight?

Recipe for Hummus

You need: 500 grams chickpeas, 2 tablespoons tahina, juice of 2 lemons, 2–3 cloves of garlic, salt and pepper, black olives

~~Putting~~ Put the chickpeas in water overnight.
In the morning they drain and boiling in fresh water for three hours.
You drain again, but you kept the water.
Then are put the chickpeas into a blender with the cooking water.
Adds the tahina, lemon juice, garlic, salt and pepper.
Now we decorate with black olives, and are serving on a shallow dish.

Extension

Write your own recipe for a famous dish from your country. If you are working in class you can make a class recipe book.

Exercise 3 Spoken instructions

A Read these written instructions for using a phone card. Put them in the right order.

USING A PHONE CARD

a) Wait for phone card to be ejected.
b) Insert phone card.
c) When call is finished, replace receiver.
d) Dial number and wait for connection.
e) Lift receiver and check dialling tone.

1 .*e*.. 2 ..... 3 ..... 4 ..... 5 .....

B Fill in the gaps in these spoken instructions for using a phone with verbs from the box. Some of the gaps are in the imperative and some are in the present simple.

come out	dial	get	need	pick up	put down	put in	tell	~~use~~

A: Excuse me, can you tell me how I *use*.this phone?

B: Well, have you got a phone card?

A: Yes, here.

B: OK, first **1** .... the receiver. 2 .... the card .... here, see? Right, now, this display 3 .... you you've got ten pounds and just 4 .... the number you want. You 5 .... to watch the display to check how much money you've got left.

A: Thanks. How 6 .... I .... my card back at the end? Will it just come out?

B: Yeah. You just 7 .... the receiver .... and your card 8 ....

Exercise 4 Written practice

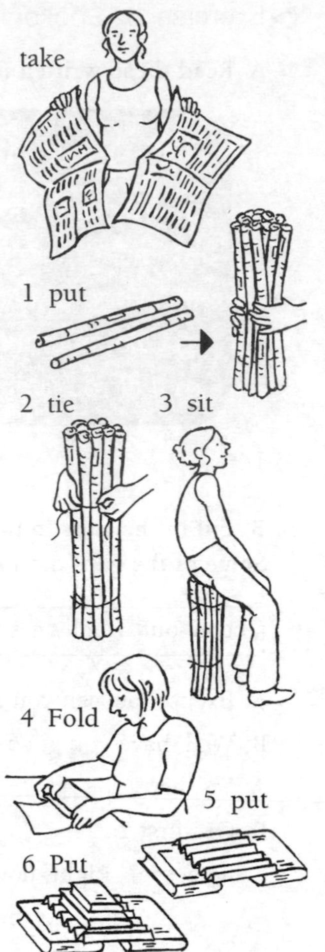

The texts below tell you how to build things out of paper. Using the pictures and verbs to help you, write the missing instructions. Then try following them!

You can use paper to build simple structures that are surprisingly strong. Try building yourself a stool out of old newspapers (you'll need about five).

Take two sheets of newspaper and roll them up.

Fix the roll with sticky tape or a rubber band to stop it unrolling. Do this again with the other sheets until you have about 20 rolls. Now **1** .... and **2** .... with string. Stand the bundle upright and **3** .... See how strong it is – it will easily take your weight.

You can use a sheet of ordinary A4-sized paper to make a supporting structure. **4** .... (make into parallel folds, each about a centimetre apart) and **5** .... two books. **6** .... and see how many it can hold before it falls down.

Classwork

1 **Divide into two groups. Group 1 looks carefully around the room and then leaves. Group 2 makes changes to the room. For example, you could turn the teacher's desk round, change pictures on the wall, turn lights on or off, move things around etc.**

2 **Group 1 returns, and each person pairs up with someone from Group 2. The person from Group 1 gives instructions to his or her partner, using imperative verbs, to put the room back to how it was. See which pair can make the most changes.**

Example:
Thierry, put the cassette player back on the teacher's desk. Turn the table round, and ...

3 **As a class, discuss who made which changes.**

Example:
Mario put the chair back under the desk.

4 **You can do the activity again, but this time Group 2 leaves the room.**

Unit 15 *Do and other auxiliaries for emphasis*

Getting started

1 **Richard Wiseman has a very unusual job. Read the interview with him and answer the questions.**

a) What is his job? ....

b) Which is the best description of Richard?

i) He believes in the paranormal (things we can't explain scientifically). .....

ii) He's still trying to find out about the paranormal. .....

iii) He doesn't believe in the paranormal. .....

What does a parapsychologist do?
We study the 'paranormal' – anything such as ghosts that cannot be explained normally.

Do you look for ghosts?
Very few parapsychologists do that. It's a very, very difficult area. You can sit in a house for a week and get nothing. Then, the moment you leave, something happens and you didn't have your camera on it. Looking for ghosts to appear is becoming less popular among parapsychologists, because it doesn't give very good results.

Have you ever been very frightened?
Not yet. I've never seen a ghost or anything like that.

So, don't you believe in the paranormal?
It may be true. We know something is going on. It may be people imagining things, or they might be seeing something paranormal. And, as other parapsychologists do report positive results, I must keep an open mind.

2 **Look at the interview again and underline any examples of *do, does, did* and their negatives, *don't, doesn't, didn't*.**

3 **Decide whether you can take out these underlined examples of *do* etc., or whether you need to keep them.**

	Keep	*Can take out*
Do you look for ghosts?	✓	
a) Very few parapsychologists do that.		
b) ... it doesn't give very good results.		
c) ... other parapsychologists do report positive results ...		

4 **If you can take out *do*, why do you think it is there?** ....

Looking at language

Do and other auxiliaries for emphasis

Use

Do can be used as a **main verb**:

I **do** *a lot of photography.*
A: *What do you* **do**?
B: *I'm a photographer.*

Do can also be used as an **auxiliary verb**:

in present simple and past simple questions: *What* **does** *a parapsychologist do?* **Did** *you see anything strange?*	in present and past simple short answers: *Do you like it? Yes, I* **do**. *Did you see him? No, I* **didn't**.
in present and past simple negatives: *... something happens and you* **didn't** *have your camera on it.* *... it* **doesn't** *give very good results.*	

See Units 2 and 4 for auxiliary *do* in the present simple and past simple.

Auxiliary *do* can also be used in **positive statements**:

I **do** *believe in the paranormal.*

Do is **not** grammatically necessary here. We often choose auxiliary *do* to emphasise (show the importance of) the ordinary verb in a positive statement. We may want to:

- **contrast** one thing with another:
  And, as other parapsychologists **do** *report positive results, I must keep an open mind.*
  (Richard has **not** had positive results; he's never seen a ghost.)
- **correct** something:
  A: *You didn't see a ghost – it's impossible.*
  B: *I* **did** *see one! David was with me. Ask him!*
- **emphasise** something:
  You **do** *look nervous!*
  This use often occurs with imperatives:
  Do *sit down.* **Do** *be quiet, will you?*

In a positive statement, *do / does / did* comes **before** the main verb:

I / you / we / they	**do**	like Spielberg's films.
She / he / it	**does**	look nice.
I / you / she / he / it / we / they	**did**	enjoy the day out.

Pronunciation

Do and all other auxiliary verbs can be stressed in spoken English to contrast, correct or emphasise:

She doesn't play the guitar but she ***does*** *play the piano.*
A: *They haven't done their homework yet.* B: *Yes, they* ***have****.*
I ***did*** enjoy the concert.

1 Read the strange story about a birthday card. Are the underlined auxiliaries used to correct or emphasise? Practise saying the sentences and stressing the auxiliaries.

It was my birthday and there was no card from my girlfriend. So I rang her and said, 'You still haven't sent me a birthday card, have you?' She said, **1** 'I <u>have</u> sent one! I posted it on Thursday.' 'Oh,' I said. 'Well, the post **2** <u>does</u> come late sometimes so maybe your card will come later.' Anyway, two weeks later the card **3** <u>did</u> arrive, with postmarks from Australia and Mexico, both on the date of my birthday ...

1 .... **2** .... **3** ....

Getting it right

Exercise 1 Choosing the best verb

A In the conversation below, two friends are talking about the paranormal. Put phrases a)–j) in the correct gaps.

a) didn't say you thought it was nonsense
b) do you think that
c) she did experience something paranormal
d) do always try to explain everything scientifically
e) don't believe any paranormal stories though
f) do believe,
g) ~~Do you believe in the paranormal~~
h) doesn't mean I think it's all nonsense
i) I do think some of the stories are true
j) didn't think about ghosts

A: What about you *g)* ?

B: I'm not sure. I've never seen a ghost or anything, but **1** ..... . A friend of mine has a strange story. She was in hospital, and two strange nurses came to see her in the middle of the night. She never saw those nurses again, but she **2** ..... or anything until two years later when she heard that two nurses had died in that room. So I think **3** ..... . I'm sure you **4** ..... .

A: Why **5** ..... ? I think I **6** ..... actually. OK, I've never seen anything myself, and I probably never will, but that **7** ..... .

B: I **8** ..... , it's just that I thought you weren't the sort of person to believe stories like that – you **9** ..... !

B Which of phrases a)–j) use auxiliary *do* for questions (q)? Which use it for negatives (n)? Which use it to emphasise the ordinary verb (e)?

a) ..... b) ..... c) ..... d) ..... e) ..... f) ..... g) ..*q*.. h) ..... i) ..... j) .....

▶ Exercise 2 Matching and pronunciation

Match the spoken extracts, 1–8, to their responses, a)–i), and underline the stressed auxiliary verbs. The stressed verbs may be in either column.

I haven't bought her a birthday present yet, but I have sent her a card. ..h)

1 I used to have hair down to my knees, you know. .....
2 I'm sure you don't remember the last time we met. .....
3 Come in. Do sit down. .....
4 You forgot to post my letter! .....
5 I do like eggs for breakfast. .....
6 She says I don't have to go. .....
7 You're not being very helpful. I'd like to speak to the manager. .....
8 She didn't walk to school this morning. .....

a) I am the manager.
b) I can. It was three years ago.
c) You didn't! I don't believe you.
d) She did walk. I saw her.
e) Yes, I'm sorry, but I did remember everything else.
f) Mmm, so do I.
g) Well, I think you should.
h) ~~Oh, that's good.~~
i) Oh, thank you.

Try saying the sentences out loud!

▶ Exercise 3 Auxiliary *do* to correct someone

In Exercise 1 you heard about a ghost story. Read the story in more detail below:

Carol: This happened while I was in hospital after an operation, and one night I was woken up by two nurses in my room. One of them touched my hair which I thought was a bit strange. The next day I told a nurse and she asked me to describe the nurses I'd seen, which I did. She looked frightened, but said nothing. I was angry and decided to find the nurses, but I couldn't and I never saw them again. It wasn't until two years later that someone told me that two nurses had been killed in that hospital ten years before.

A friend of Carol's doesn't believe the story. Fill in the gaps in Carol's replies in 1–6.

Example: You didn't really see those nurses – you just imagined it.
I did see them. One nurse touched my hair.

1 I don't think anyone touched your hair. You probably dreamt it.
.... I never remember my dreams.

2 The sister didn't believe your story, did she?
.... She was frightened.

3 I expect you didn't remember clearly what those nurses looked like.
.... I can still remember now.

4 Well, perhaps you didn't look everywhere for them.

.... ! And I asked people about them.

5 Perhaps you knew about the nurses who had been killed before you went to hospital?

.... I only found out two years later by chance.

6 You don't really believe you saw ghosts, do you?

.... They were definitely ghosts.

Exercise 4 Learning from learners

Read the interview with a learner about a course she was doing at a language school. Rewrite the underlined sections with auxiliary *do* for emphasis, or tick (✓) them if they should stay the same.

Why did you choose this course?

I could only come ....✓.......... in April, and they said, well, we don't have classes at your level in April, but we 1 have .... these new courses in April.

What do you think is different about the new course?

It's mostly spoken English. There's not much written work. But I 2 think .... it's very good for people who know some English, and want to improve on some parts of it like telephoning or report writing. I think for them 3 it's .... really good and you 4 learn .... a lot in two weeks.

Have you had a chance to tell your teachers about how your English study might relate to your work?

Yes, we have, yes. Our teacher 5 tried .... to find out what was important, and what we needed.

Classwork

1 **What do you feel is important when you are trying to learn a foreign language? Decide how you feel about the following statements, and tick (✓) the appropriate boxes.**

	Agree	Not sure	Disagree
Learning grammar is more important than practising speaking.	❑	❑	❑
The teacher should correct every error.	❑	❑	❑
Having fun in class helps you to learn.	❑	❑	❑
Learners learn best by discovering rules about language themselves, not by the teacher telling them.	❑	❑	❑
Making errors helps you to learn.	❑	❑	❑
You need to repeat new language many times in order to remember it.	❑	❑	❑

2 **Find one or two other people who agree with three or four of your opinions. Discuss why you agreed or disagreed with the statements.**

3 **Talk to someone from another group. Try to persuade him or her to agree with your opinions, but listen to his or her arguments as well, in case you want to change *your* opinion. Try to use some auxiliaries for emphasis.**

Example:

A: *You do need to know grammar first. How can you speak without knowing grammar?*
B: *I don't agree. It is possible to communicate without correct grammar, if you really want to.*

4 **Finally, tell the class how successful you were in reaching agreement.**

Unit 16

Features of spoken English

Getting started

1 **Read the conversation about the end of a relationship. Spoken language is quite difficult to read, so just try to answer this question:**

Why do the friends think the relationship ended?

....

A: Why did they split up?
B: He finished with her.
A: **He** finished with **her**?
B: Apparently she was really upset about it, she said.
A: Well she shouldn't have been looking at other men.
B: No, she shouldn't. But, I mean, I think it was a really strange situation anyway.
A: Because she left him before. Fool. Didn't know when she had a good thing.
B: He's a complete idiot, John.
A: Yeah.
B: 'Cos [because] he's really friendly, is John.
A: Oh, he is. I mean, he's really sweet.
B: Yeah.
A: Can't say I'm surprised it's ended though.

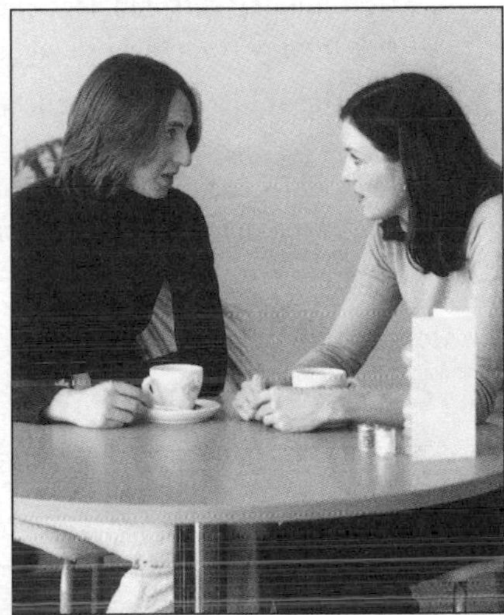

2 **Find sentences in the conversation which are similar to these sentences.**

a) John is a complete idiot. ....

b) John is really friendly. ....

c) She didn't know when she had a good thing. ....

d) I can't say I'm surprised it's ended though. ....

What are the differences?

Looking at language

Spoken English

Ellipsis (= leaving things out)

Speakers often leave out words if the situation is clear:

(Have you) Seen Margo anywhere?
(The / our) Car's broken down again.

We often leave out personal subjects (I, we) with verbs of feeling and opinion:

A: *Have we had any faxes in?* B: *No.* A: *Good. (I) Didn't **think** we would have.*
A: *How are you now?* B: *(I) **Feel** better than yesterday.*

Ellipsis is also common when speakers use fixed expressions and idioms:

(That's a) Great idea!
(That) Sounds interesting.
(It) Serves you right.
(It's) Raining cats and dogs out there.
(It's)Funny (that) you should say that.

When the subject of a sentence or clause is repeated, we often leave it, and any auxiliaries, out:

***I** got really annoyed and (I) asked him to leave.*
***She's** been home and (**she's**) gone out again.*

Heads and tails

Compare these sentences:

John's really nice.	*John, he's really nice.*	*He's really nice, John.*
(John = **subject**)	(John = **head**)	(John = **tail**)

- **Heads** are used to **introduce** and **emphasise** who or what you are going to talk about.
- **Tails** help you to **emphasise** who or what you've been talking about.

We often use ***it + be* + adjective** as a head to show our feelings about something:

***It was terrible**, that day at the beach.*
***It's lovely**, your garden.*

1 **Rewrite the sentence: 1) with *this clock* as a head, and 2) with *this clock* as a tail:**

This clock is broken.

1 .... 2 ....

2 **Which of the features of spoken English (ellipsis and heads and tails) also occur in your language?**

Getting it right

Exercise 1 Recognising spoken language

A Match the extracts, 1–6, to the types of texts, a)–d), in the box.

a) a conversation between friends b) a meeting c) a holiday postcard d) a formal letter

1 We've been having a great time, swimming every day, and visiting lots of interesting places. Mike's getting fat on the fantastic food, even though we're playing lots of tennis. I'm not looking forward to coming home because there will be too much to do. I'll try not to think about it now.

.....

2 It's great, this pizza. Why didn't you have it?
Don't know. I thought the chicken would be nicer.

.....

3 Thank you for coming today. We have quite a lot to do, so let's start with a review of last year's sales.

.....

4 Dan? Want anything from the shops?
Yeah. Can you get me a paper? And could you hurry, it always sells out of papers quickly, that shop, so don't worry if you can't get one.
OK then.

.....

5 I would be grateful if you could send me your latest brochure. I am particularly interested in travelling to South East Asia.

.....

6 Doing anything special this weekend, Sarah?
No. What about you?
Can't think of anything, no. Perhaps we ought to do something together?
Well. Nick, he's having a party, but I wasn't going to go because I wouldn't know anyone there. But we could go, I suppose.

.....

B Look at the conversations between friends in A. Find and underline examples of:

1 ellipsis (there are four examples) 2 heads (one example) 3 tails (two examples)

Exercise 2 Ellipsis

Notice how ellipsis is used in the two conversations below. Rewrite sections 1–12 to show what has been missed out.

Conversation 1

A: Hello, John.

B: Oh hi, Peter. *Been here long?* ... *Have you been here long?*

A: Not long. 1 *You OK?* ... 1 ....

B: Not too bad, thanks. 2 *Want to get some food?* 2 ....

A: 3 *Great idea*. I'm really hungry. 3 ....

4 *Seen anywhere suitable round here?* 4 ....

B: There's a Chinese restaurant just round the corner.

I've been over there and 5 *looked at the menu*. 5 ....

6 *Looks good*. Do you fancy it? 6 ....

A: 7 *Sounds fine*. 7 ....

Conversation 2

A: Oh dear. 8 *Terrible day*. 8 ....

9 *Been raining for hours*. 9 ....

B: Yes, it's awful. Never mind, though – 10 *good film on* 10 ....

tonight. I think we should just stay in and 11 *watch it*. 11 ....

Would you like something to drink?

A: Oh yes. Could I just have an orange juice?

B: Sure. 12 *Ice?* 12 ....

A: Please.

Extension

Which of the examples of ellipsis are fixed expressions?

Exercise 3 Heads and tails

Underline the heads or tails in sentences a)–g).

a) The music, it was much too loud.
b) I think it's broken, the light.
c) I didn't understand it at all, that letter from the lawyer.
d) Bees, they can find their way home from up to ten kilometres away!
e) Your mum, she's been to the new sports centre, hasn't she?
f) My dad, he's never liked flying.
g) I didn't enjoy it at all, the meal.

Now choose a sentence from a)–g) for the gap in each short conversation.

Example: A: We went to that new bar last night.

B: Oh, did you? What was it like?

A: ..a)., Otherwise it was OK.

1 A: I think we should go out somewhere this afternoon.

B: Yes, let's. .....

A: Yeah. She said it was great.

2 A: Some people are frightened of really common things. Like spiders, or heights.

B: .....

A: Really? Has he always been like that?

3 A: I think the trial is finally coming to an end.

B: I hope so. .....

A: Yes, it was confusing.

4 A: What a boring evening.

B: Yeah. ..... The film was all right, though.

A: I didn't think so.

5 A: .....

B: Is it? Are you sure it isn't just the bulb?

A: No, I've already tried changing that.

6 A: .....

B: You're full of interesting facts, you are.

A: Wish I could remember more useful information, though.

Exercise 4 Spoken English

A Ellipsis

Cross out (~~like this~~) words or phrases that can be left out of these spoken sentences.

Example: ~~Are you~~ going shopping?

1 Do you come here often?

2 I don't much like football.

3 We're not sure we can come on Monday, I'm afraid.

4 I think I'll go now.

5 Have you seen James anywhere this morning?

B Heads and tails

Fill in the gaps to complete the sentences.

Example: My teacher, her husband, *he*............ plays football for the city team.

1 My brother, his friend Sarah, ...'s got a swimming pool in her garden.

2 Her next-door neighbour, his parrot, ...'s got an orange tail and green wings.

3 It's got four doors and a more powerful engine than the old one, her new ....

4 She's not very good at cooking but she always makes a meal for the family, my ....

Classwork

1 Work in groups of four to six. You need a dice, a coin and counters for each group. The player with the highest throw of the dice starts.

2 If you land in a square with a word or phrase, throw the coin. If the coin is 'heads', make a sentence using the word or phrase as a head. If the coin is 'tails', make a sentence using it as a tail.

Example:
the sea (heads): *The sea, it was really cold.*
the sea (tails): *It was really cold, the sea.*

heads tails

If you can't make a sentence, or the group thinks you make a mistake, go back to where you came from. If you land on a dice square, throw the dice again. If you land on a blank square, you don't have to do anything. The winner is the first player to reach the end.

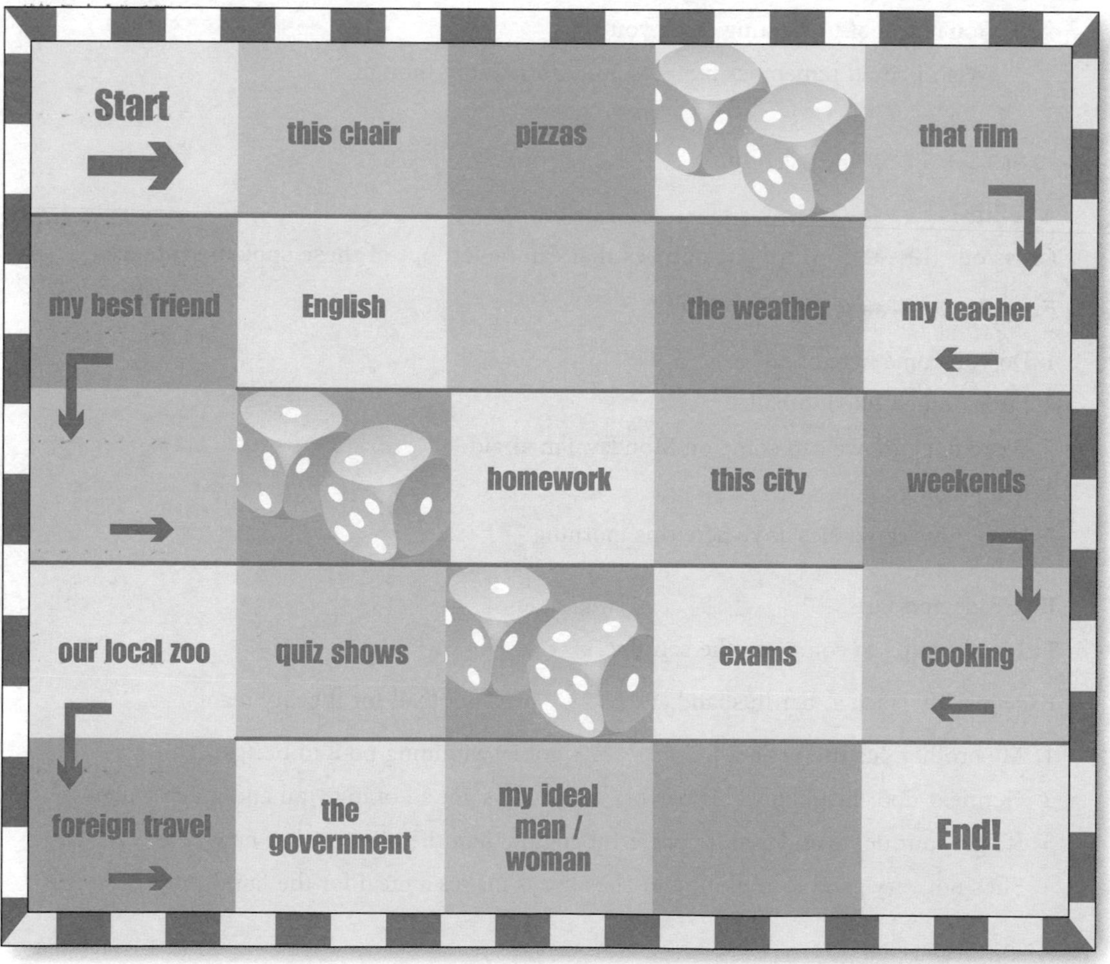

Start →	this chair	pizzas	[dice]	that film
my best friend	English		the weather	my teacher
	[dice]	homework	this city	weekends
our local zoo	quiz shows	[dice]	exams	cooking
foreign travel	the government	my ideal man / woman		End!

Unit 17

Question forms 1: basic questions

Getting started

1 **Read the questionnaire. What are *your* answers to the questions in it? Are any of them the same as Pat Cash's answers?**

QUESTIONNAIRE

Pat Cash became Australia's best tennis player at 14. He turned professional in 1982, and in 1987 became Wimbledon champion.

What is your idea of perfect happiness?
Being with my family, living on the beach in a safe environment and having a vegetable garden.

What do you most dislike about your appearance?
My hands – too fat.

Have you ever said 'I love you' and not meant it?
Yes.

Do you believe in life after death?
Yes. I look forward to moving on to the next life.

2 **Are the speakers in the conversation below friends or family? Who is who?**

....

A: Dad, what you want then?
B: You got a spoon? I'm having this, me.
A: What do you want, Amy? No, come on. What do you want?
C: Erm. Some of that, please.
A: You're quite safe. Our mother didn't make it.
What's Julie having, Mum?
D: She doesn't want anything.
A: And what you having, Mum?
D: I don't know. I'll think about it.

3 **Underline all the questions in the questionnaire and the conversation. Then complete the rules about forming questions below by underlining the correct choice.**

In written questions

a) An auxiliary verb (for example, *do* or *have*) comes *before / after* the subject.
b) The verb *to be does / does not* take an auxiliary.

In spoken questions

c) The auxiliary verb *can sometimes / must always* be left out.

Looking at language

Basic questions

In written English there are clear rules for forming questions. Spoken English often follows these rules, but not always.

Written questions

An auxiliary verb comes before the subject. The rest of the verb group comes after the subject:

auxiliary	subject	
Are	*you*	*enjoying your course?*
Have	*they*	***been living** here long?*

When there is no auxiliary in the statement, we use auxiliary **do + infinitive** in the question:

Statement	*Question*
I like Maria. *They went to Jamaica for their holidays.*	***Do** you **like** Maria?* *Where **did** they **go** for their holidays?*

We do not use *do* in a question if there is another auxiliary or modal verb, or with the verb *to be*:

*Have you **had** lunch yet?* *Can Dan **speak** Italian?* *What **is** your phone number?*

Yes / no questions begin with an auxiliary verb:

Do you want any more?

Wh- questions begin with a wh- word (*who*, *what*, *why*, *when*, *where*, *how*) and ask for information:

What do you want, Amy?

Spoken questions

It is always correct to follow the rules for written questions:

What do you want, Amy?

Sometimes the auxiliary verb is left out, or difficult to hear:

Dad, what (do) you want then?

(Have) You got a spoon?

Speakers often add answers to their own wh- questions:

*What would you like? **A Coke**?*

*Where are you going? **Home**?*

We can also use the word order of a statement to ask questions to show surprise:

You're going on Wednesday? I thought it was Friday.

You're moving in April? As soon as that?

Object and subject questions

Look at this sentence:

subject object
John *loves* ***Liz.***

Now look at these two questions:

object subject / subject object
Who does John love? *Liz.* ***Who loves Liz?*** *John does.*

Who, what and *which* can be the subject of a question. If so, we do not use auxiliary *do*:

Who came in just now? What made you wake up? Which waiter brought the menu?

Intransitive verbs always make subject questions:

What happened? Which tree fell down?

1 Read the conversation below and underline the correct question where you have a choice.

A: *Who wants coffee? / Who does want coffee?*
B: Yes, please.
A: *James, do you want coffee? / James, are you want coffee?*
C: Erm, I'd rather have tea. Is that possible?
A: Of course. So, tell us. *Who saw you at Pete's party? / Who did you see at Pete's party?*
B: Well, I saw Lucy and Simon, and Adam too.

Answers to questions

Answers to questions are usually short and are often not full sentences.

Questions	*Possible answers (falling intonation)*
Yes / no questions (rising intonation)	
Did you get a letter from Molly this week?	*No, I didn't. / Yes, I did. / Yes, got one yesterday.*
Wh- questions (falling intonation)	
Where do you live?	*In Detroit.* (*I live* is left out)
Statement questions (rising intonation)	
You don't like chocolate?	*No, I don't.* (the question is like a yes / no question)

Other points

To ask about characteristics we use *what kind / type / sort / size*:

What kind / type / sort of book is it? What size shoes do you take?

2 Write answers to questions 1 and 2, and questions to answers 3 and 4.

1 Do you like doing sport? ....
2 Who is your favourite actor? ....
3 .... ? I think Liverpool will (win the match).
4 .... ? Yes, I have (been to Singapore).

Getting it right

Exercise 1 Questions and auxiliaries

Find the auxiliary verb or modal verb in each question and write it next to the question. If the question does not have one, explain why.

Examples: Are you working hard at the moment? .... *Are*

You want anything from the shops, Fred? .... *Auxiliary left out – spoken English*

1 What sort of ice cream do you want? ....

2 Have you ever been on an aeroplane? ....

3 Where you going? ....

4 Which hotel costs the most? ....

5 What is your name? ....

6 Where do you live? ....

7 How can you say such a thing? ....

8 You think he's good-looking? ....

9 Who gave you this lovely card? ....

10 What should I do? ....

Exercise 2 Matching

Match the questions, 1–8, to the answers, a)–i).

Example: Who did you see? *g)*

1 Who saw you? .....

2 What's happened? .....

3 Which house had the best view? .....

4 Which house did you decide to buy? .....

5 Who's taken my pen? .....

6 Whose pen did you take? .....

7 Who robbed the bank? .....

8 Which bank did they rob? .....

a) I think there's been an accident, but no one's hurt.

b) The one with the best view.

c) Jane, but it's OK – no one else did.

d) Is this it? Sorry, I didn't mean to.

e) The most expensive one, of course.

f) The one I go to sometimes.

~~g) Marjorie. I shouted but she didn't hear me.~~

h) They think it was two escaped prisoners.

i) I think it was Jane's.

Exercise 3 Learning from learners

In class, learners were asked to interview a partner. Read the conversation between two learners and correct the mistakes in the questions, or tick (✓) any correct questions.

Mira: Your name is? — *What's your name?*

Lucia: Lucia Castellano.

Mira: 1 How to spell Castellano? — 1 ....

Lucia: C-A-S-T-E-L-L-A-N-O.

Mira: OK. 2 Where you are from, Lucia? — 2 ....

Lucia: Barcelona – in Spain.

Mira: Thank you. 3 What are you do? — 3 ....

Lucia: I'm a photographer.

Mira: 4 Your age is? — 4 ....

Lucia: A secret. No, really, I'm 35.

Mira: Oh, you don't look it. You look 25! — 5 ....

Lucia: Thank you.

Mira: 5 What reason you are taking this course? — 6 ....

Lucia: To improve my spoken English.

Mira: 6 Who did tell you about this course? — 7 ....

Lucia: My brother studied here last month.

Mira: OK, nearly finished. 7 What do you like to do in your free time? — 8 ....

Lucia: Oh, the usual things – shopping, cooking, cinema.

Mira: And, the last one, 8 what you hope to do in the future?

Lucia: I'd like to become a well-known photo-journalist for an international magazine.

Extension

If you are working in class, interview your partner using similar questions.

Exercise 4 Writing a survey

You work for a market research company. Use the notes below to write the questions for a survey about sport and leisure activities.

1 types of sport and leisure activity, winter / summer
2 membership of clubs / societies
3 times; weekends, evenings, other?
4 location and frequency of activities
5 spending on equipment, clothes etc.
6 individual or team sports?

1 *Do you do any sport or leisure activities? What do you do in winter and summer?*

2 ....

3 ....

4 ....

5 ....

6 ....

Extension

If you are working in class you can carry out the survey. Work in pairs. Each pair asks everyone in the class one question from the survey. Present your findings to the class.

Classwork

1 **Work in groups of four. Write four words, nouns or adjectives, on four pieces of paper. They can be objects, feelings or living things.**

Examples:

happy | soap | horse | classroom

2 **Your teacher will collect your pieces of paper and give you four new ones from another group. Do not look at these yet.**

3 **One of you looks at one piece of paper. The others must guess what is written on the paper by asking questions. You can only ask 20 questions.**

Examples:

Is it a living thing?	*No.*
Is it a feeling?	*Yes.*
Is it positive or negative?	*Positive.*
Where do you feel like this?	*Oh, it could be almost anywhere.*
When do you have this feeling?	*When I'm having a good time.*
Is the word happy?	*Yes, it is.*

Unit 18 Question forms 2: tags and indirect questions

Getting started

a Saint Bernard

1 **Read the conversation about a Saint Bernard (a kind of large dog) and answer the questions.**

a) Are the two people talking about a **real** Saint Bernard or a **toy** one? ....

b) Who do you think 'she' is?

....

A: Oh, look at it. Oh, honestly, it's like a real one. Did she get it for Christmas?
B: Yeah, although she didn't actually like it when she got it. I was really disappointed 'cos [because] I thought she'd love it.
A: Really? Was she frightened?
B: It was too big for her. But she loves it now and she just goes and lies on it, you know. But it's such a stupid thing, you know.
A: Oh.
B: I love it. I mean it's got such an amazing personality, that dog.
A: It has, hasn't it? It's almost alive, isn't it? I bet people think it's real, don't they?
B: Yeah.
A: That's what real Bernards do, isn't it? They just lie in the corner and spend most of their lives asleep.
B: Mm.

2 **Tags are phrases such as *do they*, *isn't it* and *can he* at the end of statements. Underline all the tags in the conversation above.**

3 **One of these tags is not usually possible. Underline it.**

Positive statement + negative tag	Negative statement + positive tag
Positive statement + positive tag	Negative statement + negative tag

4 **Look at these examples again:**

A: … it's got such an amazing personality, that dog.
B: It has, hasn't it? It's almost alive, isn't it?

Why are the tags used here? Tick (✓) the right answer.

a) To ask for information .....

b) To suggest a shared opinion between speakers .....

c) To check information .....

Looking at language

Tags

Use

Tags occur mostly in spoken English. Sometimes we use them to show we agree with the person we are talking to 'keep the conversation going' or to check something we're not sure about, or to ask for information.

Use	*Form*	*Intonation*	*Examples*
1 To suggest a shared opinion, and encourage the other speaker to answer	positive → negative *or* negative → positive	falling ↘	*It's almost alive, isn't it?* *You can't speak Spanish, can you?*
2 To check something we're not sure about	positive → negative *or* negative → positive *or* positive → positive	rising ↗	*I paid you back, didn't I?* *She isn't married, is she?* *You've met Jean before, have you?*
3 To ask for help or information	negative → positive	rising ↗	*You couldn't give me a hand, could you?*

Tags are added to statements, **not** to questions.
We say: *You saw him, didn't you?* We don't say: ~~*Did you see him, didn't you?*~~

A tag uses the **auxiliary** (or ***be***) and the **subject** of the statement. If there is no auxiliary, we use ***do / does / did***:

*You **haven't** been out this morning, **have** you?*
*She's here, **isn't** she?*
*She saw him, **did** she?*

Statements and tags can have the following combinations:

Statement	*Tag*	*Example*
Positive	Negative	***It's a lovely day, isn't it?***
Negative	Positive	***The food wasn't very good, was it?***
Positive	Positive	***You've met Jean before, have you?***

1 **Write two possible tags for these statements:**

1 He's here, ... / .... ?

2 She can speak Italian, ... / .... ?

3 You got back late last night, ... / .... ?

4 We've got enough money, ... / .... ?

Answers to tags

Answers to tag questions agree with the **statement**, not the tag:

A: *You're Australian, aren't you?* B: ***Yes, I am.***

A: *You **aren't** Australian, are you?* B: ***No, I'm not.***

Other points

- We use *shall we* after *Let's*:

  ***Let's** go down to the beach this afternoon, **shall we**?*
- We use *they* after *nobody*, *somebody*, *everybody* etc.

  ***Everyone's** here, aren't **they**?*
- The tag for *I'm* is *aren't I*:

  *Sorry. **I'm** late again, **aren't I**?*

Indirect questions

We can ask questions and express thoughts in an indirect way. Compare:

Excuse me. Where's the Red Lion Hotel? (direct)

*Excuse me. **Do you know where** the Red Lion Hotel **is**?* (indirect)

Indirect questions help us to sound more polite by making a question sound more like a statement. Notice the word order and the two parts of the question:

Do you know *Can you tell me* *Could you tell me* *I wondered* *I was wondering*	**+ wh- + subject + verb** *where the Red Lion Hotel is?* **+ *if* + subject + verb** *if the Red Lion Hotel is near here?* **+ *if* + subject + verb (past tense)** *if you wanted to see a film tonight?*

2 Correct the word order in these indirect questions.

1 Do you know what time is it? ....

2 I was wondering when could I see you? ....

3 Can you tell me where has Pete gone? ....

If you need to ask more than one question, we often **start** indirectly and **then** use direct questions:

A: *Excuse me, **can you tell me** how to get to the station from here?* (indirect question)

B: *Yes, you just go straight on and take the first left.*

A: *Thank you. And **what about** a cash machine – **is there** one on the way?* (direct question)

Getting it right

Exercise 1 Thinking about use

Look at the tags in the conversation extracts below. Write the 'Use' number, 1–3, on page 102, after each tag and mark the intonation.

Example: A: Peter's really good to work for.

B: Yes, he's really helpful, *isn't he?* 1↘

1 A: You couldn't open the door for me, *could you?* .....

2 A: Do you know how often trains go to Birmingham?

B: Mike should know, *shouldn't he?* ..... He travels a lot.

3 A: You know Pat and Neil? They never say hello when I see them.

B: Yes, they're really unfriendly, *aren't they?* .....

4 A: You haven't got a hammer, *have you?* .....

B: Yes, I'm sure I have somewhere.

5 A: I'm next in the queue, *aren't I?* .....

B: No, I'm afraid it's me next, actually.

6 A: Have you noticed how people are always great when there's a problem?

B: Yes, they are, *aren't they?* .....

Now practise saying the conversations, paying attention to intonation.

Exercise 2 Learning from learners

Add six tags to the learners' conversations below, in places where they make the conversations sound more natural. You may need to delete some words.

A: So, what shall we do tonight? You said you wanted to try the Mexican restaurant, *didn't you?*
B: Yes, I did. What do you think?
A: Well, only if it's not too expensive. It's very expensive to live here.
B: Yes, I agree, for most things. I bought some CDs the other day, and they were twice as expensive as they are at home.
A: But some things are cheaper. Clothes are reasonable.

A: This is more difficult than the first exercise.
B: Oh, I don't know. I think it's OK.
A: You've finished, Marcel. What did you put for number 5?
C: Number 5? It could be 'has been'.
A: Oh yes, it is. And you couldn't tell me the answer to number 8?
C: That's 'has gone'.

Exercise 3 Using tags

Complete each conversation with a statement and a tag. The conversations are examples of Uses 1–3 on page 102.

Use 1

Example: A: It's much warmer here than I expected.

B: Yes, *it's very hot, isn't it?*

1 A: Nice day today.

B: Yes, ... , ... ?

2 A: I didn't like the ballet very much.

B: No, it .... , ... ?

3 A: .... , ... ? Sally told me.

B: Yes, just a month ago. The old house was much too small.

4 A: I need some advice about holidays in Greece.

B: Try John. He's .... , ... ?

Use 2

5 A: Sydney .... , ... ?

B: No, no, Canberra is the capital.

6 A: There isn't any chocolate left! You .... , ... ?

B: Oh, er, sorry. Yes.

Use 3

7 A: I couldn't .... , ... ?

B: Yes, in a minute. Just let me look up a couple of words first.

8 A: .... , ... ?

B: Yes, I have, actually. She's in the garden.

Exercise 4 Writing indirect questions

Complete each conversation with a suitable indirect question.

Example: A: Excuse me. *Could you tell me how far it is to the city centre?*

B: Yes, of course. It's about three kilometres. You're nearly there.

A: Thanks very much.

1 A: Excuse me. .... ?

B: No, I'm sorry, I'm afraid I don't. You could go to Tourist Information. They have a list of all the hotels in the area.

2 A: Hello, Ollie, how are you?

B: I'm fine. .... ?

A: Oh, that's very kind of you, but I'm afraid I'm busy tonight. How about tomorrow?

3 A: Have you heard from Deborah recently?

B: No, I haven't actually. .... ?

A: No, I don't. She said she'd phone me if she got the job, but she hasn't called.

4 A: Martin, have you got a minute?

B: Yes, sure. What's up?

A: Oh, nothing really, but ....

B: Oh yes, I found out last week. 'CE' means cost effectiveness.

5 A: And I've only got one more question. .... ?

B: 25 March.

A: Oh, so your birthday is tomorrow!

6 A: Hello, can I help you?

B: Yes, ... ?

A: Yes, we've got a single room on 20 February.

Classwork

1 **Work in teams of two to four. Team 1 has one minute to prepare a sentence or exchange using a topic and a tag from the squares below.**

Example:

Topic: eating out   Tag: will you

A: *Sorry, that was a terrible meal.*

B: *Yes, you won't take me there again, will you?*

If the sentence or exchange is grammatically correct, Team 1 'wins' the squares. If it is not grammatically correct, the squares can be used again.

2 **Team 2 has a turn, but cannot use any squares already won.**

3 **The winning team is the one with the most squares.**

TOPICS

a holiday	the weather	animals
a friend	some news	television
a gift	grammar	a good book

TAGS

would you	isn't it	wasn't it
can't he	haven't we	weren't they
do they	aren't I	don't you

Unit 19

Reported speech 1: say, tell, ask

Getting started

1 **Read the article about a robbery and answer the questions.**

a) Who was the painting of? ....

b) How did the thief escape with the painting? ....

GUNMAN STEALS £650,000 PICASSO

A thief stopped a taxi outside the Hilton hotel at midday yesterday and asked to go to the Lefevre Gallery in central London. Giving the driver a £10 tip to wait, he walked into the private gallery and asked the value of Picasso's *Tête de femme*. The portrait of Picasso's girlfriend, Dora Maar, was painted in 1939 and is valued at £650,000.

'He seemed very civilised until he pulled out his gun,' said Camilla Bois, one of two assistants in the gallery when the thief entered.

He demanded the picture from the other assistant, Jacqueline Cartwright. 'He looked like an art student with long hair,' she said. He told her he had a gun and he wanted the picture. He told her to get it off the wall, but she said she could not. The man then pulled the picture from the wall and ran out of the gallery. The whole operation took 35 seconds.

At the taxi, the thief pointed the gun at the driver and demanded to be taken to Wimbledon, south-west London.

2 **Find and underline two examples of direct speech (words in quotation marks) and two examples of reported speech in the text.**

3 **Look at these examples of reported speech from the text:**

a) *He told her he had a gun and he wanted the picture.*

b) *… she said she could not.*

Which of the sentences below, i) or ii), do you think were the original words?

a) i) 'I've got a gun and want the picture.' .....

ii) 'Do as I say because I've got a gun. Give me that picture now.' .....

b) i) 'I can't.' ..... ii) 'I'm sorry, I can't do that.' .....

Looking at language

Say, *tell* and *ask*

Direct and reported speech

When we want to report someone's **exact words** we use **direct speech**:
She said, 'I'm afraid I don't know him – I've never met him before.'
When we want to report the **general meaning** of what someone said, we use **reported speech**:
She said she didn't know him.

Time and tense

We often move the tense of a verb one step back in reported speech because the original words happened before the reported speech:

original words	reported speech
*'I'm sorry. I **can't** do that.'*	*She **said** she **couldn't**.*
present tense	past tense

Here are some possible tense changes:

Original words	*Reported speech*
Present simple / present continuous: *'I'**m going** to the supermarket to buy food for the party.'*	Past simple / past continuous: *She said she **was going** shopping.*
Past simple / past continuous: *'He **went** in to work late yesterday.'*	Past perfect simple / continuous: *She told me he'**d gone** into work late yesterday.*
Present perfect simple / continuous: *'I'**ve had** a terrible cold, but I'm better now.'*	Past perfect simple / continuous: *She said she'**d had** a really bad cold.*
Past perfect simple / continuous: *'**I'd been having** loads of trouble with my washing machine so I finally got the plumber in yesterday.'*	Past perfect simple / continuous: *She told me she'**d been having** trouble with her washing machine but she's had it fixed now.*
Will: *'My mother **will water** my plants whilst I'm away.'*	*Would*: *She told me her mother **would look after** her plants until she gets back.*
Be going to + verb: *'They'**re going to have** a big celebration.'*	*Was / were going to* + verb: *She said they **were going to have** a big party.*

Often we don't need to change the tense because:

- what we are reporting is still true:
  They said that it's going to be very hot tomorrow.
- the reporting verb is in the present:
  She says she's going to be late.
- the original words were in the past simple or past continuous:
  'I loved him.' → *She said that she loved him.*

1 **Match the reported statements or questions, 1–5, to the probable tenses used in the original words, a)–e).**

1 She asked me if I wanted to go to the cinema. .....
2 They told me I'd have to pay before the start of the course. .....
3 She said that she'd been to New York. .....
4 The Prime Minister said he was going to give more money to education. .....
5 We were told he'd been seeing that girl for ages. .....

a) present perfect
b) present simple
c) present perfect continuous
d) *will* + verb
e) *be going to* + verb

Tell and *say* + *that*

Tell is followed by an object:
They told us (that) their holiday was great.
Say is not followed by an object:
They said (that) their holiday was great.
You do not have to use *that* after the reporting verb.

Reported questions with *ask*

Yes / no questions:
Have you been to the States before? → *She* ***asked if I'd been to the States before.***
Wh- questions:
Where have you been? → *She* ***asked me where I'd been.***

Reported speech in informal spoken English

In spoken English the reporting verb can be in the past continuous, especially to report newsworthy information and gossip:
Tracy ***was saying*** *(that) Diane and Marty have got engaged.*
Carla ***was telling*** *me (that) her home town doesn't have a cinema any more.*

2 **Here are some reported questions. Write the original questions.**

1 They asked me where I was going. ....
2 She asked me what I was thinking about. ....
3 He asked her if she was married. ....
4 I asked them whether they'd liked it. ....

Getting it right

Exercise 1 Thinking about context

Look at the original words and the reports below and answer the questions.

Example: Original: 'Why are you looking so miserable? What's happened to make you so depressed today?'
Report: He asked me why I was so depressed that day.
Was this report said on the same day, or a week later? A week later.

1 Original: 'Have you been to Hong Kong, David?'
Report: Sarah asked David if he'd been to Hong Kong.
Is there a tense change in the report or not? ....

2 Original: 'We're having friends round for dinner on Saturday.'
Report: He said they're having friends round on Saturday evening.
Is there a tense change in the report or not? ....

3 Original: 'They're going to buy that house in Bournemouth. You know, the lovely old cottage with the pretty garden.'
Report: Sue was saying they've decided to buy that cottage in Bournemouth.
Is this report spoken or written? ....

4 Original: 'Can I bring two friends to your party?'
Report: She's asked if she can bring two friends to the party.
Was this report said before or after the party? ....

5 Original: 'We're really lucky – we've got tickets for the opening night of the show next Saturday.'
Report: She told me they'd got tickets for yesterday's opening night of the show.
Was this report said before or after the opening night? ....

6 Original: 'We went to an excellent play last night.'
Report: Martin said they went to the theatre last night.
Was this report said on the same day as the original or later? ....

7 Original: 'I've won two tickets for a weekend in New York!'
Report: She says she's won a weekend for two in New York!
Was this report made soon after the original words or some time later? ....

8 Original: 'Apparently Denmark only has about 5,000,000 people.'
Report: Pete was saying that the population of Denmark is only about 5,000,000.
The tense is the same in the original and the report. Why? ....

Exercise 2 Learning from learners

Correct any mistakes in the learners' sentences below.

Examples: She said ~~us~~ that she felt tired.

asked me if I was

My boss ~~said was I~~ going to work late.

1 She said last night that she isn't going to come to the party, but look, she's over there.
2 They said me they had been waiting for a long time.
3 He told that he had had a wonderful holiday.
4 I asked him what did he do.
5 Miguel was telling that you're thinking of changing your job.
6 I missed the lecture, so I asked Sheena what had they done.
7 I asked him was he free on Friday night but he said he was busy unfortunately.
8 He asked me when did the film start.

Exercise 3 Completing a conversation

Use the direct speech on the left to fill in the missing reports in the conversation on the right.

A: 'Helen, my sister, isn't very well.' **Jenny:** 'I know. I met her in the supermarket.' **A:** 'That's strange because my sister's too ill to go out.' **Jenny:** 'She only had a cold, that's all.'	A: How are you, Carolyn? B: I'm fine. What about you? A: Well, not too bad, although I had a bit of a funny day yesterday. B: Why, what happened? A: I met Jenny and I told her *that Helen, my sister, wasn't very well*. She said 1 .... already .... because .... Well, I said I thought 2 .... because my sister was too ill to go out. Jenny said 3 ....
A: 'Have you been shopping in the last few days?'	B: Did you ask your sister about it? A: Yes. That afternoon I went round to her house and she was still in bed. I asked her 4 .... and she looked at me as if I was mad. Then that evening I met an old colleague of mine who said that
Colleague: 'Oh, by the way, I saw your sister, Helen, on Monday.' **A:** 'Really? Did you speak to her?' **Colleague:** 'No, I only waved.'	5 .... too. I asked him 6 .... and he said 7 .... B: Maybe Helen has been so ill she can't remember what she's been doing. A: It looks like it, yes.

Exercise 4 Reporting and quoting

Read the conversation below between Lucy and a newspaper reporter. Then complete the newspaper article. Use reported speech or direct speech.

Example: Conversation: I'll never forget it.
Direct speech: She said, 'I'll never forget it'. *or*
Reported speech: She said she would never forget it.

Reporter: So what happened exactly?
Lucy: Well, he held a gun to my face and told me to hand over the money in the till.
Reporter: Can you remember what he looked like?
Lucy: Well, he didn't look like a thief. He was old – probably 65, with grey-white hair – and he looked very ordinary.
Reporter: Did he hurt anyone? Was he violent at all?
Lucy: No. In fact he was quite polite and thanked me when I gave him the money.
Reporter: Why hasn't he been caught, do you think?
Lucy: Maybe just because he looks like anybody's grandad!

THIEF 'LOOKS LIKE GRANDAD'

A THIEF who has robbed six times in the last year is proving difficult to catch because he looks so ordinary. The elderly man blamed for the robberies generally walks into a store, gets out a gun and demands cash from the cashiers. Lucy Dray, a cashier at a Birmingham department store, said **1** .... She described him as **2** .... He appears to be quite a polite man. According to Ms Dray, **3** .... The police are finding it very difficult to catch him. Ms Dray told reporters **4** ....

Classwork

1 **Think of three pieces of personal information about yourself. Two should be true, but the other should be untrue. Tell the student next to you the information, and listen to theirs.**

2 **Join up with a different person, and report the information you heard about your first partner.**

Example:
Jania said she'd been to the USA twice, that she's one of four sisters, and that she's going to study law.

3 **Decide together what you think is true and untrue.**

4 **Go back to your first partner and see if you were right.**

Unit 20

Reported speech 2: reporting verbs

Getting started

1 **Read the article about an attempt to fly round the world in a balloon and answer the questions.**

a) What did the crew throw away by mistake? ....

b) Do you think the journey was successful? ....

Branson's crew throws away $2,000

Richard Branson's* crew threw $2,000 from their round-the-world balloon without realising it, in their efforts to lighten their load over Algeria on Wednesday.

The cash had been placed in a flight bag for use after an emergency landing, but none of the crew knew anything about it until technicians told them it had gone missing.

'We didn't know it was aboard,' Mr Branson said yesterday. 'We just threw it out with most of the other unnecessary things – water, food, oil, everything.'

Per Lindstrand, who was at the controls at the time, remarked that he had suggested that Mr Branson throw out his wallet.

Speaking on the crew's return to London, Mr Lindstrand admitted that the balloon's operating systems had never been properly tested before Tuesday's take-off from Morocco.

*Richard Branson is a famous British businessman

2 **Find two examples of reporting verbs that could be replaced by *said*.**

3 **Here is another reporting verb from the text:**
... he <u>had suggested</u> that Mr Branson throw out his wallet.

What do you think Per Lindstrand's original words were? ....

Looking at language

Reporting verbs

In Unit 19 you used *say*, *tell* and *ask* to report the **overall meaning** of what someone said, rather than the **exact words**. Reporting verbs such as *invite*, *admit* and *suggest* show the overall meaning of what someone said more precisely.

Compare:

*She **asked** him if he would like to go out for a drink.*
*She **invited** him out for a drink.*

Here are some other reporting verbs. Notice the form of the following clause. Some verbs can be followed by more than one form of clause.

Reporting verbs with (*that*) + clause

agree	*They **agreed (that)** the match had been disappointing.*
admit	*He **admitted (that)** they had cheated in the exam.*
complain	*She **complained (that)** the service was bad.*
deny	*He **denied (that)** he had done anything wrong.*
promise	*We **promised (that)** we would try to see them the following week.*
suggest	*He **suggested (that)** he throw away his wallet.*
warn	*She **warned** me **(that)** he would be late.*

Reporting verbs with an infinitive

agree	*I **agreed to** come back later.*
advise	*He **advised** her **to** see a doctor.*
demand	*We **demanded to** see a specialist.*
encourage	*My parents **encouraged** me **to** practise the piano.*
offer	*She **offered to** help her with her homework.*
promise	*They **promised to** get me some money.*
refuse	*He **refused to** do what I asked.*
remind	*He **reminded** me **to** go to the meeting at 2.00.*
warn	*He **warned** me **not to** go out with her.*

Notice that when *warn* is followed by the infinitive, *not* is always used.
The verbs *agree*, *advise*, *demand*, *promise* and *remind* can also be followed by *not* + infinitive.

Reporting verbs with *about*

advise	*She **advised** me **about** my decision.*
apologise	*He **apologised about** the service.*
complain	*She **complained about** the food.*
remind	*He **reminded** me **about** my meeting at 2.00.*

Reporting verbs with *-ing* form / noun:

accept	*He accepted the invitation.* (not usually used with the -*ing* form)
admit	*He admitted cheating in the exam.* *He admitted his guilt.*
deny	*He denied doing anything wrong.* *He denied responsibility.*

1 **If you have problems with a computer or software you can usually phone a helpdesk. Why are the helpdesk stories below funny? Put a reporting verb in each gap.**

A helpdesk technician 1 .... his customer to put a floppy disk back in the drive. The customer asked him to wait a moment and was heard opening the door and going outside. The customer returned to the phone to say it was OK, the floppy disk was outside on the drive just next to the car.

A customer called up the helpdesk when her words disappeared in the middle of typing. When the helpdesk technician asked her to check if the computer was plugged in, she said it was too dark to see. When the technician 2 .... that she turn the lights on, the customer said she couldn't because there was a power failure!

Reported requests and orders

We use *ask* / *tell* (+ object) + infinitive:

'Can you open the window?' → ***He asked me to open** the window.*

'Get up at once! It's 10.00.' → ***She told me to get up** immediately.*

2 **Report these requests and orders.**

1 'Could you phone me later?' → She ....

2 'Put the camera down!' → He ....

3 'Can you two help us for a few minutes?' → They ....

Getting it right

Exercise 1 Identifying functions

Match the sentences, 1–10, to the reporting verbs, a)–k).

Example: 'I don't think the food in your restaurant is very good.' *d)*

1 'I don't think you should tell him about this conversation.' .....
2 'I'm fed up with you being late every day.' .....
3 'Don't forget to get some milk on your way home.' .....
4 'I'm sorry, but I can't accept your offer.' .....
5 'Can I help you?' .....
6 'Would you open the window for me, please?' .....
7 'I know it was a stupid thing to do.' .....
8 'Why don't we go out somewhere tomorrow night?' .....
9 'I really think you should learn to drive.' .....
10 'Don't touch it! It's hot!' .....

a) remind
b) ask
c) encourage
~~d) complain~~
e) complain
f) refuse
g) offer
h) suggest
i) advise
j) admit
k) warn

Extension

Report sentences 1–10.

Example: *She complained about the restaurant.*

Exercise 2 Learning from learners

Complete the sentences from learners with endings a)–i) and correct the mistake in each sentence. Some verbs are not in *Looking at language*. Use a dictionary to check their meaning and the form of their following clause.

Example: He complained ^*to* me about the facilities in the school but *b)*.

1 Peter invited me out to dinner last week but .....
2 The police accused to him of helping the escaped prisoner but .....
3 In the film they asked him if he had seen the questions before the show and .....
4 She complained about that the food was cold and .....
5 It was very kind of him to offer help me with my suitcase and .....
6 I got a letter asking me to fill in a questionnaire but .....
7 Jason asked us if we wanted to go to the pub tonight but .....
8 My secretary reminded me about my appointment and .....

a) we suggested to go to the cinema instead.
~~b) I insisted that they are of the highest standards.~~
c) eventually he admitted to have done it.
d) I'm refusing do it because it's so long.
e) I had to refuse going because I was already doing something.
f) I accepted his help happily.
g) I admitted that completely forgetting about it.
h) he denied doing it.
i) the waiter apologised to her.

Exercise 3 Using reporting verbs

Rewrite the sentences and phrases in *italics* using different reporting verbs.

A: I met Joe on the way home. *He asked if we'd like to go round to their house for dinner next Saturday night.* **1** *I said, yes, we'd love to.* I hope that's OK.

B: Yes, we're not doing anything. **2** *Did you tell him we'd bring some wine?*

A: Yes, and **3** *I told him that we would be late.*

He invited us round to their house for dinner next Saturday night.

1 ....

2 ....

3 ....

A: How was work today?

B: Oh, another pretty awful day, actually. **4** *A customer said the food was disgusting* and **5** *said that he had to see the manager.* **6** *I said I was very sorry about the food*, but that just made him angrier. The manager gave him his money back in the end.

4 ....

5 ....

6 ....

A: What did you say to Frances?

B: **7** *I said that she should arrange a meeting with Max.*

A: **8** *Did you tell her not to forget to take the photos?*

B: Yes, and she's going to phone us as soon as she's seen him.

7 ....

8 ....

Exercise 4 Writing a summary

A 'syndicate' is a group of people who put their money together to buy lottery tickets. The syndicate below won a lot of money and are meeting to decide how to spend it. Read the conversation and then write a summary of the meeting, using some of the reporting verbs in the box on the next page if you can.

Sarah: Wow! Twenty-five thousand pounds! What are we going to do with it?

Dave: Well, I think the best idea is to invest it all together. Think about the long-term future.

Chris: Yeah, Dave's right. It's a good idea.

Anna: Wait a minute. We always follow Dave's decisions, and this time I don't agree. I think we should share the money out equally and do what we like with our own share.

Sarah: What do other people think?

Marion: Well, I know it's selfish but … I like Anna's idea of taking our own share. I'm sorry if some of you don't like it but, well, I want to get a new computer.

Dave: Careful, everyone! Once you've spent it, it's gone!

Chris: Oh, we're never going to agree. Don't forget we said we should think about it for a month if we ever won a big prize. Why don't we meet again next week when we've all had a chance to think about it?

admit	advise	agree	ask	complain	remind	suggest	warn

NOTES FROM MEETING 28 MAY

Present: Sarah, Dave, Chris, Anna, Marion

Sarah started by asking for ideas, and Dave suggested that ....

....

....

....

....

....

....

....

Classwork

1 **Work in pairs. On a piece of paper write a reporting verb.**

Example: deny

2 **On a different piece of paper write a sentence in direct speech that matches the verb on your new piece of paper.**

Example: I didn't break those glasses!

Your teacher will collect both pieces of paper.

3 **Your teacher will give you either a reporting verb, or a sentence in direct speech. Walk around the class to find the person with the matching piece of paper.**

Example:

A: *I've got 'deny' on my paper. What have you got?*

B: *I've got 'I didn't break those glasses!', so you're my partner.*

4 **Sit down with your new partner and write a report of the sentence in direct speech using the reporting verb.**

Example:

He denied breaking the glasses.

5 **Read out your report. The class should decide if it is correct or not.**

Unit

21 Defining relative clauses

Getting started

1 **You're going to read three stories about a cat, a dog and some monkeys. Which animal(s), do you think, could go in each headline?**

a) .... go to prison b) .... eats money c) .... is hurt by automatic feeder

Now read the three stories to find out which animals were really involved.

A Southampton dog lover who rescued a lost dog returned home to find it had eaten £800 he had saved for a new car.

MONKEYS which annoy people in the northern Indian state of Punjab are being locked up in a special jail and held until they are ready for release back into society.

A cat feeder, probably for people who secretly hate their cats, was introduced in 1979. It was a plastic machine that made feeding the cat a simple job. You put food into the feeder and it would automatically give it to the cat. Great idea for a pet owner – but not so great for the cat. The lid of the feeder would often fall down while the cat was eating and hit it on the nose.

2 **Find these words in the texts: *who*, *which* and *that*. Which of these words.**

a) is used for people? ....

b) are used for things and animals? ....

3 **Read the spoken version of the dog story and answer the question.**

'There was this man that loved animals, and one day he found a dog wandering around in the street and he took him home with him. He left the dog in his house while he went out shopping and when he came home he had a bit of a shock. The stupid dog had eaten £800 that he had been saving to buy a new car!'

Can *that* be used for things **and** people? ....

4 **Using the answers to 2 and 3 above, complete this sentence:**

a) .... and b) .... can be used to describe people, and c) .... and d) ....can be used to refer to things or animals.

Looking at language

Defining relative clauses

Relative clauses give information about a noun or noun phrase. There are two types:

- **defining relative clauses** give information to help us identify a specific person, animal or thing:
  *Monkeys **which annoy people in the northern Indian state of Punjab** are being locked up in a special jail.* (not *all* monkeys in the Punjab, just these specific monkeys)
- **non-defining relative clauses** give additional information which does not identify the person, animal or thing:
  *The painting was by Picasso, **who died in 1973**.* (we are not identifying this Picasso from any other Picassos)

(See Unit 22 for more on non-defining relative clauses.)

Words like *who*, *that*, and *which* in relative clauses are called **relative pronouns**. The chart below shows what they refer to.

Relative pronoun	*Refers to:*
who (or *whom* in formal English when it replaces an object); *that* (usually in spoken English)	people (and sometimes pet animals): *There's the woman **who / that** told me.* *There are several people **whom** I need to talk to.* *It was my dog **who / that** chased the cat, not yours.*
which and *that*	things: *Flowers **which / that** attract bees are good for gardens.*
where (= *in which*)	places: *It's a place **where** time seems to stand still.* Also in descriptions of stories and films: *There's a scene **where** the hero nearly dies.*
when	nouns of time: *It was just after 9.00 **when** he got back.*
whose	possessives: *The people **whose** daughter I look after are moving away.*
why	after the noun *the reason*: *And that's the reason **why** we're leaving.*

In defining relative clauses you can leave out the relative pronoun when it refers to the **object** of the verb in the clause.
Compare:

subject — verb — object

The man who visited us was a salesman.

Here *who* cannot be left out.

object — subject — verb

The man who we went to visit was a salesman.

Here *who* can be left out:

The man we went to visit was a salesman.

But be careful:

*The man with a large expensive house and fast car (**who**) we went to visit was an insurance salesman.*

If you leave out *who* here, the sentence is unclear because the relative clause is a long way from the noun (*the man*) it replaces.

1 In the text below, can you leave out the relative pronoun in the underlined relative clause? Why / why not?

Lamine Martori, the French boy who last year stole £8,500 from his parents for a luxury holiday at Disneyland Paris, has stolen again. Lamine, 12, took £750 for a three-day visit. After he returned, his mother Jeanne said: 'I'm relieved he's home but I'm sure he'll do it again.'

....

....

Other points

- *What* generally means 'the thing(s) that':
  *We went out again to get **what** we needed.*
  *That's **what** I thought.*
- After prepositions we use *whom* and *which*. Prepositions come before the pronoun in formal language:
  *The order **to which** I referred in my previous letter has not arrived.*
  *The relative **with whom** I went to India stayed there for another month.*
  Prepositions come at the end of the clause in informal spoken English:
  *Careful with that! It's the bag (**which**) I keep my keys **in**.* (informal / spoken)
- *Whom* is rare in spoken English.

Getting it right

Exercise 1 Relative pronouns

Underline the relative pronoun in the sentences below. Explain what it refers to, and decide whether it can be left out.

Relative pronoun	*Refers to:*	*Can it be left out?*
Example: I don't know the man that Sarah's talking to, do I?	*the man*......	*yes*..............
1 What's the name of that TV channel which shows classic films?	....	....
2 As a vegetarian, there aren't many things that I can eat in that restaurant.	....	....
3 What do you think now about the things that you did in your youth?	....	....
4 Did you hear about the man who's trying to fly round the world in a balloon?	....	....
5 What's the best holiday that you've ever had?	....	....
6 The doctor has given me some new antibiotics which are better than the old ones.	....	....
7 Jane is someone that I get on really well with.	....	....
8 That's the woman who told me about the job.	....	....

Exercise 2 Link up

Match the two halves of the sentences and link them with a suitable relative pronoun.

Example: This is one occasion *when*......*h)*

1 Who's that woman ....
2 Do you know ....
3 According to reporters at the scene ....
4 You know the earrings I bought ....
5 She's someone ....
6 The trainer gave him some exercises ....
7 Do you remember the time ....
8 I can't remember ....

a) I mean?
b) I feel you can trust.
c) we went swimming and that boy pushed you in the water?
d) were really expensive? Well, I lost one of them.
e) saw the event, the police overreacted.
f) she said.
g) were aimed at improving his fitness.
h) ~~we should work together for the good of the company.~~
i) always waits at the bus stop?

▷ Exercise 3 Learning from learners

Look at this learner's story. Sentences 1–8 all contain a relative clause. Two relative clauses are correct, but the others each have a mistake. Find and correct the mistakes.

It was late in the evening and I was travelling home by train after a long weekend in the north of the country. I had been speaking to the woman whom was sitting next to me when suddenly the man opposite interrupted our conversation. **1** He was quite polite, telling us that he was looking for a friend which he had lost touch with. **2** He was trying to find him, because another friend whose they had both known had died and left them some money.

3 I asked him to tell me more about the person which he was looking for. **4** He said that it was someone from the town in where he grew up. **5** He said that this man for whom he was looking was called François Dumont.

6 I had listened to his story quietly, but when I heard the name of the man that he was looking for him I couldn't help feeling excited. **7** I asked him the name of the place which he had known this missing man. And he answered as I had hoped.

And so I told him that my father's name was François Dumont. **8** And after this meeting my father became quite rich because the long-lost dead friend had left a will which gave my father a lot of money.

▷ Exercise 4 Completing conversations

Complete each conversation with a suitable relative clause.

Example: A: Do you want to go out tonight?
B: I'd love to, but there are a few things which *I have to do.*

1 A: Look over there! That's him.
B: Who?
A: You know! The man who ....
B: Are you sure? Shouldn't we call the police then?

2 A: I've decided what I want for my birthday. I want that blouse I told you about. The one that ....
B Oh, well, I'm afraid I've already got your present.

3 A: Are you going anywhere nice during the holidays?
B: Yes, we are actually. We're going to a lovely place where ....

4 A: I saw Mike yesterday.
B: Who's Mike?
A: He's the one whose ....
B: Oh yes, she does that news programme on Friday nights, doesn't she?

5 A: Have you seen any good films lately?
B: Yes, I saw a good one on TV last week. There was a brilliant scene where ....
....

6 A: I saw a woman with a small dog which ....
B: Oh, how strange.
A: Yes, and she was wearing a coat the same colour!

7 A: I can't decide which ....
B: I think the black ones will look nicer with your new leather jacket.

8 A: What are you listening to?
B: It's the CD that ....
A: Oh yes, of course. I'm glad you like it. I couldn't decide what to give you, but when I heard this I thought it would be ideal.

Extension

Look at the relative clauses again and decide which relative pronouns can be left out.

Classwork

1 **Choose someone in the class for each sentence below and write a relative clause that you think is true for them.**
Example: I think Jeanne generally likes people who are extrovert and sociable.

I think …

1 .... generally likes people who ....
2 .... likes things that ....
3 .... doesn't like food which ....
4 .... often goes to places where ....
5 .... never goes to see the kind of films where ....
6 .... finds activities in which you have to .... difficult / easy.
7 .... listens to the kind of music which ....
8 .... knows someone who ....

2 **Read out your sentences one by one and let the person you have named say if they are true or not. If they are true you get a point. The winner is the person with the most points.**

Example:
A: *I think Jeanne generally likes people who are extrovert and sociable.*
Jeanne: *Yes, that's probably true. You can have a point.*

Unit

22 Non-defining relative clauses

Getting started

1 Read the article about a businessman, Reuben Singh. What is unusual about him?

....

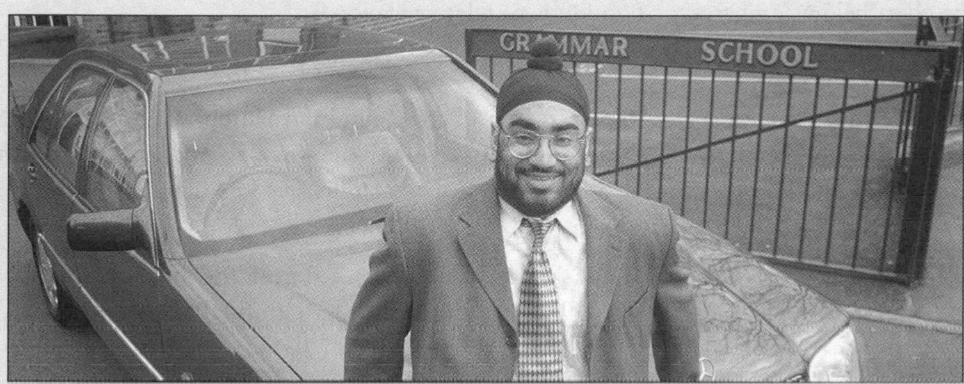

Reuben Singh, who is worth about £14 million, hands the phone to his accountant. 'Most newspapers,' says the accountant, 'state that Reuben is worth 15 million. We are a bit conservative and say 14 million. It is still rather a lot ... especially for a 19-year-old,' he adds before passing the phone back to the teenage businessman, who coughs quietly.

Singh is the owner of the Miss Attitude Retail Group, which supplies fashion jewellery and accessories. He is also a student at Manchester Metropolitan University, studying for a degree in financial services. Last year, when he was still only worth ten million, he was running his own business while studying for exams at William Hulme Grammar School in Manchester.

He opened the first Miss Attitude shop in Manchester less than a year ago; now he has 14 shops with another 16 planned for next year. He points out that he is the only teenager who has set up a company for his own age group.

(adapted from an article by Douglas Kennedy in *The Independent*, 9 December 1995)

2 Find and <u>underline</u> all the clauses starting with *who*, *which* and *when*.

3 Answer the questions about the clauses in 2.

a) Which clauses have commas (,)? ....

b) Which clause gives essential information, and **cannot** be left out? ....

....

Looking at language

Non-defining relative clauses

Look at the **relative clause** in this sentence:

Reuben Singh, ***who is worth about £14 million****, hands the phone to his accountant.*

The **non-defining relative clause** gives **extra** information. The sentence is still meaningful without it:

Reuben Singh hands the phone to his accountant.

Compare it with this **defining relative clause** (see Unit 21):

... he is the only teenager ***who has set up a company for his own age group****.*

This relative clause is essential to make the sentence meaningful. It distinguishes this teenager from others.

The chart below compares the two kinds of relative clauses.

Defining relative clauses:	*Non-defining relative clauses:*
identify something or somebody: *Reuben Singh is the teenager* ***who runs his own retail business****.*	give extra information: *Last year,* ***when he was still only worth ten million****, he was running his own business.*
do not have commas (written English) or pauses (spoken English).	are separated from the main clause by commas (written English) or pauses (spoken English).
can use *that* instead of *who* or *which*: *Reuben Singh is the teenager* ***that runs his own retail business****.*	do not use *that*: *Reuben Singh,* ***who*** *is worth about £14 million, hands the phone to his accountant.* We don't say: ~~*Reuben Singh, that is worth about £14 million...*~~
can sometimes (see Unit 21) leave out the relative pronoun: *The business (****which****) he started is now worth £14 million.*	have to have the relative pronoun: We don't say: ~~*The business, he started five years ago, owns a chain of shops*~~. We say: *The business,* ***which*** *he started five years ago, owns a chain of shops.*

Notice how the meaning of a sentence changes according to the type of relative clause:
Non-defining: *The man, who was wearing a lime green hat, seemed a little strange.* (there is only one man)
Defining: *The man who was wearing a lime green hat seemed a little strange.* (there is more than one man, and I want to talk about the one in the lime green hat)

Other points

- *Which* can refer to a whole clause, often with ***be*** **+ adjective**:
  *We spent a week high up in the mountains, **which was wonderful**.*
- Non-defining relative clauses come in the middle or at the end of a sentence:
  *The man, **who was wearing a lime green hat**, seemed a little strange.*
  *The policeman spoke to the girl, **who did not appear to listen**.*

1 In the story below, all the commas have been removed. Underline the three relative clauses in the story and add commas where necessary.

A 45-year-old woman has won a major modelling contract after having ten children. Annette Edwards whose last child was born only 19 months ago will appear in advertisements for a face cream. Mrs Edwards who weighs 58 kg claims she has the same figure that she had at 15.

(adapted from an article by Richard Smith in *The Independent*, 3 March 1997)

Getting it right

Exercise 1 Defining and non-defining relative clauses

Underline the relative clause in each sentence, and say if it is defining or non-defining. Then answer the question about the sentence.

Example: The course, which was very tiring, passed very quickly. *non-defining*

Which is the main information, a) or b)?

a) The course was very tiring. b) The course passed quickly. *b)*

1 My mother, who had been sitting still for a very long time, finally spoke. ....

Does the sentence make sense if you leave out the relative clause? ....

2 The woman who was standing in the corner finally left, but the other women stayed behind. ....

Is the sentence OK if you leave out the relative clause? ....

3 A boy, who was wearing a jacket, was seen running away from the burning car. ....

Which is the main information, a) or b)?

a) The boy was wearing a jacket.

b) The boy was seen running away from the burning car. .....

4 I've got a new job which is wonderful. ....

What is wonderful, a) or b)?

a) The job itself. b) Having a new job. .....

5 The chairs, which at first looked old and dirty, were very valuable. ....

Which is the main information, a) or b)?

a) The chairs were old and dirty. b) The chairs were very valuable. .....

....

Exercise 2 Adding relative clauses

In the story below all the relative clauses have been removed. Put clauses a)–g) in the gaps and add commas where necessary. In some places more than one clause will be suitable.

River rescue

A quick-thinking cyclist ......c)....... today received an award for his actions.

Steve Kimberley was cycling home one day last year when an anxious woman asked him to help a man **1** .... Steve **2** .... initially tried to pull the man out with a dog lead. Then, as someone else rang for the police, he tried to keep the man calm and alert by asking him questions. Eventually a police officer threw a rope to the man **3** ....

Mr Kimberley **4** .... was today being presented with the Tom Mogg Trophy by the Royal Lifesaving Society. Mr Kimberley **5** .... had been taught by the society's Rescue Unit **6** ....

a) who lives in Bath
b) who had recently had a series of three life-saving lessons
c) ~~who helped save the life of a man who fell into an icy river~~
d) who had fallen into the river
e) who works as a computer webmaster
f) which meets at Culverhay Sports Centre
g) which he was able to climb up

Exercise 3 Learning from learners

Rewrite each learner's extract as one sentence using a defining or non-defining relative clause.

Example: While I was there I met a really interesting man. He told me all about his travels in Asia.
While I was there I met a really interesting man who told me all about his travels in Asia.

1 We went to this wonderful holiday complex. There was a huge pool and a fitness centre.

....

2 The pool was used for training by Olympic athletes. It was over 100 metres long.

....

3 Our room had a fantastic view over the beach. The room had a jacuzzi and a large balcony.

....

4 There were lots of insects. They kept me awake at night with their buzzing and biting.

....

5 Fiji has beautiful golden beaches and warm, clear blue sea. The beaches are often empty.

....

6 We went to a place up in the mountains. It had a monastery and amazing views.

....

Exercise 4 Building sentences

Make sentences by joining the boxes using non-defining relative clauses.

Examples:

	coat	new	green	*His coat, which was new, was green.*
	hotel	£200 per night	expensive	*The hotel costs £200 per night, which is expensive.*
1	story	interesting	too long	....
2	mobile phone	Japan	tiny	....
3	plant	flowers are yellow	rare	....
4	John	job	good	....
5	man	two young daughters	76	....
6	Sarah	American	yoga	....

Extension

Copy the words in boxes onto pieces of paper and mix them up in three piles, one for the first boxes, one the second etc. Turn over one from each pile and try to make a sentence including a relative clause.

Classwork

1 **Write a) below on a piece of paper. Add a relative clause to it:**
One day a man called Joe, who was wearing a ridiculous pair of trousers

2 **Fold the top of the paper over so you cannot see your writing, and pass it to the next student.**

3 **Copy b) in the same way, add a relative clause to it and pass it on.**

4 **Continue like this until sentence f) is completed. Unfold the paper and read the stories. Whose is the funniest?**

a) One day a man called Joe
b) met a woman called Miranda
c) in the
d) He asked her to go to a restaurant
e) She said she'd prefer to go to the cinema
f) In the end they got married and had four children

Review unit

2 Units 13–22 Sentences

Exercise 1 Mixed structures Units 13–22

Match the grammar areas, 1–10, to the example sentences, a)–k).

Example: Using information about time to start a sentence ..d)

1 Imperative for instructions .....
2 Auxiliary *do* for emphasis .....
3 A tail .....
4 A wh- question .....
5 A tag question to check something we think we know .....
6 An indirect question .....
7 Reported speech using *tell* .....
8 Reported speech using another reporting verb .....
9 A defining relative clause .....
10 A non-defining relative clause .....

a) They advised me not to go there because it's been quite politically unstable recently.
b) I was wondering if you could lend me 50 pence?
c) He's a bit strange, my brother.
d) ~~At first she didn't like her new job.~~
e) I know you don't trust her, but she did help me a lot in the past.
f) Five boys who were seen in the area just before the robbery have now been arrested.
g) The paintings, which went on sale yesterday, are on show at the local gallery.
h) You don't live here, do you? Otherwise you'd know about the village festival.
i) What time are you meeting Sam?
j) First fill the kettle with water, and then put a teabag in your cup.
k) Her teacher told me she hadn't been seen all day.

Exercise 2 Imperatives Unit 14

Fill in the gaps with verbs from the box. Then follow the instructions.

add	multiply	choose	take	take	~~think~~	think	turn

Example: ..Think.. of a number between 1 and 10 and

1 .... it by 9.
2 If the answer is a two-digit number, ... these digits together to give a new number.
3 .... 5 away from the new number.
4 .... this number into a letter from the alphabet where A=1, B=2, C=3 etc.
5 .... the name of a country beginning with this letter.
6 .... the second letter in the country name and .... of a mammal that begins with that letter.

What have you got?

Exercise 3 Questions and answers in jokes **Units 17–18**

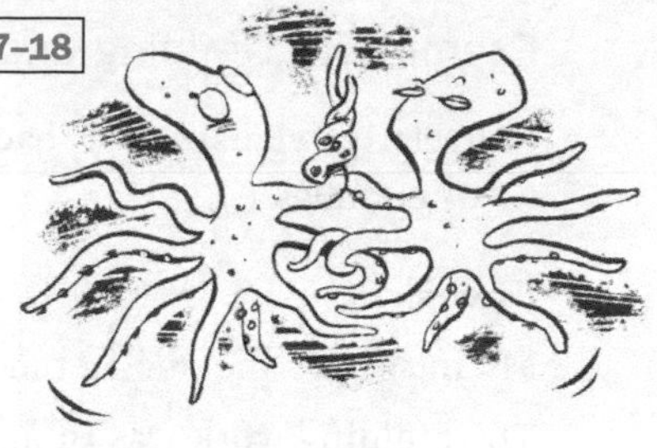

In the jokes below, put the words in questions 1–6 in order, and find the appropriate answers from a)–g).

Example:
Waiter! steak got you Why on thumb my your have? c)
Waiter! Why have you got your thumb on my steak?

1 is high Why sky the? ....
2 be long How the Oxford will train to? ....
3 you that Why are making at funny-looking faces dog? ....
4 octopus to the did say boyfriend What her? ....
5 a and green is pea small Why? ....
6 say work What when do from they get bees home? ....

a) I want to hold your hand, your hand, your hand.
b) So that birds don't bump their heads.
c) ~~I don't want it to fall off the plate again.~~
d) Because if it was large and red it would be a tomato.
e) 'About 200 metres,' said the station master.
f) Well, he started it.
g) Honey, I'm home.

Exercise 4 Mixed structures **Units 14–22**

Fill in the gaps in this phone conversation between a young woman and her mother.

A: Hi, Mum. It's me.
B: Oh, hello! I wasn't expecting you to call. Where are you?
A: We arrived in India yesterday, and an amazing thing happened this morning which I just had to tell you about.
B: Oh, what?
A: Well, you remember the Prices, 1 .... used to live next door when I was ten or eleven? Well, I met Jamie Price this morning, in the same hotel!
B: You didn't, 2 .... ?
A: Yeah, and he looked just the same. I told him he looked familiar and he said I did too, and when he told me his name I immediately remembered him. You still write to them at Christmas, 3 .... ?
B: Yes. Well, how amazing. What 4 .... in Delhi?
A: He's doing what I'm doing, travelling for a year. Anyway, I'd better go in a minute, but before I do, I 5 .... if I could ask you a favour?
B: Of course. Go on.
A: You couldn't ring my bank and check they sent the money I asked for, 6 .... ?
B: Yes, all right. And what about letters? 7 .... you want me to open them?
A: Only if they look urgent, and then 8 .... me any important news. There are Internet cafés everywhere. Must go, Mum. Great to speak to you. I'll ring again in a couple of weeks. Bye.

Exercise 5 Defining and non-defining relative clauses **Units 21–22**

Put relative clauses a)–l) back into sentences or phrases 1–10. Add any necessary full stops (.) or commas (,).

Examples:

My husband's the one, *d)* not me.

The building work *i)* was running late as well.

1 There were only three people in the queue.
2 The place is France.
3 Our car was damaged by the storm.
4 I don't know anyone, do you?
5 The weather was lovely.
6 We chose the house
7 Our old flat was very airy and big.
8 We've tried to arrange the meeting at a time
9 Moira Fisher was left homeless.
10 The one was a bit bigger than this one.

a) which was good as we wanted to stay outside
b) I asked for
c) which was brand new at the time
d) ~~who does all the cooking~~
e) that gets on well with him
f) who was only 16 at the time
g) that had the bigger garden
h) that I like best for family holidays
i) ~~which was already over budget~~
j) which was on the fourteenth floor
k) which is convenient for everyone
l) which wasn't many for that time of day

Exercise 6 Reported speech **Units 19–20**

Read the two texts and then write what you think the original words were in 1–8.

When Martin *invited* me to visit his family with him, I 1 *agreed* to go because I'd heard so much about them. On the way down there he 2 *warned* me not to talk about politics. I 3 *asked* him what the problem was, and he 4 *said* that they all disagreed with each other!

Example: *Would you like to come and visit my family with me?*

1 ....
2 ....
3 ....
4 ....

David 5 *reminded* Deborah to take her medicine. She's always forgetting to take it and then wonders why she isn't getting any better. I 6 *suggested* she set an alarm to help her remember, but she 7 *refused* to do that. She 8 *said* it was a crazy idea.

5 ....
6 ....
7 ....
8 ....

Unit 23

Verbs followed by the infinitive or the -ing form

Getting started

1 **Read the reviews for the book *Harry Potter and the Philosopher's Stone* by J.K. Rowling. Underline one word in each review that shows the speaker liked the book.**

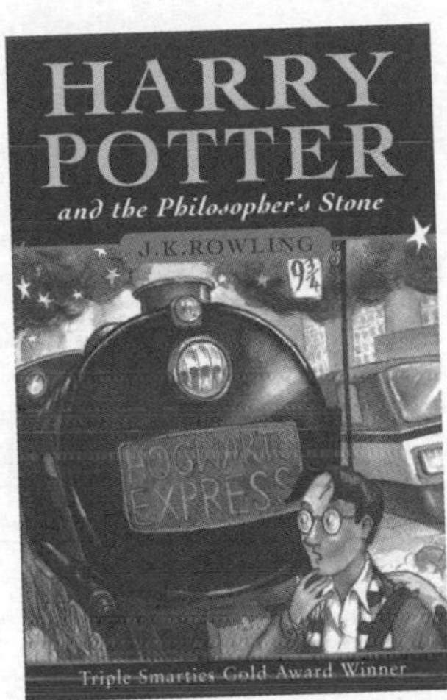

'I think *Harry Potter and the Philosopher's Stone* is brilliant. Once you start reading you can't stop. My Mum kept telling me off because every night I was using up the electricity very late. I didn't want to stop until I'd reached the very end.'

'I love *Harry Potter and the Philosopher's Stone*. Before I read this book my parents had to force me to read anything. I preferred watching TV or playing computer games. Now I want to read all of the Harry Potter books.'

'*Harry Potter and the Philosopher's Stone* is a spectacular book. The story goes straight into your head. It's very funny. It made me wish I was a wizard. I'd love to make up magic spells.'

2 **These verbs in the texts – *start, keep, want, force, prefer, make, love* – are all followed by another verb. Put them in the right column in the chart.**

Verb + to + *infinitive*	*Verb* + *object* + to + *infinitive*

Verb + -ing *form*	*Verb* + *object* + *infinitive*

Looking at language

Verbs + infinitive or *-ing* form

When you use two verbs together in English you need to decide whether the second verb should be the infinitive with or without *to*, or the *-ing* form. The structure you use depends on the first verb.

Verb + *to* + infinitive

These verbs are followed by ***to* + infinitive**:

agree appear arrange ask attempt choose decide encourage
expect fail hurry learn manage offer prepare promise
recommend refuse seem tell tend try want warn

We can group some of these verbs like this:

- **Reality verbs**: *appear*, *seem*:
  *He **seems to like** music.*
- **Effort verbs**: *try*, *attempt*, *fail*, *manage*:
  *She **failed to reach** the final of the competition.*

***Tend* + *to* + infinitive** means you **usually** or **often** do something.

*I **tend to get up** earlier when the weather's good.* *I **tend not to drink** coffee in the afternoon.*

Verb + object + *to* + infinitive

These verbs are followed by an **object + *to* + infinitive**:

ask choose encourage expect tell want warn

*I **wanted the sun to shine** on my birthday.*

Many of these are **reporting** verbs: *ask*, *tell*, *encourage*, *warn*:

*She **asked him to speak** more quietly.* *I **told her not to leave** the room until I came back.*

Verb + object + infinitive without *to*

Make and *let* are followed by an **object + infinitive without *to***:

*My mother **made me wear** the most awful clothes.*
*She **let me stay** out later than most of my friends though.*

Verb + *-ing* form

These verbs are followed by the ***-ing* form** of the second verb:

avoid can't help can't stand consider deny enjoy feel like
finish give up hate imagine keep like love mind
practise prefer put off suggest understand

We can group some of these verbs like this:

- **Like and dislike verbs**: *like*, *love*, *mind*, *can't stand*, *enjoy*, *hate*, *prefer*:
  *I **don't like getting up** early.*
- **Time verbs**: *start*, *stop*, *continue*, *begin*, *put off*:
  *I **began taking** singing lessons as a child.*

Verbs that can take *to* + infinitive or *-ing* form

Some verbs – *like, love, begin, start, continue* – can be followed by either the infinitive or the *-ing* form.

*I **like sailing**. / I **like to sail**.*

*She **began having** lessons. / She **began to have** lessons.*

With some verbs, different meanings are expressed through these two structures:

Verb	+ to + *infinitive*	+ -ing *form*
go on	*They **went on to talk** about their travel arrangements.* (They did something new.)	*They **went on talking** after the waiter brought the bill.* (They continued doing the same thing.)
need	***I need to repair** my washing machine.* (I will do the job.)	*My washing machine **needs repairing**.* (Someone else will do the job.)
remember / forget	*I **remembered to buy** the milk.* (I remembered and then I bought the milk.)	*I **remember buying** the milk.* (I bought the milk and now I remember doing it.)
stop	*He **stopped to talk** to me.* (He stopped in order to talk to me.)	*He's **stopped talking** to me.* (He's not talking to me any more.)
try	*I'm **trying to lose** weight.* (I'm trying something difficult.)	*I'm **trying eating** just fruit for breakfast.* (I'm trying something new.)

Sense verbs: *hear, see, feel, notice*

These verbs can either be followed by the infinitive without *to* or the *-ing* form but there is a difference in meaning. Compare:

*I **heard** a dog **bark**, and then a car started and drove off.* (I heard the whole of the barking.)

*I **heard** a dog **barking** as I went past the house.* (I heard part of the barking.)

Other points

- With some of these verbs there is a choice of negative with different meanings. Compare: *I **didn't ask** him to leave* (I didn't ask him, but he left) and *I **asked** him **not to leave*** (I said, 'Please don't leave.').
- We use the *-ing* form after a preposition: *We talked **about starting** earlier.*

1 Read the text about a musician and answer the questions.

Shy ten-year-old pianist

It is lunchtime and the pianist comes to the end of a long practice in preparation for a performance tonight. He has played his Mozart, Beethoven, Schumann and Janacek but can't seem to stop himself. It looks as if someone will have to make him stop. The pianist is ten years old. Lukas Vondracek has come with his mother to play at a music festival. 'At a rehearsal, one of the players was so affected by Lukas's playing that she forgot to play,' said the conductor. Lukas began playing when he was two and was at first taught by his parents, musicians in their home town in the Czech Republic.

1 Why is he extraordinary? ....

2 Find examples of these verb patterns:

a) Reality verb + *to* + infinitive: ....

b) Time verb + *-ing* form ....

c) Verb + object + infinitive (without *to*): ....

d) Verb that can be followed by *to* + infinitive or by *-ing* form with different meanings:

....

Getting it right

▶ Exercise 1 Thinking about meaning

Decide which beginning, a), b), or both, matches each ending and tick (✓) your choice.

Example:

a) They liked playing cards in the evening ..✓..	but that night they decided to go out instead.
b) They liked to play cards in the evening ..✓..	
1 a) They stopped to have a drink	because they were thirsty.
b) They stopped drinking	
2 a) He remembered buying some sugar	but he couldn't remember where he'd put it.
b) He remembered to buy some sugar	
3 a) Oliver tried taking some aspirin	but it didn't make him feel better.
b) Oliver tried to take some aspirin	
4 a) The prisoner went on to say that	she was innocent, again and again and again.
b) The prisoner went on saying that	
5 a) She started to talk just	at the same moment as me.
b) She started talking just	
6 a) Simon heard someone screaming	once and then everything went quiet.
b) Simon heard someone scream	
7 a) He began playing the guitar	when he was 12 years old.
b) He began to play the guitar	
8 a) I heard the tap drip	and the noise started to send me to sleep.
b) I heard the tap dripping	

Exercise 2 Learning from learners

Correct any mistakes in the sentences, or write *correct* if there is no error.

Example: My mother made me to keep my room tidy.
My mother made me keep my room tidy.

1 I wanted that he tell me the news. ....
2 You should stop to work so hard. ....
3 I enjoy to go to the cinema. ....
4 He avoided talking about it. ....
5 They won't let us to watch TV late. ....
6 I look forward to receive your reply. ....
7 The university doesn't let students bring food into the classrooms. ....
8 We talked about to go out for a meal one night, didn't we? ....

Exercise 3 Choosing the correct form

Read the stories and fill in the gaps with verbs from the box in the correct form.

chew	give up	go	~~hop~~	keep away	know	lie	smoke	feed

The doors were just about to close on my underground train when I saw a pigeon hop.. in. The tourists wanted 1 .... it with crisps, but the bird wasn't interested. It appeared 2 .... where it was going and as soon as the doors opened at the next station, it flew out.

If you want to give up 3 .... , you are recommended not 4 .... electrical cables to help. An Australian builder chewed almost a metre of cable a day for ten years, and found it had a 'sweet and pleasant taste'. Unfortunately the cables he was eating contained lead and last year doctors found the lead levels in the man's blood were three times the safety limit. Fortunately, his blood is now back to normal but he has failed 5 .... smoking.

On 29 January a worried resident of Tilehurst, Berkshire saw a cobra 6 .... motionless by the side of the road. He rang the local animal hospital who told him not 7 .... near it. As the man waited for help he warned other people 8 .... When a man arrived from the animal hospital in full protective clothing and approached the snake, he realised it was an old car exhaust pipe.

Exercise 4 Text completion

Fill in the gaps with the correct form of a verb from the box, followed by an appropriate form of the verb in brackets ( ).

begin begin go on go on keep manage need remember tend try ~~want~~

Have I ever told you about the time I ruined a new engine? Well, I ...*wanted to get*... *(get)* a bigger car because the children 1... *(get)* bigger, so we 2... *(look)* and we 3... *(find)* one quite quickly. A few days after I bought it I 4... *(put)* some fuel in it, so I stopped at a petrol station and started to fill it up. I 5... *(not notice)* what I'm doing in petrol stations and I 6............... just .... *(fill up)*, paying and driving off. Soon the engine 7... *(make)* the most awful noise, and I 8... *(stop)* and starting a couple of times but it just 9... *(get)* worse, so I pulled in at another garage and of course found out that I'd put diesel in a petrol car. Because I'd 10... *(drive)* the engine needed 500 pounds' worth of work. Only a week or two old, too.

Classwork

1 **Copy these sentences onto a piece of paper and complete them about yourself using another verb and any other necessary information.**

I began .... when I was ....
I stopped .... when I was ....
I tried .... but ....
I love ....
I hate ....
I go .... (how often?).
I remember .... when I was a child.
My parents made me ....

2 **Fold your piece of paper, and put everyone's pieces together.**

3 **Take a different piece of paper. Try to decide who wrote the sentences, and return the piece of paper to its owner.**

Unit 24 First, second and zero conditional sentences

Getting started

1 **Match Extracts 1, 2 and 3 to the correct headlines, a), b) or c).**

a) **What a winner!** b) **Jupiter, saviour of the world** c) **Baby talk**

1 Headline: .....

If a large comet hit the Earth, humans would very soon die out. If it hit the land, it would cause earthquakes worldwide, knocking down almost every building. If it landed in the deepest ocean, it would send waves thousands of feet high over surrounding continents. A minimum of a billion people might die. But Jupiter helps to stop such disasters.

2 Headline: .....

MARGARET JONES, 56, can't seem to stop winning. She has won two out of the three competitions she's entered this year, and now she's won the lottery too! OK, so she didn't win the top prize, but she's not unhappy with her £50,000. 'Margaret's amazing. If she enters a competition, she wins!' says husband Mike.

3 Headline: .....

Rosanna Della Corte was 62 when she gave birth to a son in 1994. Now she's trying for another child. If Rosanna gives birth soon, she'll be nearly 80 when all the teenage problems start!

2 **Find the sentences with *if* and number them 1–5. Write the numbers of the sentences which match a), b) and c) below.**

	First clause	*Second clause*	
a)	*If* + present tense	*will* / *can* + verb	....
b)	*If* + past tense	*would* + verb	....
c)	*If* + present tense	present tense	....

3 **Which of the *if* sentences describe real, possible situations?** ....

Which describe unreal or imaginary situations? ....

Do any refer to the past? ....

Looking at language

Conditional sentences

Conditional sentences usually have an *if* clause (the condition) and another clause (the result): *If a large enough comet hit the Earth* (condition), *humans would very soon die out* (result). The *if* clause can come either before or after the result clause.

Use and form

1 The **zero conditional** describes something that **is** or **was** generally true:

If I eat fish, I get ill. *If I didn't eat my meals, Mum got cross.*

Form: ***If*** **+ present tense, present tense** or ***If*** **+ past tense, past tense**

If means 'whenever' in a zero conditional sentence.

The imperative (see Unit 14) is often used with the zero conditional:

***Tell** her about the party **if** you **see** her.*

2 The **first conditional** describes **real** or **probable** future situations:

If it rains, I won't go out.

Form: ***If*** **+ present tense, *will* + infinitive**

The present simple, present continuous, present perfect simple or continuous (**not** *will*) can be used to talk about the future in the *if* clause:

*If you're **going** shopping, **will** you **buy** me some milk?*

*If he's **had** enough, he'**ll stop**.*

When and *as soon as* can replace *if* in a first conditional sentence. Compare:

If I see her, I'll tell her. (Perhaps I won't see her.)

***When / As soon as** I see her, I'll tell her.* (I know I'll see her.)

Will can be replaced to show something is less certain:

*If you go now you **may / might** see her.* (It is possible but not definite.)

*If I pass my exam, we **can / could** celebrate.* (We can celebrate if we want to.)

In spoken English, we often use *going to* in the *if* clause to suggest a previous arrangement (see Unit 11):

*If your sister's **going to be** there, I'**ll** definitely go.*

3 The **second conditional** describes **imaginary** or **unlikely** situations:

If I knew, I'd tell you.

Form: ***If*** **+ past tense, *would* + infinitive**

In a more formal style we use *were*, not *was*, after *if*:

*If I **were** you, I'**d apply** for the job.*

*If he **were** here, what do you think he'**d do**?*

Would can be replaced to make the situation in the result clause less certain:

*If I **went** to Africa, I **might** see wild elephants.* (It is possible but not definite.)

*If I **had** enough money, I **could go** round the world.* (If I wanted to.)

Conditions are not always stated. Some sentences do not include an *if* clause: it is just suggested:

***I'd love** to meet your brother.* (If you let me.)

1 **Match the sentence beginnings, 1–6, to the endings, a)–f). Are the sentences examples of first, second or zero conditionals?**

1 If Deborah rings, ...
2 If I were you, ...
3 In those days girls only went to school .....
4 She'll be really upset .....
5 If they're watching television, ...
6 We'd have no countryside left .....

a) if she doesn't get the job. ....
b) they won't notice anything. ....
c) tell her to come round at 7.00. ....
d) if everybody lived in big houses. ....
e) if they came from a rich family. ....
f) I'd find a new girlfriend. ....

Other points

The choice of first or second conditional often depends on the speaker's view of the situation.

Example: Two people buy lottery tickets every week. One says:

If I win, I'll give up my job. (first conditional; he thinks he can win)

The other says:

If I won, I'd move to the country. (second conditional; she thinks it's unlikely she'll win)

Getting it right

Exercise 1 Choosing the best form

In situations 1–8 below, which conditionals are possible? Tick (✓) a), b), or both if they are both possible.

Example: The farmer wants to sell the field behind our house to property developers.

a) If they build houses there, it ruins the area. .....
b) If they build houses there, it'll ruin the area. ✓

1 That politician Steven Brown has been offered some money by a businessman.
a) What will you do in his situation? .....
b) What would you do in his situation? .....

2 The interview went well, actually. I think they liked me.
a) If they offer me the job, I'm going to accept it. .....
b) If they offered me the job, I'd accept it. .....

3 It's a simple law of physics.
a) Water boils if you heat it to 100 °C. .....
b) Water would boil if you heated it to 100 °C. .....

4 I can't believe more people are getting on this bus.
a) If any more get on, it'll never be able to move. .....
b) If any more got on, it would never be able to move. .....

5 She's phoned twice already today.

a) If she phones again, I'll tell her what I think. .....

b) If she phoned again, I'd tell her what I thought. .....

6 I think I know how it works.

a) If you pushed this, the drink would come out. .....

b) If you push this, the drink comes out. .....

7 Elvis died in 1977, didn't he?

a) If he's still alive today, do you think he's still singing rock'n'roll? .....

b) If he was still alive today, do you think he'd still be singing rock'n'roll? .....

8 Their baby is due next month.

a) If it's a girl, they're going to call her Emily. .....

b) If it was a girl, they would call her Emily. .....

Exercise 2 Getting the form right: first conditional

In the conversation below, two friends are putting a new piece of furniture together. Fill in the gaps with the correct form of the verb in brackets.

A: So where do you think this bit goes?

B: Well, if we .put.. (*put*) it here, this piece will fit (*fit*) onto it perfectly.

A: Yes, but if you **1** .... (*do*) that, how **2** .... you .... (*get*) the doors on?

B: Good point. Perhaps we should do the doors first. Yes, if we **3** .... (*attach*) the doors now, we **4** .... (*be able to*) stand it upright.

A: But how **5** .... we .... (*get*) the top on if we **6** .... (*do*) that? It **7** .... (*be*) too tall to reach.

B: Hmm. OK. Let's put the top on first then.

A: Yes. Good. Now, if we **8** .... (*stand*) it upright, we **9** .... (*be able to*) fix the doors and put the shelf in, and it **10** .... (*be*) finished.

B: Not quite. What's this bit?

A: Ah, that's easy. If you **11** .... (*read*) the instructions, you **12** .... (*see*) that it's a spare shelf – we don't need it.

What is the piece of furniture? Choose from pictures a)–e) below. .....

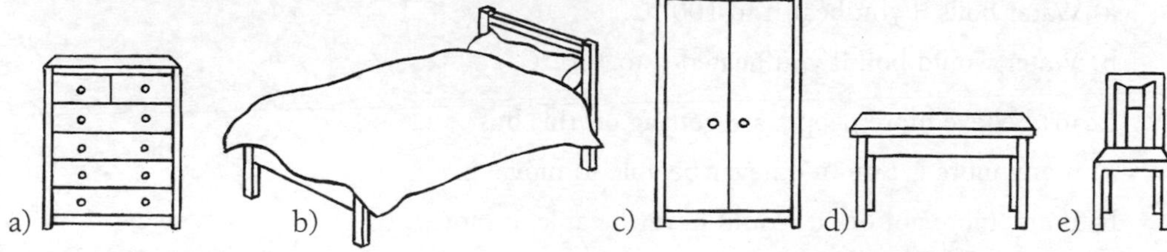

Exercise 3 Getting the form right: second conditional

Write answers for questions 1–4 below, and write suitable questions for answers 5–8.

Example: How would your friend feel if you always wore the same clothes as him / her?

He'd probably get quite annoyed with me.

1 What would you do if you found £500 in the street?

....

2 What would you say if your mother asked what you thought of a new dress and you hated it?

....

3 What would you tell your teacher if you hadn't done your homework?

....

4 Where would you live if you could live anywhere in the world?

....

Example: *How would you feel if you came top in all your exams?*

I'd be really happy, but I'd probably feel a bit sorry for my friends who didn't do as well as me.

5 ....

I'd probably scream and run away, although actually I don't believe in things like that.

6 ....

I wouldn't touch it. I'd call for help and move away from it.

7 ....

I'd walk up to them and ask him / her what he / she was doing, and then tell him / her our relationship was over.

8 ....

First I'd buy a big house with a swimming pool and then I'd invest the rest of it.

Extension

Extend your answer to either question 1 or 4 into a short paragraph giving more information about what you would do and why. If you are working in class, your teacher can read out your paragraphs and other students can guess who wrote them.

Exercise 4 Learning from learners

Two language students are talking about their plans for the future. Decide if their use of conditionals in 1–10 is right or wrong, and put a tick (✓), or correct those that are wrong.

Pietro: I'm thinking of moving to Oxford next month.
Suzi: Really? Why do you want to do that?
Pietro: Because I think if I will stay here, 1 I might get bored. — *stay*
Suzi: But you might not like Oxford. What 2 will you do then?

1 ....

2 ....

Pietro: Oh, I know I'll like it because I've been there before.
Suzi: Have you? You seem to have been everywhere. I've hardly been anywhere since I arrived.

Pietro: Where 3 would you like to go? 3 ....
Suzi: Oh, lots of places – 4 I like to go to Scotland, and I'd love to see Oxford and Cambridge, of course. 4 ....
Pietro: Well, if 5 I will decide to move to Oxford, 6 come and visit. 5 .... 6 ....
Suzi: Thanks. When 7 do you know for sure if you're moving? 7 ....
Pietro: Well, if 8 I didn't pay for the course by next week, 9 I'll have to wait until next month. 10 I'd let you know what happens if you like. 8 .... 9 .... 10 ....

Classwork

1 **Work in pairs. Write a first conditional sentence on a piece of paper. Then give it to your teacher.**

Example:

If the weather's good tomorrow, we could go to the beach.

2 **Make a circle. Your teacher gives Player 1 one of the conditional sentences. Player 2 (on Player 1's right) has to use something from Player 1's result clause to make a new sentence. Continue round the circle.**

Example:
Player 1: *If the weather's good tomorrow, we could go to the beach.*
Player 2: *If we go to the beach, I'll try windsurfing.*
Player 3: *If you go windsurfing, you'll fall in the sea a lot.*
Player 4: *If you fall in the sea …*

3 **You're out if:**
you can't think of a new sentence
or you repeat an idea
or the class agree you've made a conditional mistake.

4 **Start again with a new sentence each time someone loses. The winner is the last person left.**

Unit

25 The third conditional, wishes and regrets

Getting started

1 **Read the articles about lucky rescues and choose the correct sentence, a) or b), to finish each article.**

a) 'I don't know what would have happened to me if he hadn't heard me.'
b) If rescuers had delayed another 24 hours, he would have used up his supply of oxygen.

ALIVE – after four days under a boat

IT WAS, he said, like heaven. Four days after his yacht capsized in the icy Southern Ocean, Tony Bullimore was finally rescued yesterday. He had spent four days under his yacht in one of the world's most dangerous seas. Waiting in complete darkness, he survived through determination and bits of chocolate. Two days ago he ran out of water. .....

Talking parrot saves trapped van driver by crying out 'help'

A parrot rescued a man who was trapped under the wheels of a van by copying his calls for help. 'I thought I was going to be stuck under the van all night long,' Mr Stone, 58, said. 'Although I cried and shouted for help, no one seemed to be able to hear me.' But 100 metres away, at the Broadway Caravan Park, Sonny, the parrot, heard him and repeated his shouts which alerted two men who work at the park. 'Sonny is a real life-saver,' said Mr Stone. .....

2 **What is the form of the third conditional? Label the <u>underlined</u> parts of the sentence below using phrases from the box.**

would *if* past participle past perfect *have*

....

<u>If</u> rescuers <u>had delayed</u> another 24 hours, he <u>would</u> <u>have</u> <u>used</u> up his supply of oxygen.

3 **<u>Underline</u> the correct alternative in each sentence.**

The third conditional talks about **1** *the past / the present / the future*. It describes **2** *what really happened / what might have happened*. The *if* clause comes **3** *before / after / before or after* the possibility clause.

Looking at language

This unit looks at ways of expressing how things could be or could have been different, and how to express wishes about the present and the past.

The third conditional

The third conditional describes possibilities in the past that did not happen. Look at these examples:

Conditional sentence	*What actually happened?*
If rescuers had delayed another 24 hours, he would have used up his supply of oxygen.	Rescuers did **not** delay; he did **not** use up his supply of oxygen.
I wouldn't have met my husband if I hadn't gone to Italy.	I **did** meet my husband because I **did** go to Italy.

We can make the possibility less certain by using *might* or *could* instead of *would*:

*We **might** / **could** have won the match if Williams hadn't been injured.*

Form

If **+ past perfect,** ***would(n't) / might(n't) / could(n't)*** **+** ***have*** **+ past participle**

If I hadn't gone *to Italy,* ***I wouldn't have met*** *my husband.*

The *if* clause can come either before or after the possibility clause. When the *would* clause begins the sentence, we do not use a comma:

I wouldn't have met *my husband* ***if I hadn't gone*** *to Italy.*

Other points

We can mix third with second conditionals (see Unit 24):

If I hadn't gone *to Italy,* ***I wouldn't be*** *married now.*
past possibility present result

1 Fill in the gaps in the third conditional sentences below.

1 They .... (*finish*) by now if they .... (*start*) the job on time.

2 What .... she .... (*do*) if her parents .... (*not like*) her new boyfriend?

3 I'm sure lots of people .... (*apply*) for the job if they .... (*hear*) about it.

Wish

We use *wish* to talk about something in the present or past that is or was not true, but we would like it or would have liked it to be true.

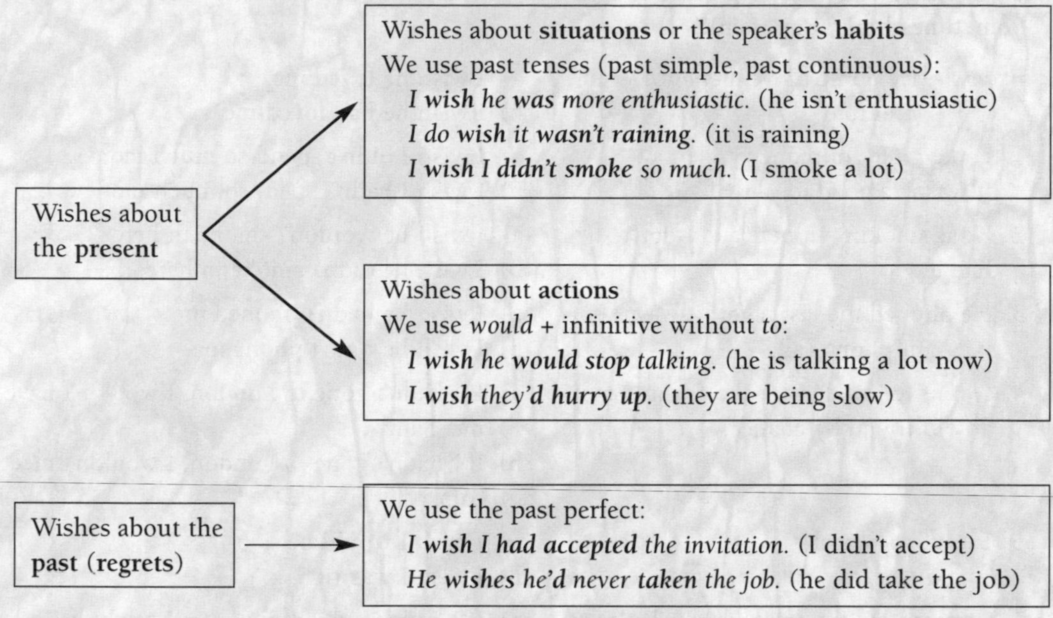

Wishes about the **present**

Wishes about **situations** or the speaker's **habits**
We use past tenses (past simple, past continuous):
*I wish he **was more enthusiastic**.* (he isn't enthusiastic)
*I do wish it **wasn't raining**.* (it is raining)
*I wish I **didn't smoke** so much.* (I smoke a lot)

Wishes about **actions**
We use *would* + infinitive without *to*:
*I wish he **would stop talking**.* (he is talking a lot now)
*I wish **they'd hurry up**.* (they are being slow)

Wishes about the **past** (regrets)

We use the past perfect:
*I wish I **had accepted** the invitation.* (I didn't accept)
*He wishes **he'd never taken** the job.* (he did take the job)

Other points

If only can be used in the same way as *wish* (both present and past). It is slightly stronger and more dramatic:
If only I could drive. (I can't drive.)
If only I'd seen you earlier. I could have warned you about the traffic. (I didn't see you earlier.)

2 Look at the cartoon. What do you think the missing words are?

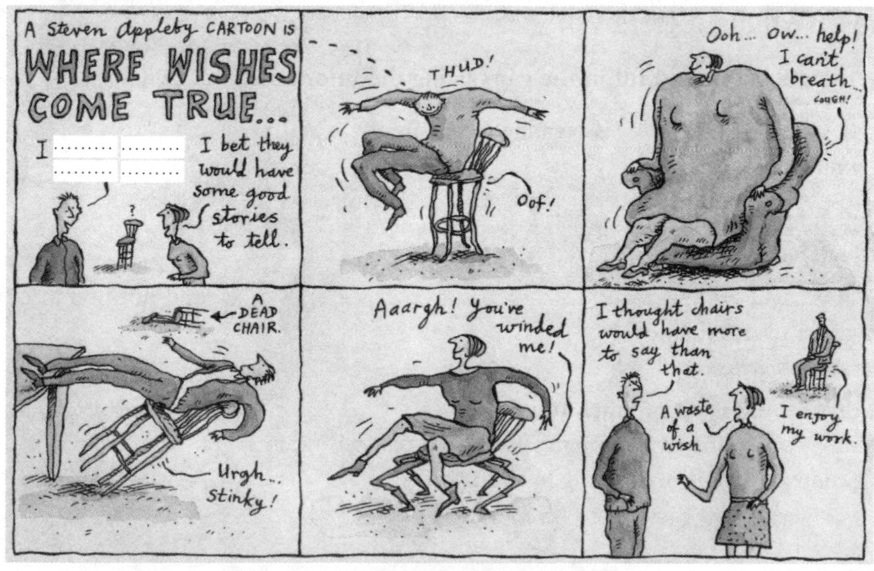

Getting it right

Exercise 1 Choosing the best form

Decide if a) or b) best expresses the idea of sentences 1–8, and tick (✓) your choice. Sometimes both are possible.

Example: He doesn't love me, but I want him to.
a) I wish he loved me. ..✓..
b) I wish he had loved me. .....

1 I spent a lot of money yesterday. It wasn't a good idea.
a) I wish I didn't spend so much money. .....
b) I wish I hadn't spent so much money. .....

2 He is smoking in here and I don't like it.
a) I wish he wouldn't smoke in here. .....
b) I wish he didn't smoke in here. .....

3 He phoned me last night. It wasn't a pleasant phone call.
a) I wish he hadn't phoned me. .....
b) I wish he didn't phone me. .....

4 I went to London for the day and met an old friend by chance.
a) If I hadn't gone to London, I wouldn't have met Sam. .....
b) If I hadn't gone to London, I wouldn't meet Sam. .....

5 I want to be rich.
a) I wish I would be rich. .....
b) I wish I was rich. .....

6 I missed my train, which was lucky, as it crashed.
a) If I hadn't missed the train, I might be in hospital. .....
b) If I hadn't missed the train, I would have been in hospital. .....

7 I want Mike to write to me more often.
a) I wish he wrote more often. .....
b) I wish he would write more often. .....

8 Abigail is making a mess all over the floor with her toys.
a) I wish she didn't make such a mess. .....
b) I wish she wouldn't make such a mess. .....

Exercise 2 Writing regrets

Read the regrets below and fill in the gaps using the information in *italics*.

Example: If *I'd passed my exam*, I'd be a lawyer by now.
I didn't pass my exam.

1 If I'd left home ten minutes earlier, I .... !
I didn't catch the bus.

2 Maybe if .... , and not literature, I would have a more useful job now.
I didn't study science.

3 I wouldn't have wasted so much time if .... the exams were going to be so hard. I wish I'd realised that earlier.
I didn't know the exams were going to be so hard.

4 Maybe if .... as a child, I wouldn't be so scared of dogs now.
I didn't have a pet dog.

5 I do sometimes wish .... I would've been able to travel more.
I got married quite early.

6 Where are Dave and Susannah? The dinner's going to be completely ruined.
I wish ....
They're always late.

7 I wish .... to work. This awful uniform makes me look ridiculous.
I can't wear my own clothes.

8 My sister wishes ....
I always borrow my sister's clothes and she hates it.

Exercise 3 Learning from learners

Learners were asked to talk in groups about their wishes and regrets. Rewrite the underlined mistakes they made with *wish* and the third conditional.

A: Is there anything you regret, Kyoko?

B: Sometimes I think about my career. If I would've listened to my parents, I might've become a violinist. How about you?

A: Actually, 1 I wish I can speak Japanese. I might like to go and work in Japan one day. Oh, and 2 I wish my sister married her boyfriend. The whole family wants her to.

C: A regret of mine is about an ex-boyfriend. 3 I wish now I didn't spend so much money on him. If I'd known how he was going to treat me 4 I would be more careful. Stefan, you're very quiet. Any regrets?

D: Only about food. I was a very fussy eater as a child. 5 I wish I discovered good food earlier In my family, though, it's my mother who has the regrets. 6 She wishes she would have had the opportunities I had

Example: If I'd listened ....

1 .... 4 ....

2 .... 5 ....

3 .... 6 ....

Extension

Write two regrets that you have.

▷ Exercise 4 Writing people's comments about the past

Read the stories about lucky escapes below and add an appropriate comment using the third conditional. One story is about luck but not a lucky escape. Which one? .....

Example: A robber broke into Mrs Jakeson's house, tied her up and started to look around for valuable items to steal. But luckily for Mrs Jakeson her nephew arrived unexpectedly. The robber ran off without stealing anything. 'If John, my nephew, *hadn't arrived, the robber might have stolen everything valuable*,' she told a reporter.

1 When Sarah Donaldson got to the check-in desk, they asked her if she would stay one more day because they had overbooked the flight. They offered her a room in a luxury hotel, and she agreed as she had no urgent appointments back home. She didn't realise how lucky she was until she read that everyone on the plane had become ill with food poisoning. 'If I ....'

2 Mike Watson and his girlfriend Deborah Willis had a lucky escape from their car yesterday. They were driving through town when they saw a friend of theirs walking along, so they decided to park and say hello. One minute after stepping out of their car, it exploded. 'If we ....'

3 Last week Sheila Dunnock decided not to play the lottery for the first time in over a year. She had never won anything in the past. She was horrified when her numbers were chosen that week, but then her husband Dick told her he had bought the ticket himself. 'If Dick ....'

Classwork

1 **Read the amusing article below about a robbery that went wrong.**

2 **Work in teams of three or four. In ten minutes, write as many third conditional sentences about the story as possible.**

Example: If the men hadn't got lost, they wouldn't have returned to the same gas station.

3 **At the end of ten minutes, the group with the most correct sentences wins.**

Two men drove into a petrol station in Vancouver, Canada, pointed guns at the cashier, and drove away with $100. But 20 minutes later, they realised they were lost. They decided to ask for directions, so they pulled into another petrol station.

Somehow they didn't realise that they were at the same station they had robbed earlier, and they asked directions from the same cashier. He stayed cool, gave them directions, and, as soon as they left, he began calling the police.

Then the robbers returned yet another time. This time their car wouldn't start and they needed a mechanic. When they learned that there was no mechanic available until eight the following morning, they kept trying to start the car themselves. The police finally arrived and the men were still there. This time they were on the phone, trying to call a breakdown service. Their car battery was flat.

Unit

26 The passive

Getting started

1 **Read one of the extracts from an article about a burglary. Then answer this question:**

Why was the burglary unusual?

....

Extract 1

Police? I want to report a burglary. Somebody has stolen my house.

'I WENT to put the key in the door and the door had gone,' Mr McSharry said yesterday. 'Not only that, but somebody had taken the stone around the door too. Inside there was almost nothing left and I thought there must have been a terrible mistake. It is the worst theft I have ever seen. There was nothing left but the walls.'

The police believe an organised gang carried out the theft.

'It is important the police catch them,' said Mr McSharry. 'You can replace a door, but you can't replace a whole house.'

Extract 2

Police? I want to report a burglary. My house has been stolen.

'I WENT to put the key in the door and the door had gone,' Mr McSharry said yesterday. 'Not only that, but the stone around the door had been taken too. Inside there was almost nothing left and I thought there must have been a terrible mistake. It is the worst theft I have ever seen. There was nothing left but the walls.'

The police believe the theft was carried out by an organised gang.

'It is important they are caught,' said Mr McSharry. 'You can replace a door, but you can't replace a whole house.'

2 **Read both extracts and <u>underline</u> any differences you notice.**

3 **Look at the two headlines. Which headline makes the house more important than the thief? How does it do this?** ....

Looking at language

The passive

Use

In English a verb can be **active** or **passive**:

Active: The starting point of a clause is the person or thing that did something (the 'doer'): *Somebody* ***has stolen*** *my house.*	**Passive:** You can use a different starting point, not the 'doer': *My house* ***has been stolen.***

1 The passive can be used when the 'doer' is understood, or not important:
*It is important they **are caught**.* (we **know** it is the police who will try to catch them)
This use of the passive is typical:

- to describe processes – the emphasis is on **how** something is produced, not **who** does it:
  *Tea **is grown** on south-facing hillsides, and **is harvested** twice a year. It **is packed** locally before **being sent** to ...*
- in formal writing, especially impersonal letters which focus on **what** happens, not **who** does it:
  *The statement **was sent** to you at the end of January, and you **were asked** to repay the loan by the middle of March. This **was not done**.*

2 We can use the active or the passive to keep the starting points of two clauses the same, even when the 'doer' changes. Compare:

starting point		same starting point	
'doer'		'doer'	
She	*opened the door and*	*(she)*	*shouted to a friend.*

The starting point stays the same. Both clauses are **active** because 'she' is the 'doer' in both clauses.

starting point		same starting point	passive + *by* + new 'doer'
'doer'			
She	*opened the door and*	*(she)*	***was seen by*** *one of her neighbours.*

The starting point stays the same, but the second clause is **passive** because 'she' is not the doer.

1 Answer the questions.

1 In the two clauses in the sentence below, is the 'doer' the same or different?
He walked into the room and was asked to sit down. ....

2 Is the second clause active or passive? ....

Form

The passive is formed with ***be* + past participle**:

	Passive	
Tense / verb form	*be*	*Past participle*
Present simple	***It is***	*cooked*
Present / past continuous	***I am / was being***	*watched*
Present perfect	***She has been***	*seen*
Will future	***They will be***	*sold*
Going to future	***They are going to be***	*sold*
Future perfect	***She will have been***	*elected*
Past simple	***He was***	*arrested*
Past perfect	***We had been***	*asked*
Infinitive	***I wanted to be***	*noticed*
-ing form	***I hate being***	*watched*

Verbs that do not have an object (intransitive verbs) do not have a passive form: We say: *The plane took off.* We don't say: ~~*The plane was taken off*~~.

2 Change the active verb forms into passive forms.

Example: gives is given take is / are taken

1 does ....

2 is watching ....

3 has read ....

4 caught ....

5 was carrying ....

6 had eaten ....

7 will teach ....

8 to make ....

9 will have seen ....

10 going to ask ....

Other points

In spoken English, ***get* + past participle** can also be used to make the passive, with verbs expressing **change** or **something happening**:

My house ***got broken into / was broken into*** *last night.*

If there is no change, or nothing happens, we use ***be* + past participle**. We don't say: ~~*The meal got enjoyed by everyone*~~. We say: *The meal* ***was enjoyed*** *by everyone.*

Getting it right

Exercise 1 Choosing the best form

Underline the correct verb form.

Example: The gallery has over 1,000 paintings. *These have been collected / have collected* during the last 100 years.

1 He was a collector as well as an artist. He *collected / was collected* nearly 1,000 paintings.

2 The first pocket calculator weighed almost a kilogram. Its inventor *invited / was invited* to trade fairs all over the world.

3 Jonathan is starting a new job next week. He *is going to pay / is going to be paid* much more than before.

4 These beautiful clocks *assemble / are assembled* by hand.

5 Visitors *are advising / are being advised* to stay away from the city centre at night.

6 The five prisoners who escaped last week *have caught / have been caught*.

7 Welcome to the conference. After this meeting *you'll give / you'll be given* a welcome pack with details of the talks and your accommodation.

8 I'm fed up with always *asking / getting asked* the same question by unfriendly journalists.

9 I am pleased to report that your visa application has been successful and that your passport *has been returned / has returned* by the Immigration Office.

10 A young couple, whose parents *were not allowed / didn't allow* them to see each other because of an argument between the two families, have married in secret.

Exercise 2 Active or passive?

Fill in gaps 1–9 in the statistics below about Coca-Cola with the verb in brackets. Use the active or passive in a suitable tense.

500 million servings of Coca-Cola (*consume*) ....*are consumed*.... worldwide every year.*

94 per cent of the world's population 1 (*recognise*) .... the Coca-Cola trademark.

109 is the number of years since Coca-Cola **2** (*invent*) ....

148 litres 3 (*consume*) .... by the average Brit every year.

The average American **4** (*drink*) .... 275 litres every year.

195 is the number of countries where Coca-Cola 5 (*sell*) ....

Seven billion servings of Coca-Cola's products (these include Cherry Coke, Lilt, Fanta, Sprite, TAB Clear, Five Alive) **6** (*consume*) .... in Britain last year.

The 40-foot Coca-Cola bottle in Times Square, New York, 7 (*take*) .... seven seconds to open, float a straw and empty itself.

773 million servings of Coca-Cola products **8** (*drink*) ....every day around the world.

Nine billion litres of Coca-Cola 9 (*sell*) .... in Britain last year.

*all these statistics are from 1995

Exercise 3 Explaining choices

Say if verb forms 1–6 in the stories below are active or passive and tick (✓) the correct explanation for the choice, a), b) or both.

Story 1

BEN BEECH, a bookseller in Scarborough, was amazed recently when *someone offered him* a box of old books containing a poetry book that he had won as a 14-year-old schoolboy. **1** *My mum threw it out one day*, Mr Beech said. The book still had the name of Mr Beech's old school in Derby, 150 miles away. **2** *It was given to* Mr Beech for a poem he wrote about a fish tank.

Example:

.active....... a) *Someone* is the 'doer'. ..✓..

b) *Someone* is not the 'doer'. .....

1 .... a) The starting point and 'doer' are the same. .....

b) The starting point and 'doer' are different. .....

2 .... a) It is understood who gave Mr Beech the book. (The school.) .....

b) The starting point is the same as in the sentence before. .....

Story 2

■ A teenage couple who fell in love but **3** *were separated* by World War Two **4** *were married* yesterday after a chance meeting 56 years later. Tom Bryant, 73, and Ivy Butler, 71, met in 1941, but lost touch when Tom **5** *was called up* for the army. **6** *Both married* other people and settled in different places. Back in his home town of Ellesmere Port this year, Tom saw Ivy shopping.

3 .... a) The starting point (the couple) is the same in this clause as the one before. .....

b) We don't know what separated them. .....

4 .... a) The couple is the 'doer'. .....

b) You need a 'doer' (often a priest) to join two people in marriage. .....

5 .... a) The 'doer' is understood. .....

b) Tom is the 'doer'. .....

6 .... a) *Other people* is the 'doer'. .....

b) *Both* is the 'doer'. .....

Exercise 4 Text completion

Read Extract 2 in *Getting started* again. Then fill in gaps 1–8, choosing the active or passive voice. The box of nouns / pronouns and verbs will help you.

Nouns / pronouns: a door the door ~~house~~ I they a whole house
Verbs: carry out catch go replace replace see ~~steal~~ take think

Police? I want to report a burglary. My house has been stolen **.**

'I went to put the key in the door and 1 .... ,' Mr McSharry said yesterday. 'Not only that, but the stone around the door 2 .... too. Inside there was almost nothing left and 3 .... there must have been a terrible mistake. It is the worst theft I 4 .... There was nothing left but the walls.'

The police believe the theft 5 .... by an organised gang.

'It is important 6 .... ,' said Mr McSharry. 'You can 7 .... , but you can't 8 ....'

Classwork

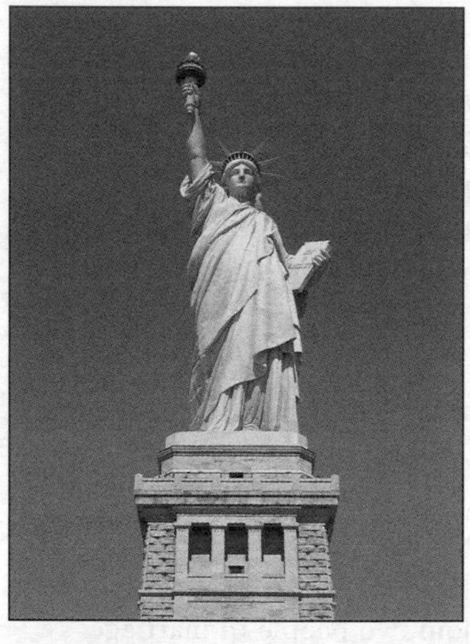

Think of a book, film or building. Describe it to the others in your group, always using the word *it* as the starting point of the sentence. The others have to guess what you are talking about.

Examples:

It was built about 100 years ago in New York. It's very tall, and it was designed to show people that they had arrived in New York. (Statue of Liberty)

It was written by a Russian over 100 years ago, and it's very long. It has been made into a film more than once, I think. (War and Peace)

It was directed by Quentin Tarantino, and it was made in the States. It was very violent. (Pulp Fiction)

Unit

27 Verbs confused with the passive

Getting started

1 **Read the strange story about a ship, the *Baychimo*. Which is true, a), b) or c)?** .....

a) The ship was stolen by some Inuit.
b) The ship sailed for many years without any people on board.
c) The ship's crew said there was a ghost on board.

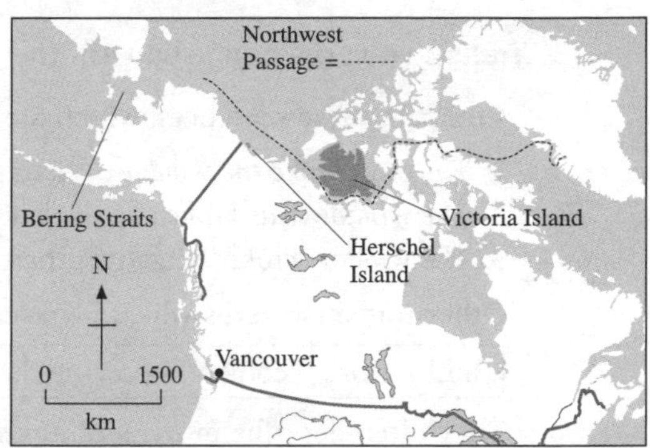

On 6 July 1931, the *Baychimo* left Vancouver, Canada, under the command of Captain John Cornwall. Passing through the Bering Straits, the ship entered the Northwest Passage. The captain spent hundreds of thousands of dollars buying furs along the Victoria Island coast. On the return journey the ship was caught in early winter ice and was unable to move. With the ship in danger of being crushed, Captain Cornwall and his crew made a camp on safer ice closer to shore and prepared to wait there until the spring.

After a storm in November the temperature rose, enabling the men to leave the camp. They found that the *Baychimo* had broken free of its ropes and disappeared. Captain Cornwall learnt that some Inuit had seen the missing ship 45 miles away. Captain Cornwall and his crew managed to find the ship and remove most of its furs, but before they could finish, the *Baychimo* vanished again.

The following spring the ship was seen 300 miles further east near Herschel Island. Since then the *Baychimo* has been seen frequently. The last time was in 1962 when fishermen found the ship in the same area. The *Baychimo* has disappeared since then, but it will turn up again.

2 **Without looking back at the story, tick (✓) the phrases below which were in it.**

a) the temperature was risen .....
b) the temperature rose .....
c) the *Baychimo* was vanished .....
d) the *Baychimo* vanished .....
e) The *Baychimo* has been disappeared since then .....
f) The *Baychimo* has disappeared since then .....

3 **Now check your answers to Exercise 2 in the story. Do any of the correct answers look strange? Why?** ....

....

Looking at language

Verbs confused with the passive

This unit looks at verbs which are easy to confuse with the passive because the 'doer' (the thing that did or caused the action) is not mentioned. There are two types: some are transitive, and can be used in three ways, and others are intransitive.

Transitive verbs confused with the passive

Compare these sentences, which are all possible in English:

1 *The boys broke the window.* (Active: the boys are the 'doers')
2 *The window was broken by the boys.* (Passive: the boys are the 'doers')
3 *The window broke.* (Ergative: there is no 'doer'; the window appears to have broken itself.)

Other transitive verbs which behave like *break* are:

boil	close	cook	freeze	melt	open	sink	smash	start	stop

They often describe movement or change.

1 Active	*2 Passive*	*3 Ergative*
*A guard **opened** the door.*	*The door **was opened** by a guard.*	*The door **opened**.*
*I **started** the car.*	*The car **was started** by James.*	*The car **started** first time.*
*Mary **boiled** the water.*	*The water **was boiled** by Mary.*	*The water **boiled**.*

In the examples in the third column, the subject of the sentence (*door*, *car*, *water*) is not the 'doer'. The 'doer' is not mentioned. (We don't say: ~~*The door opened by a guard*~~.) When the 'doer' is mentioned, the passive is used: *The door was opened by a guard.*

These verbs can be useful to avoid taking responsibility in embarrassing situations. You can say: *The glass has broken* (rather than *I've broken the glass*).

1 Use the words to write sentences for columns 1–3 above.

Example: Tim rang the bell

Tim rang the bell. The bell was rung by Tim. The bell rang.

1 the sun melted the ice

....
....
....

2 the storm sank the ship

....
....
....

Intransitive verbs confused with the passive

Compare these sentences:

1 *An accident* ***happened*** *late last night.*

2 *A careless driver* ***caused*** *an accident late last night.*

Sentence 1 may sound strange because we often expect the subject of a sentence to be the cause of an action.

There is a group of intransitive verbs in English which behave like *happen* above:

crash	die	disappear	fall	happen	land	rise	take off	vanish

The passive is **not** possible with these verbs because they do not have an object:

We say:	*We don't say:*
Something terrible happened yesterday. *My cat disappeared last week and hasn't been seen since.* *Her father died peacefully in the night.* *The plane took off safely during a storm.*	~~*Something terrible was happened.*~~ ~~*My cat was disappeared last week and hasn't been seen since.*~~ ~~*Her father was died peacefully in the night.*~~ ~~*The plane was taken off safely during a storm.*~~

2 Fill in the gaps with a verb from the box above to give a similar meaning to the active, transitive sentences 1–4.

1 The pilot flew the plane out of the airport.	The plane ....
2 I couldn't see my friend anywhere.	My friend had ....
3 The gas lifted the balloon into the air.	The balloon .... into the air.
4 The bad driver caused an accident.	An accident .... because of the bad driver.

Other points

To talk about problems with cars we can say: ***I can't / couldn't start the car*** or ***The car won't / wouldn't start***, but we don't usually say: ~~*The car doesn't / didn't start.*~~

Getting it right

▶ Exercise 1 Getting the form right

In 1–10 below, tick (✓) the sentences which are grammatically correct and put a cross (✗) next to those that are wrong.

Example: All of a sudden the strange shape was disappeared. ..✗..

1 At last the sun rose and it suddenly seemed a lot warmer. .....

2 The chicken is cooking at the moment, but it will be ready in ten minutes. .....

3 The ice melted by the heat. .....

4 In the battle the ship was sunk by sailors from its own navy. .....

5 She was died peacefully last year after a long illness. .....

6 She was fallen in love with him almost as soon as she saw him. .....

7 The car crashed into a tree. .....

8 This story was happened in 1988 to my father. .....

9 My glasses have broken again so I'll have to get a new pair. .....

10 Anna will happen an accident if she continues to drive so fast. .....

Extension

Correct the sentences that you marked wrong.

Example: ....*the strange shape disappeared.*

▷ Exercise 2 Choosing the best form

In the strange story below, underline the best form of the verb in 1–10.

The events I'm going to tell you about *was happened* / *happened* ten years ago when I was a student. I was about to set off for home from college, but my car 1 *wouldn't be started* / *wouldn't start*. It was about five in the evening and dark. When I got out of the car, the door 2 *was closed* / *closed* behind me without me touching it. When I tried to open the door, I couldn't, so I stood there for about ten minutes wondering what to do. Then I saw a man coming towards me, so I asked him to help me try to open the door. But suddenly he 3 *was disappeared* / *disappeared*. And then, all of a sudden, I heard a noise and the door 4 *was opened* / *opened*. I looked around but there was no one there. I got back into the car and this time it 5 *was started* / *started* straight away.

On the way home I had to stop because of an accident. Two cars 6 *had been crashed* / *had crashed*. A policeman told me the accident 7 *had been happened* / *had happened* a few minutes earlier and that one of the drivers 8 *had been died* / *had died*. I had been saved from the accident because my car 9 *had been broken down* / *had broken down*. After that I 10 *was started* / *started* believing in guardian angels.

▷ Exercise 3 Learning from learners

In the extracts from learners' ghost stories below, there are mistakes with the verbs you have studied in this unit, or the passive is chosen wrongly. Find the mistakes and correct them.

Extract 1

I saw a girl standing by the side of the road and I ~~was stopped~~ stopped the car to offer her a lift. She got in and I drove her down the road to a farm house. When we got there I got out of the car, but the girl was disappeared completely. A man and a woman came out and I said I had brought their daughter home but she had just been vanished. They looked very surprised and a little scared and told me their daughter was died ten years ago.

(three more mistakes)

Extract 2

The hand without an arm came towards him and was held his hand. He couldn't move or speak but he was terrified.

(one mistake)

Extract 3

My friend dreamt she saw her uncle who was died two months earlier. She told her parents the next day and they went to his grave and found that his grave stone was broken.

(one mistake)

Extract 4

Jenny woke up one night because her bed suddenly was shook violently. There was no one in the room. Suddenly it was stopped as quickly as it was started. She moved out of the flat the next day.

(three mistakes)

Extension

Write a story about something strange that has happened to you or someone you know.

Exercise 4 Rewriting questions

Rewrite sentences 1–8, using the verbs in brackets, so that you avoid claiming responsibility for a difficult situation.

Example: Oh, look! I've pulled the curtain down. (*come down*)
Oh, look! The curtain's come down.

1 I've broken your vase. (*break*)

....

2 Unfortunately, I dropped the glass and smashed it. (*fall / smash*)

....

3 I just walked past the car and I set the alarm off. (*go off*)

....

4 I've burnt the rice. (*burn*)

....

5 I couldn't start the car this morning. (*start*)

....

6 I caused an accident early this morning. (*happen*)

....

7 I've torn my trousers. (*tear*)

....

8 I was trying to cut the cheese but I bent the knife. (*bend*)

....

Classwork

1 **In small groups, write five sentences, of at least ten words each, one with the verb *disappear*, one with *happen*, one with *die*, one with *stop* and one with *rise*.**
Example: I need to take some notes, but my pen has disappeared.

2 **Choose one word in each sentence (not the verb) to miss out. Replace your word with the word *blank*.**
Example: I need to take some notes, but my blank has disappeared.

3 **Take it in turns to read a sentence with the word *blank* to the other groups. The other groups guess the missing word and write it on a piece of paper. Each group holds up their piece of paper. A group scores a point if they guessed correctly, but they must get exactly the right word, not just any word which is grammatically correct.**
Example: pencil is incorrect, and only *pen* gets a point.

4 **The winning group is the one with the most points at the end.**

Unit 28 Get / have something done

Getting started

1 **Read the newspaper article and answer the questions.**

a) What was the good news for the woman in the article?

....

....

b) Where did the woman find the brooch?

....

....

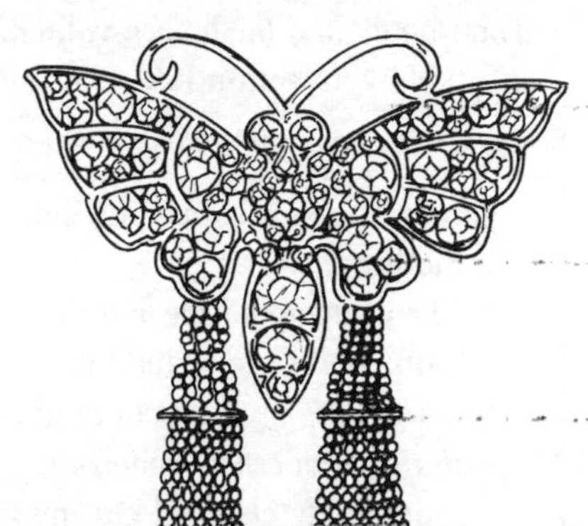

Woman sells 50p brooch for £13,000

A HOUSEWIFE who feared losing her home sold a brooch bought for 50p for £13,225 at auction yesterday. She had been going through serious financial problems after divorcing her husband.

The buyer bought the diamond butterfly-shaped brooch at auctioneers, Phillips, in west London.

The woman noticed the brooch in the corner of a shelf at her local second-hand shop about a year ago. Her local jewellers told her the diamonds were not real.

When the woman had the brooch valued, Phillips' jewellery specialist, Keith Pearson, told her it would sell for up to £10,000 at auction.

2 **Look at this sentence from the text, and answer the questions.**

When the woman had the brooch valued, Phillips' jewellery specialist, Keith Pearson, told her it would sell for up to £10,000 at auction.

a) Who valued the brooch, the woman or Keith Pearson? ....

b) What is the form of the underlined phrase, i) or ii)? .....

i) *have* + object + past participle ii) *have* + past participle + object

Looking at language

Get / have something done

Use

Look at these sentences about the brooch:

*Keith Pearson **valued the brooch**.* Active: We know the 'doer' and want to put him first.

*The brooch **was valued**.* Passive: The 'doer' is not important or not known.

*The woman **had the brooch valued**. Have something done*: We want to put the person *affected* by an action first, not the 'doer'.

So *get / have something done* is used when:

1 you arrange for somebody else to do something: *The woman **had** the brooch **valued**.* (somebody else valued it) ***I'm getting** my hair **cut** at a new place in the town centre tomorrow.* (somebody else will cut my hair) *They've **had** their house **repainted** since our last visit.* (somebody else has painted it)	2 something happens to you, often (but not always) something unpleasant: *She **got** her hat **blown off**.* *I've **had** my house **burgled** three times now.* *If she's lucky, she'**ll have** her business plan **accepted**.*

We use *get* (not *have*) *something done* when no one / nothing else is involved:

*I **got** my finger **stuck** in the bottle.*

*He **got** his hat **caught** in the branches.*

Note that *get something done* is not usually used in the present perfect tense. We say: *I've had my hair cut.* We don't say: ~~*I've got my hair cut.*~~

1 **Underline four examples of *get / have something done* in the conversation below. Are they examples of Use 1 or 2 above?**

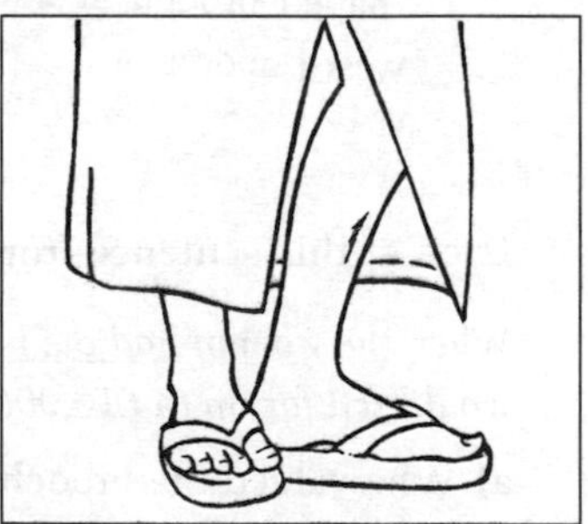

A: What's that scar you've got on your leg?

B: That's from an accident I had a few years ago. It all happened when I was having a new patio built and I came out with cups of tea for the workmen. I got my sleeve caught on the door handle and the cups flew out of my hands. Then I fell over onto a bit of broken cup. The workmen were great, and I wasn't hurt badly, but I've still got this scar on my leg. I even had a piece of the cup built into the patio.

A: Is it still there?

B: Sadly, no. I had to have the patio redone last year.

1 ..... 2 ..... 3 ..... 4 .....

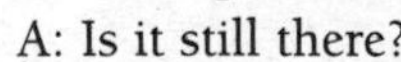

Form

Tense	Get / have	Object	Past participle
Present simple	*He gets / has*	*everything*	*delivered to his home.*
Present perfect	*She's got / had*	*her hair*	*done.*
Will future	*They'll get / have*	*their computer*	*upgraded soon.*
Past simple	*I got / had*	*new windows*	*put in.*
Past perfect	*We'd got / had*	*the carpets*	*cleaned.*

Notice that *have* is a main verb in *have something done*, so don't use contractions.
We say: *I had my eyes tested.* We don't say: ~~*I'd my eyes tested*~~.

Getting it right

Exercise 1 Thinking about meaning

For sentences 1–10, write *m* if I did the action myself, or *sb* if somebody else did it. For one, both are possible.

Example: I had my hearing checked last week. I was worried about it. ...sb...

1 I had my hair cut this morning. What do you think of it? ....
2 I've mended your bike. It should be OK now. ....
3 I got my thumb broken in a rugby match. ....
4 I fixed the broken food mixer last night. Try using it again. ....
5 I've had the computer repaired. I hope it's all right. ....
6 I had to clean the car before we could leave. ....
7 I got my handbag stolen when I was on holiday. ....
8 I got the cake made to save some time. I've been so busy! ....
9 I had mended the lamp before he even noticed it was broken. ....
10 By the time they got there I had already put in the new kitchen sink. ....

Exercise 2 Getting the form right

Fill in the gaps using a *get / /have something done* phrase. Use the correct forms of the verbs and noun phrases in the box.

Noun phrases	all his meals ~~his eyes~~ the film her hair my hair his hi-fi her paintings her dress his diaries
Verbs	accept catch cut develop make pay for publish steal ~~test~~

Example: I think he got his eyes tested................ because he kept getting headaches.

1 She's going to .... this afternoon. I wonder what style she'll have this time!

2 I .... yesterday. There are some really good photos of you and the children.

3 She's .... for the exhibition. I'm so pleased. There are some quite famous artists taking part.

4 He's .... again. He's really annoyed because he'd just bought it.

5 Did you know that he's won a holiday to Spain? He's won two weeks in a luxury hotel and he'll even ....

6 Her father died last year, but she's hoping to ....

7 Pat, can you help me a minute? I .... on my brooch and I can't get it free.

8 Fiona's spending a lot on her wedding. She .... by a top designer.

Exercise 3 Completing a conversation

Fill in the gaps in the conversation about a holiday with words a)–g) and the correct form of *get / have something done*.

a) some new photos / take
b) money / send
c) new passport / issue
d) it / fix
e) passport / steal
f) ~~his feet /cover~~
g) my camera / catch

Angus: How was your holiday? What did you do?

Katie: Well, on the first day we went swimming, and Luke got his feet covered in oil on the beach. It took us ages to get them clean.

Luke: And the next day Katie **1** ....

Katie: So I had to **2** .... , and go all the way to the capital to **3** .... at the embassy.

Luke: And that wasn't all. I 4 .... in the lift door in the hotel and it broke. I tried to 5 .... but it cost too much, and anyway we were having money problems.

Katie: Yes, we had to 6 .... from our bank at home because no one would take our credit card. Somehow we enjoyed ourselves though!

Exercise 4 Learning from learners

Seven of sentences 1–8 below contain a mistake involving *get / have something done*. Correct the mistakes and tick (✓) the one correct sentence.

Example: I think in some countries you can ~~have delivered shopping~~ *have shopping delivered* to your home.

1 Oh, that's nice. You've cut your hair.

2 If you use a digital camera, you don't need to develop the film at a shop.

3 A: What have you done today?

B: The garage had fixed my car this morning, and then I did a bit of shopping.

4 Do you like my new ring? It didn't fit when I tried it on at first, so I had enlarged it.

5 A: Did you ever have a fight at school?

B: Only once, and I got my nose broken.

6 We want to sell our house so we valued it last week. It's worth much more than we thought.

7 You haven't been well for ages. I think you should get your blood pressure check.

8 I want the invitations to look professional, so I'm going to find somewhere where I can get printed them.

Classwork

1 **Think about the town or city you are studying in. What would you like to get done to improve the area?**

Example:
I'd have the main street pedestrianised. I'd get museum entrance fees reduced.

2 **Work in three groups. Prepare a list of ideas, and think about how to present your ideas to the class. You have ten minutes. Then present the ideas to the class.**

Example:
At the moment there's too much traffic in the city centre, so we'd have the main street pedestrianised, and then people could walk around the shops safely. We would also …

3 **Which group has the most ideas, and which group has the best ideas? As a class, vote on the three best ideas for the town.**

Unit

29 Be / get used to

Getting started

1 **Do you think there are some jobs that men do better than women and some that women do better than men? Which ones?**

....

2 **In the article about a woman bus driver, find two things she likes about the job and one thing that she found difficult at first.**

....

....

It's a power thing. Rosalyn Clark enjoys life as a bus driver

I've always loved driving. For some reason I find it relaxing, so driving a bus is ideal. Some of the male bus drivers were a bit funny at first and I think it took them a while to get used to the fact that I was a woman. I could see it in their faces that they were a bit shocked.

I like being in control of a big vehicle. Perhaps it's the power. I don't find London traffic stressful, and I don't let anyone annoy me. I've learnt to manage when people start being rude.

I think I'm quite a good driver, although some days are better than others. Changing back to driving cars when I'm not

working was a bit difficult at first. I kept forgetting how wide the car was, but I'm used to it now.

3 **Find and underline two examples of *be / get used to something* in the article.**

4 **Underline the correct statement.**

a) *Be / get used to something* means that something is:
   i) no longer new and strange   ii) finished and no longer true

b) *Be / get used to* is followed by:
   i) the infinitive   ii) a noun / pronoun or the *-ing* form

5 **What does *it* refer to in this sentence from the text:**

I kept forgetting how wide the car was, but I'm used to it now.

....

Looking at language

Be / get used to

Use

We use *be used to something* to show that something is familiar (not strange or new) now because you have done it or experienced it many times:

*I kept forgetting how wide the car was, but **I'm used to it** now.* (now I know how wide the car is)

*We asked them to stay. **We were used to having lots of visitors**.* (we often had visitors)

The negative (*be not used to something*) is very common:

***I'm not used to the food** in this country. It's too spicy for me.*

We use *get used to something* to show that something that was strange is becoming familiar:

*It took them a while to **get used to the fact** that I was a woman.*

*I find the accent here difficult to understand, but **I'm getting used to it**.*

***I couldn't get used to the long hours**, so I resigned.*

Note that *used to* + verb is completely different; this means you did something regularly in the past but don't do it now:

***I used to watch** a lot of television, but I prefer radio these days.*

(See Unit 6.)

1 **Does *used to* in the sentences below refer to something familiar (this unit) or a past habit (Unit 6)?**

1 I don't eat meat much these days, but I used to. ....

2 They never went abroad in the past, but now they're used to it. ....

3 Molly was used to going everywhere by car, so she's finding it hard without one now.

....

4 Paolo used to live in the United States. ....

5 I haven't had a cigarette for four months and I'm getting used to not smoking now.

....

6 We always used to go to the same place for our summer holiday. ....

Form

We use *be / get used* to with a noun, pronoun or the *-ing* form. You can use it in most tenses.

Tense	*Example*
Present simple	*I'm used to it.* We don't usually use ***get used to*** with the present simple except in the expression *you get used to it* (you = anyone).
Present continuous	We don't usually use ***be used to*** with the present continuous. *I'm **getting** used to my new job.*
Present perfect	*She's **been** used to moving house every year, so she can't settle down.* *They've **got** used to their son's behaviour.*
Will future	*They'll **be** used to it after a few months.* *They'll **get** used to people staring at them.*
Past simple	*He **was** used to being treated like a prince.* *She **got** used to driving a bus.*
Past perfect	*We'd **been** used to a much simpler life.* *I'd **got** used to buying whatever I wanted.*

Negatives

With ***get*** *used to something* we usually use *can't* or *couldn't* in present and past tenses:

*I **can't** get used to this awful weather.*

*I **couldn't** get used to driving on the left.*

With *will* future we often use *never* instead of *not*:

*I'll **never** get used to his strange ways.*

Pronunciation

Used to is usually pronounced /**juːstə**/.

Other points

Something ***took some getting used to*** is a common expression:

*The climate is completely different here. It's hot and humid. It **took some getting used to**.* (It took a long time to get used to it.)

Getting it right

Exercise 1 Thinking about meaning

For sentences 1–8, tick (✓) the sentence, a) or b), which is true. In one sentence both a) and b) are true.

Example: I expect they'll get used to living in the countryside but it will take some time.
a) They have always lived in the countryside. .....
b) They haven't lived in the countryside before. ..✓..

1 I'm not used to people shouting at me.
a) People shouting at me is unusual. .....
b) In the past people shouted at me a lot. .....

2 I used to eat a lot of junk food.
a) I don't eat a lot of junk food now. .....
b) I eat a lot of junk food these days. .....

3 They've just moved here and they're not used to so much traffic.
a) There was a lot of traffic where they lived before. .....
b) There wasn't much traffic where they lived before. .....

4 I just can't get used to the idea that Marianne is married.
a) Marianne isn't married. .....
b) I find it strange that Marianne is married. .....

5 In China I thought I'd never be able to eat with chopsticks, but I got used to it.
a) Using chopsticks is still difficult for me. .....
b) I can now eat with chopsticks. .....

6 At first Laura couldn't understand their accent. It took some getting used to.
a) Their accent was strange at first. .....
b) Laura can understand their accent now. .....

7 Sabine is finding it hard to take orders from someone, but I'm used to it.
a) I've taken orders from people before. .....
b) Sabine has taken orders from people before. .....

8 It took me a while to get used to getting up early every day.
a) I always got up early in the past. .....
b) Getting up early was new for me. .....

Exercise 2 Describing changes

Read about changes in two people's lives and complete sentences 1–6 using the correct form of *be / get used to (something)*.

A I live in Canada now, but I was born in Ireland and lived there until I was 15. Although it was quiet there, I was happy. Things are completely different in Vancouver where we live now. The people are nice, but they aren't as friendly as they were in Ireland. When we first arrived I found it quite strange that when I said hello to someone in the street they said nothing. My school is much bigger. There are 40 students in a class. I found that difficult at first, but it's starting to feel normal. The noise seemed very strange when we arrived. We lived in a quiet village before, but Vancouver is a very noisy city, though I find that quite exciting now.

Example: I was used to living in a quiet place.

1 People aren't as friendly here, but I've .... now.

2 I .... big classes.

3 Vancouver is a noisy city, but I .... now.

B Marcus changed his job recently. The new job is quite different from his old one and it took him a while to feel comfortable with his new workmates. In the old job he was working with just three other people in a small family company, but now he's responsible for 100 workers. He doesn't know them well, which is completely different from before and he finds that hard. He'd like to be friends with them all, but of course it's impossible.

4 At first he .... his new workmates.

5 He .... with a small number of colleagues.

6 He can't .... not .... friends with his colleagues.

Exercise 3 Learning from learners

A teacher recorded a conversation with two learners about things that were strange when they first arrived in Britain. After the conversation the teacher noticed eight mistakes with *be / get used to*. Underline seven more mistakes and correct them.

Teacher: What did you find strange when you arrived here in Scotland?

Paloma: Oh, many things, actually. First, of course, the weather. I used to sunny weather nearly all the year, but here it's the opposite! I still can't be used to the cold and rain.

Anna: Yes, that's the same for me. I didn't expect the weather to be so bad. You're used so you don't find it hard, but for us it's strange.

Teacher: Well, we don't like the rain either, you know. Anything else?

Anna: Yes, the time you eat your meals. We're used to eat at about nine or even ten in the evening, but my family here eat their evening meal at seven. It's awful for me. I'm no used to it.

Paloma: Yes, it's the same for me. My Scottish family eat at six! And another thing that's strange? Your taps! Why do you have two separate taps for hot and cold? I got used to it now, I suppose.

Teacher: What about the traffic? Has that been a problem for you at all?

Anna: Well, driving on the left side of the road took some getting used.

Paloma: Yes, the same for me, but I'm used now and probably when I go home I'll have problems there.

Example: *I'm used to sunny weather.*

1 ....

2 ....

3 ....

4 ....

5 ....

6 ....

7 ....

▷ Exercise 4 The lottery

Find one sentence in each row that can be rewritten with a similar meaning using *be / get used to*. Rewrite it in the right box. The first row has been done as an example.

1 I always played with dolls when I was a child.	2 When I started typing, my fingers ached, but they don't any more. *I've got used to typing.*........	3 I can't play tennis very well. ....
4 When I was a student I sang in a choir.	5 I work in a pub and go to bed late every night, which isn't a problem for me.	6 My friends all think I'm mad wanting to be a farmer. ....
7 It didn't take long before I was familiar with the new car.	8 Leslie has never been abroad.	9 Some of the animals in the zoo once lived in the wild. ....
10 What do you usually do in your summer holiday?	11 Is it still strange for you living in your new house?	12 It was a difficult exam, but I think I did OK. ....

Look at the numbers of the sentences you have rewritten. Which is the winning lottery ticket? .....

a) 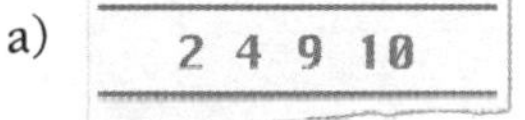

b) 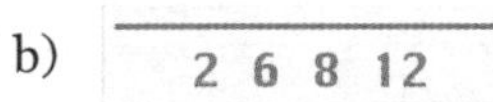

c) 2 5 7 11

Classwork

1 **Divide into two or three groups. Tear up a piece of paper into ten pieces and on each piece write either a noun, verb, adjective or adverb.**

Example: banana beautiful eat

2 **Pass your words to another group, face down so that they cannot see them. In each group, Learner 1 takes a piece of paper. He / she looks at the word but does not show it to anyone else. Then he / she draws pictures to explain the word. The rest of the group guesses it. When they have guessed it correctly, the whole group writes a sentence using the word and *be / get used to*.**

Example: I'm used to eating bananas because they're very cheap in my country.

3 **Then Learner 2 takes another piece of paper and the group guesses that word. The group with the most correct sentences in ten minutes is the winner.**

Review unit

Units 23–29 Other verb forms

Exercise 1 Mixed structures [Units 23–29]

Underline the correct choice in *italics*. Sometimes both choices are possible.

Example: *If it rains* / *If it will rain* again tomorrow, I'm not even going to try to go out.

1 I think he *expected to fail* / *expected failing* the exam, so he was very pleased when he heard he'd passed.
2 I didn't enjoy the meal last night. If *I felt better* / *I'd felt better* I might have had a better time.
3 A: What a lovely vase! Is it very old?
B: I think it *made* / *was made* at the end of the eighteenth century.
4 A: You look miserable. What's the matter?
B: *I had turned down my suggestion.* / *I had my suggestion turned down.*
5 I'm sorry I'm late. Something *had happened* / *was happened* on the main road and there was a long traffic jam.
6 I spoke to her several times, but she continued *causing* / *to cause* trouble.
7 You look nice. *Have you cut your hair?* / *Have you had your hair cut?*
8 I hated the long train journey to work at first, but I guess *I'm used to it* / *I used to it* now.
9 I saw Janice on the way home so I *stopped seeing* / *stopped to see* how she was.
10 Have you heard the news? This plane *just vanished* / *was just vanished* over the Atlantic.

Exercise 2 Mixed structures [Units 23–29]

Fill in the gaps in the conversation with words from the box.

been doing ~~had~~ leave to to do travelling used 'll (will)

A: Hey, you've *had* your hair cut! It's really nice.
B: Oh, thank you. It's rather different, isn't it?
A: Yes. What made you decide 1 .... have it short this time?
B: I just felt like 2 .... something different. It's a bit of a shock every time I look in the mirror but I'm getting 3 .... to it. How are you anyway?
A: I'm fine, thanks. I've just 4 .... offered a new job.
B: Great! Where is it?
A: It's with a big company in London. It's a long journey, but I don't mind 5 .... I really needed 6 .... something new.
B: When do you start?
A: Well, my company won't let me 7 .... until March. Then, if I can afford it, I 8 .... have a couple of weeks' holiday.

Exercise 3 Conditionals **Units 24–25**

Fill in the gaps in these conditional sentences with the correct form of the verb in brackets.

Example: If you're going to help tomorrow, I 'll get up. (*get up*) a bit later.

1 Don't worry. If I needed your help, I .... (*ask*) for it.
2 If I .... (*stay*) in the sun too long, I get a headache.
3 If I .... (*know*) you were coming, I would've kept some food for you.
4 I'd tell the truth if I .... (*be*) you.
5 If we keep saving like this, we .... (*be able to*) move to a bigger house.
6 United could have won if the referee .... (*not make*) so many bad decisions.
7 If you press this button, the motor .... (*start*).
8 I won't answer the phone if you .... (*not want*) me to.
9 I .... (*recognise*) you if you hadn't worn that hat.
10 If you leave the lights switched on, it .... (*waste*) electricity.

Exercise 4 Conditionals and wishes **Units 24–25**

Match the sentence beginnings, 1–10, to the endings, a)–k).

Example: I'm upset about not getting the job, but if I had got it .c).

1 Well, we're looking forward to seeing you tomorrow. Just let us know .....
2 If my sister was as unkind as yours .....
3 There are some amazing coincidences in life. I wouldn't be talking to you today .....
4 If Jake was ever rude to his parents .....
5 I wouldn't want to live on a tropical island for the rest of my life .....
6 Michael gave me some really sensible advice. If only I'd listened to him .....
7 He's broken my heart and now I just wish .....
8 I've got a headache and I wish .....
9 If they'd known what she was going to be like .....
10 What do you think you'd do if .....

a) I'd never speak to her again.
b) they would never have offered her the job.
c) ~~I'm not sure I would have accepted it anyway.~~
d) if I hadn't missed that plane.
e) even if I could.
f) I hadn't ever met him.
g) you were alone in a foreign country and you had your passport stolen?
h) he was sent to his room.
i) I wouldn't be in this mess today.
j) he'd stop talking so loudly.
k) if you think you're going to be late.

Exercise 5 The passive **Units 26–27**

Learners were asked to write something about their country. Correct the mistakes in the underlined passive structures 1–9, or write a tick (✓) if the use is correct.

A

My country is famous for its tea. The tea are made in the mountainous area in the centre of the country. The leaves 1 is picked by hand and taken to the factory where they 2 dry and then 3 crush. They 4 are then packed into packets by the factory workers. You should buy tea from my country because it is delicious.

B

If you look at the rug on the floor in your house you may discover it 5 made in my country. They 6 are often made in mountain villages, but they 7 are sell all over the world. It can take a long time to make one rug. Some 8 are taken five years or more. The rugs 9 is often made by women. They have different patterns and colours from different areas.

is made ....

1 ....

2 ....

3 ....

4 ....

5 ....

6 ....

7 ....

8 ....

9 ....

Exercise 6 *Get / have something done* and *be / get used to* **Units 28–29**

Use language from Units 28 (*get / have something done*) or 29 (*be / get used to something*) to rewrite the phrases in *italics*, but try to keep the meaning the same.

Example: I left the door to my car unlocked and unexpectedly *somebody stole the stereo.*

I *had my stereo stolen*. ....

1 I was quite surprised when she first talked about her beliefs but *I'm familiar with her funny beliefs* now.

....

2 We needed new pictures for the passports so *we paid someone to take our photos* again.

....

3 I've lived here six months now and *I'm starting to feel that being cold is normal.*

....

4 I took my camera back to the shop and *someone fixed it for me.*

....

5 In my country we have dinner late in the evening, so *it's still strange to be eating so early*.

....

6 I went to the dentist and *she took one of my teeth out*.

....

Unit

30 Articles 1: general introduction

Getting started

1 Read the article and answer the questions.

a) What happened at the prison?

....

b) How did the prisoner do what he did?

....

PRISONER COPIED KEYS FROM MEMORY

A PRISON spent thousands of pounds changing locks after a prisoner with a photographic memory copied a vital set of keys.

The prisoner memorised the shape and size of the set of keys after seeing them for only a few seconds. He then made the copies from a plastic mirror.

The alarm was raised when a guard uncovered at least three keys hidden in his cell. As soon as they were found, managers at the prison ordered a complete change of locks in order to reduce the chances of an escape.

(adapted from *The Independent*, 3 March 1998)

2 ***A, an* and *the* are articles – they come before a noun. Underline any that you find in the text above.**

3 A prisoner (paragraph 1) changes to the prisoner (paragraph 2). Why?

....

4 Why a vital set of keys (paragraph 1) but the set of keys (paragraph 2)?

....

Looking at language

Articles

Articles show whether we are:

- talking **generally** about something
- talking about one or more **unidentified** examples of something. We don't know which one(s).
- talking about one or more **identified** examples of something. We **do** know which one(s).

Talking generally

To talk generally about something, we use **no article + plural / uncountable noun:**

Copying keys from memory is very difficult. *Tea is produced in Malaysia.*

(We are talking about keys and tea **in general**.)

We use ***the*** **+ adjective** to talk generally about groups of people:

***The unemployed / the poor / the young** need more money from the government.*

Unidentified / identified

We use ***a / an*** **+ singular noun** to talk about something our reader / listener doesn't know about (it's **unidentified**).

We use ***the*** **+ singular / plural / uncountable noun** to talk about something we and our reader / listener knows about (it's **identified**). Compare:

A prisoner with a photographic memory copied a vital set of master keys. (we don't know which prisoner)

***The** prisoner memorised …* (we know which prisoner because we have already mentioned him)

Something is unidentified when:

- we mention it for the first time in a story, as above
- we are naming or labelling:

  A: *What sort of car is that?*

  B: *I think it's **a** Toyota.*
- we mean *any*:

  *Can you bring me **an** apple?* (any apple; it doesn't matter which)

Something is identified because:

- it has been mentioned **before**:

  ***A** writer and **some** artists live there. **The** writer is French but **the** artists are all Italian.*
  first mention — second mention
- it is identified **later**:

  ***The** writer of this book lived in Italy for most of his adult life.*
- There is only one possible example of something that you can be referring to:

  ***The** Prime Minister spoke for nearly an hour.* (a country has only one Prime Minister)

  ***The** moon rose just after midnight.*

Pronunciation

The is usually unstressed and pronounced /ðə/. Before a vowel sound, however, it is pronounced /ði/.
Compare:

*Have you got **the** keys?* *Have you read **the** article?*
/ðə/ /ði/

The letter *u* often has the consonant sound /j/ at the beginning of words, as in *university*. Before /j/, *the* is pronounced /ðə/.

A and *an* are pronounced /ə/ and /ən/.

Other points

- We use *an*, not *a*, before vowels (*a, e, i, o, u*): we say ***a** prisoner,* but ***an** artist.*
- In spoken English, *this* can mean *a(n)* in stories.
  ***This** (a) prisoner, he copied keys just using his memory.* (See Unit 33.)
- We **must** use an article with a singular countable noun, even when there is also an adjective. We say: *He is **an** interesting man.* We don't say: ~~*He is interesting man*~~.

---

1 Match the sentence beginnings, 1–6, to the best endings, a)–f).

1 I think football .....
2 I think the football .....
3 The boy that lives next door .....
4 A boy at college .....
5 A few years ago I used to read a lot of .....
6 The best book I ever read was .....

a) thrillers.
b) – I don't know who – has won some money.
c) a thriller.
d) is always playing loud music.
e) is a bit boring.
f) needs more air in it.

Getting it right

Exercise 1 Thinking about use

Read the texts and answer the questions.

Example: As we sat there *the moon* came up in *the east*.

Why do we say ***the moon*** and ***the east***? *There is only one moon and one 'east'.*

Text 1

An officer from the Prison Service said: 'Yes, some keys were stolen, but the situation has now been dealt with.' No one at the prison would comment on the cost of replacing the locks, but *a Prison Service officer* said that nothing similar would be allowed to happen in future.

Do you think the same spokesperson for the Prison Service spoke each time, or a different one?

....

Text 2

Waiter: Are you ready to order?
Woman: Yes, I think so. I'll have *the chicken* with stir-fried vegetables.
Waiter: And for you, sir?
Man: Yes, *the vegetarian lasagne*, and a green salad.

Why do the customers ask for ***the chicken*** and ***the vegetarian lasagne***?

....

Text 3

It was just after seven in the evening when *a stranger* stepped into *a bar* in a quiet Parisian side-street. *The bar* was nearly empty, and it wasn't too hard for the barman to recall the face of *the stranger* and describe him to the police the following day.

Why does ***a stranger*** and ***a bar*** change to ***the stranger*** and ***the bar***?

....

Text 4

Orangutans are found on the islands of Borneo and Sumatra. They live in *trees* and eat mainly *fruit*. They are closely related, genetically, to *humans*, and their name means 'man of the forest'.

Why is there no article with the nouns in *italics* in this extract?

....

Text 5

This government seems to be helping *the rich*, while life for *the poor* gets worse and worse.

Why does this speaker talk about ***the rich*** and ***the poor***?

....

Exercise 2 *A, an, the* or no article

Fill in gaps 1–15 with an article, or '–' if there is no article.

A bank robber passed **1** .... note to **2** .... employee of **3** .... large bank. **4** .... note said the things that **5** .... bank robbers usually say. He had **6** .... gun and he wanted **7** .... employee to fill **8** .... bag with cash. But then **9** .... robber did something rather different from usual bank robberies. Noticing all the video cameras around **10** .... inside of the bank, he told **11** .... employee he would wait outside for **12** .... cash. He asked him to bring **13** .... bag out when he was ready. He went outside, and **14** .... police officer, seeing **15** .... gun, immediately arrested him.

Exercise 3 Learning from learners

In Extracts A and B below, learners write about themselves. Decide if the underlined article choices are right (✓) or wrong (✗). If they are wrong, correct them.

A

I work as an accountant in the foreign company. My duties are to prepare (no article) budgets and financial reports and also to maintain 1 the bank accounts of 2 (no article) company. At present, I am in charge of 3 a big project to build 4 the factory in a small town. I will have to prepare cost reports for 5 the project on a monthly basis.

..... ✗ a ....

.... ✓ ....

1 ....

2 ....

3 ....

4 ....

5 ....

B

My family and I live in 6 a town. Although it is a small place, everyone does interesting things and helps each other. I cannot imagine that I will ever leave 7 a town. I work in 8 a aircraft engineering company as a production clerk. Every day I come home at around 7.30, except for Tuesday and Thursday when I have 9 a class at 10 a language school. My teacher at 11 (no article) language school is very kind, and I have 12 a good friend in the class who comes from Turkey.

6 ....

7 ....

8 ....

9 ....

10 ....

11 ....

12 ....

Exercise 4 Text development

Add a suitable sentence (or part of a sentence) to the extracts below using the words in brackets to help you. Think carefully about whether to use *a*, *an*, *the* or no article.

Example: A loud, constant noise filled the air. *He thought it was a plane* (*he / think / it / plane*), but as it got louder he saw it was three helicopters.

1 It was a beautiful day. .... (*sun / shine*), and there wasn't a cloud in the sky.

2 When she arrived, she put a key on the table and walked out again. .... (*he / pick up / key*) and thoughtfully turned it over in his hand.

3 Wooden spoons are excellent toys for children, and so are .... (*plastic bottles / cardboard boxes*). Expensive things from the best shops may not make the best toys.

4 When Elaine got home, ... (*carry / large shopping bag*). The bag was full of clothes from different stores.

5 Visitors to India may be surprised to see .... (*cows / Hindu temples*). Cows are important in the Hindu religion and allowed to go where they want.

6 .... (*coffee room / not be / available*) between 2.00 and 5.00 today. We apologise to staff for any inconvenience.

7 You know .... (*dress / I / wear / yesterday*)? Well, it was my mother's when she was my age!

8 I'm really hungry. Would you mind .... (*get / me / banana*) from the kitchen?

9 My parents have just bought a new car. .... (*It / small / Renault*).

10 I work in a big insurance company with about 1,500 employees. In fact, ... (*I / Managing Director / company*).

Classwork

1 **Work with a partner. Write three sentences, each including an article. One of the sentences must have a mistake in the use of the article.**

Examples:
My father works as an accountant. (*Right.*)
Let's meet on a corner of Bridge Street and Park Lane at 7.00. (*Wrong – **the** corner.*)

2 **Pass your sentences to another pair, who should try to find the mistake.**

3 **Pass the papers back. Did they find the mistake? Did they find the right mistake?**

Unit 31

Articles 2: special uses

Getting started

1 **Read the advertisement for two holidays and answer the questions.**

a) Which holiday would be more suitable for someone who likes to visit places of natural beauty? ....

b) Which holiday would you choose? ....

MARRAKESH – four nights by air from Gatwick Airport

In Marrakesh the present-day traveller can see an old unchanged Africa. The High Atlas mountains supply water to the city, making Marrakesh an oasis on the main caravan routes from the Sahara. Our weekends in Morocco include a guided tour of Marrakesh, and a full-day trip to the High Atlas mountains. The five-star Hotel Imperial Borj has a café, bar, restaurant and a swimming pool.

CAIRO – four nights by air from Heathrow Airport

The Pharaohs believed that the goddess, Nut, gave birth daily to the sun as it travelled from east to west. So the Ancient Egyptians lived on the east bank of the Nile and died on the west. Our weekends in Egypt include a guided tour of the Pyramids at Giza and a guided tour of Cairo including the Egyptian Museum. The Mena House Oberoi is an elegant, traditional, deluxe hotel, near the Great Pyramid.

2 **Underline all the proper nouns (nouns starting with capital letters, such as *Pharaohs*) in the advertisement.**

3 **Do the types of proper nouns in the box need *the* or not? Put them in the correct column in the chart and add an example from the advertisement.**

~~airports~~	cities	continents	countries	deserts	hotels
mountain ranges	museums	nationalities	rivers		

Nouns with the	*Example*	*Nouns without* the	*Example*
		airports	*Heathrow Airport*

Looking at language

Articles

Special uses of *the*

1 Some **names** (proper nouns) always use *the* and some do not:

Nouns with the	*Examples*	*Nouns without* the	*Examples*
Deserts	*the Sahara, the Gobi*	Airports	*Heathrow, JFK*
Many famous / historical buildings	*the Pyramids, the White House*	Castles and palaces	*Buckingham Palace*
Hotels	*the Hilton, the Oberoi*	Cities and towns	*Riyadh, Athens*
Island groups	*the Canary Islands*	Companies	*Sony, Samsung*
Mountain ranges	*the Himalayas*	Continents	*Africa, Asia*
Museums and art galleries	*the British Museum, the Louvre*	Countries	*Germany, New Zealand*
Nationalities	*the French, the British*	Days, months, years	*Tuesday, April, 2009*
Newspapers	*the* Independent	Individual islands	*Crete, Sicily*
Oceans and seas	*the Atlantic*	Individual mountains	*Everest*
Rivers and canals	*the Amazon, the Suez Canal*	Languages	*English, Cantonese*
Theatres and cinemas	*the Globe*	Squares and streets	*Red Square, Oxford Street*
		States and regions	*California, Wales*

Noun phrases containing a proper noun and *of* usually need *the*:
the Palace of Westminster / the King of Spain / the University of Bath

1 Can you think of another example for each of the noun types that need *the*?

1 a desert ....
2 a hotel ....
3 a mountain range ....
4 a nationality ....
5 an ocean / sea ....
6 a theatre or cinema ....
7 a famous / historical building ....
8 an island group ....
9 a museum ....
10 a newspaper ....
11 a river / canal ....

2 We use *the* to talk about:
- playing a musical instrument:
  I didn't know you could ***play the guitar.***
  but *I didn't know you* ***had a guitar.***
- periods of time in history:
  The Beatles were famous in ***the sixties.***
  The 1990s *were difficult for many people around the world.*
  Mozart lived in ***the eighteenth century.***
- inventions:
  The camera *was first used in the second half of the nineteenth century.*

3 We use *the + most* for superlatives (see Unit 43):
It was ***the most interesting*** *holiday I've had in years.*
Team A scored ***the most goals*** *in the whole competition.*
but **without** *the* to mean the majority / nearly all:
Most *people have a television.* (nearly all people)

4 We use *the* with the names of some countries:
the *United States* (but ~~the~~ *America*), ***the*** *United Kingdom* (Britain), ***the*** *Philippines.*

Special uses of *a(n)*

We use *a(n)* with:
- hundred, thousand, million, billion etc.:
  There are ***a hundred*** *names on the list.* *There are* ***a thousand*** *people.*
- occupations:
  She's a student / a nurse etc.

Other points

- Places
  We use *the* to talk about most local, familiar places:
  I'm going to ***the shops / the bank / the supermarket.*** *Can I get you anything?*
  School, university, hospital, prison and *church* are different.
  We use **no article** to talk generally:
  A long stay in ***hospital*** *can be very boring;*
  or when someone is a pupil, student, employee, patient, prisoner or churchgoer:
  It's terrible. ***Brian's in prison*** *again.* ***Sally*** *starts* ***school*** *soon.*
  But we use *the* with these nouns to talk about particular (identified) places:
  They live near ***the prison,*** *just outside the city.* *She's going to* ***the school I*** *went to.*
- *Bed, work, home*
  We don't use an article with these words:
  Grandad's still in ***bed.*** *What time do you go to* ***work?*** *Let's go* ***home.***
- School subjects
  We don't use an article with school or university subjects:
  I'm studying ***computer science*** *at university.*

2 In the spoken extracts below, decide whether or not *the* is needed in the gaps.

'Well, school – I never really liked 1 .... school. I only went there basically to meet my friends and things. But I would've liked to have done well at 2 .... school.'

'Even though we had a photocopy of a map and instructions we still got lost. We went round and round. We asked five different people and they all said different things. Finally at ten to one I said 'There you are. There's 3 .... school on the right', so we just made it in time.'

'There's an open day at Trent University which I want to go to, so I hope my mum will take me to 4 .... university and then she'll have three or four hours to look round the town.'

'No, I didn't really enjoy my time at 5 .... university. I know you're supposed to, but I'm afraid I just didn't very much.'

Getting it right

Exercise 1 Explaining article choice

For each sentence, 1–10, complete the rule about the use of articles.

Example: **Samsung** has over 200,000 employees!

Don't use the *with* company *names.*

1 Didn't you know? My brother's **a doctor**.
Use a *with* ....

2 I'm flying from **Heathrow Airport** very early tomorrow.
Don't use the *with* .... *names.*

3 The country with **the most** televisions per person is the USA.
Use the *with* ....

4 **Most people** in the USA have at least one television.
Don't use the *when* most *means* ....

5 **English** is used as the language of commerce in more and more countries.
Don't use the *with* ....

6 I wish I could play **the piano**. *Use* the *to talk about* .... *musical instruments.*

7 I was a schoolgirl in **the 1990s**. *Use* the *to talk about* ....

8 K2 is the second highest mountain in **the Himalayas**. *Use* the *with* ....

9 A multinational team is planning to climb **K2** without oxygen later this month.
Don't use the *with* .... *names.*

10 I've heard **the Philippines** is beautiful. .... *countries need* the.

Exercise 2 *A, an, the* or no article

Why do you think the name 'Dorothy Comm' might be special? In gaps 1–10 write *a*, *the* or – if you think there is no article.

Dorothy Bell Comm is wondering what all the fuss is about. In the past three months the quiet 68-year-old from ..–.. California, **1** .... English professor and mother, has become **2** .... international celebrity with appearances on television, and now, in her favourite newspaper, **3** .... *Times*.

Her name is the reason for her fame. Dorothy, known to her friends as Dot Comm, rose to instant fame in **4** .... October when she was 'discovered' by **5** .... Excite, an Internet media company.

6 .... name Dot Com is heard several times an hour on television and radio stations throughout **7** .... North America, and increasingly **8** .... world, as **9** .... companies who do business on **10** .... Internet publicise their web addresses. The vast majority of these addresses start with *www* and end with *.com* (*dot com*).

Exercise 3 Learning from learners

Read these descriptions of famous places written by learners. They made some mistakes with articles. Correct the underlined phrases or tick (✓) them if they are correct. What cities are they describing?

River Seine flows through this city. It's famous for its tower which gives a wonderful view across the city. It's called 1 the Eiffel Tower. There's a world famous art gallery called 2 Louvre. Just outside this city is 3 Palace of Versailles. **City name:** ....

This city is divided into two by 4 the Bosphorus Sea. Half of it is in 5 the Asia and half in 6 the Europe. It has many beautiful old buildings, including 7 the Blue Mosque and 8 the Topkapi Palace. It used to be called 9 the Constantinople. **City name:** ....

This city is famous for its cathedral, 10 the Duomo, and the bridge over 11 Arno River called 12 the Ponte Vecchio. There are almost 13 hundred museums and art galleries in this city. 14 Most famous art gallery is 15 Uffizi. **City name:** ....

✗ The ....
1 ....
2 ....
3 ....
4 ....
5 ....
6 ....
7 ....
8 ....
9 ....
10 ....
11 ....
12 ....
13 ....
14 ....
15 ....

Exercise 4 Correcting a text

A schoolchild wrote the following geographical description of Britain, but a computer error removed all examples of *the*. Add *the* in 17 more places (after the example).

The
United Kingdom is an island surrounded by English Channel, Atlantic,
^
Irish Sea and North Sea. It is made up of four regions: England, Scotland, Wales and Northern Ireland, and although London is capital of whole country, each region has its own capital city (London, Edinburgh, Cardiff and Belfast). Best-known rivers are Thames, which flows through London, Severn which divides England and Wales, and in north of England, Humber and Mersey. Highest mountains in United Kingdom are found in Scotland (Grampians) and North Wales (Cambrian Mountains), while England's major range is called Pennines. English is spoken everywhere in Britain, although there are other languages such as Welsh and Gaelic, but there are also a lot of distinct regional accents.

Classwork

1 **Work in groups of three or four to answer the quiz questions.**

1 Where is Mount Everest? ....
2 What is the longest river in the world? ....
3 Name another language spoken in Spain apart from Spanish. ....
4 What is the name of the long range of mountains in South America? ....
5 What is the name of the famous square in Moscow? ....
6 What is the name of an airport in New York? ....
7 Where is the Taj Mahal? ....
8 In which decade did the Beatles become famous? ....

2 **Your teacher will tell you the correct answers. Which group got the most right?**

3 **Now write four questions of your own. The answers should include language you have studied in this unit – deserts, mountains, cities etc. Ask the other groups your questions. You might like to give points for the first correct answers. Which group is the class winner?**

Unit

32 Personal, possessive and reflexive pronouns

Getting started

1 **The text below describes robots designed to think like people. Read the text and answer the question.**

How are the robots **different** from humans?

....

March of the machines

We built lots of little robots on wheels. We gave them 'eyes' to see with, a tiny brain to learn with – the same sort that humans have, but much less powerful. And the rest we let them find out for themselves.

We didn't programme them; we didn't give them instructions. And what did they do in the new world they found themselves in? Like children, they learned.

One of them became a 'leader'. When they wanted to, they chose a new leader. And when one of these little robots became weak, with a low battery, the others 'bullied' him. They built up a whole social order of their own. Yet they were machines with less brain power than a bee. A brain's power can be measured by the number of cell connections in it. Our robots have 50. A human brain has a billion.

We humans, their creators, gave our robots just one basic instinct – survival. The rest they found out for themselves.

2 **Are the pronouns underlined in these sentences correct or not? Look back at the text to check.**

a) *We didn't programme they; we didn't give they instructions.* ....

b) *... the others 'bullied' he.* ....

c) *They built up a whole social order of their own.* ....

d) *The rest they found out for theirselves.* ....

3 **In the text, who or what is:**

a) we .... b) it .... c) they ....

Looking at language

Pronouns

Form

Pronouns replace nouns. Here are the main types:

Type	*Form*
Personal subject pronouns	*I, you, she, he, it, we, they*
Non-subject pronouns	*me, you, her, him, it, us, them*
Possessive pronouns	*mine, yours, hers, his, ours, theirs* (no ~~*its*~~)
Reflexive pronouns	*myself, yourself, herself, himself, itself, yourselves, ourselves, themselves*

For the possessives *my, your, her, his its, our, their* + noun, see Unit 33.

Use

Subject pronouns come before verbs:
We built lots of little robots on wheels. *Like children, **they** learned.*
Non-subject pronouns can come after verbs and prepositions:
*We gave **them** 'eyes' to see with.* *One of **them** became a 'leader'.*
Possessive pronouns replace a possessive (see Unit 33) and a noun:
*We made the robots, but they weren't **ours**. (our robots)*
Notice the structure **noun + *of* + possessive pronoun**:
a friend of mine / those keys of yours / something of his
Reflexive pronouns are necessary when the subject and object are the same:
*And what did they do in the new world **they** found **themselves** in?*

The first three types of pronouns help you to avoid repeating nouns:
And when one of these little robots became weak, with a low battery, the others circled and 'bullied' him. They built up a whole social order of their own. Yet they were machines with less brain power than a bee. A brain's power can be measured by the number of cell connections in it.

1 Use lines and circles to show the words or phrases that the <u>underlined</u> pronouns refer to.

A CLEANER in a hotel was asked to clean a lift. The job took <u>him</u> four days.

His confused supervisor asked him why <u>it</u> had taken so long. The cleaner replied, 'Well, there are 12 lifts, one on each floor, and sometimes some of <u>them</u> aren't there.'

Apparently, the man thought each floor had a different lift, so <u>he</u> went to each floor and cleaned the same lift 12 separate times.

Other points

Written and spoken English

- Reflexive pronouns can also be used to emphasise the subject or object, with the meaning 'nobody or nothing else':
  *The rest **they** found out for **themselves**.*
  (they found out, nobody else)
- *It* can replace whole phrases, sentences and ideas:
  *We want to get another telephone line, but **it*** (getting a telephone line) *can take a long time.*
- *You* is often used to mean 'everybody', including yourself:
  *When do **you** leave school in your country? When **you**'re 16.* (Not ~~*When I'm 16*~~.)

Mainly spoken English

- The reflexive pronoun *yourself* is common after some imperatives (see Unit 14) that need an object:
  ***Help yourself** to tea or coffee.*
  Enjoy yourself.
- *They* often means 'people in power' or experts, but you don't know exactly who:
  ***They** say that the world is getting warmer, don't **they**?*
- *They* and *them* can replace *he or she* or *someone* when you don't know if a person is male or female:
  *I saw someone outside, but I don't know if **they*** (he or she) *saw me.*

2 **Match the nouns or noun phrases, 1–5, to their possible replacement pronouns, a)–d).**

a) she b) they c) it d) we

1 somebody .....
2 the beautiful girl .....
3 finding a job .....
4 Janet and I .....
5 the government .....

Getting it right

Exercise 1 Which use?

Match the pronouns in *italics*, 1–8, to the best rule, a)–i), below.

Well, I looked at *myself* in the mirror, and thought my hair looked terrible. So I cut it **1** *myself*.

2 *You* can find anything on the Internet these days. **3** *You* use the Internet a lot, don't you, Peter?

I saw someone come into the theatre, and **4** *they* told us to keep quiet. Then the show began, and the children loved it. **5** *They* all started clapping.

They earned high salaries for years, but **6** *it* didn't make them happy. I was happy the day I found $10. I picked **7** *it* up and walked home smiling.

Have you heard? **8** *They*'re going to build a new road right behind the school.

a) *they* = he or she
b) *you* = everybody
~~c) *myself* because the subject and object are the same~~
d) *it* = whole phrase
e) *myself* for emphasis
f) personal *they*
g) personal *you*
h) *it* replaces singular / uncountable noun
i) *they* = people in power or experts

..c).. 1 ..... 2 ..... 3 ..... 4 ..... 5 ..... 6 ..... 7 ..... 8 .....

Exercise 2 Learning from learners

Read the letter to a language school. In 1–9, choose a pronoun to replace the underlined word or phrase, or to fill in the gap.

Dear Mrs Brown

I am writing to find out about courses at your school for my daughter. My daughter is 16 years old and can come to your school in July. I would like 1 my daughter to live with a British family, as I hope that 2 living with a family will give her more opportunities to practise her English. A friend of 3 ____ knows someone who studied at your school. 4 Her friend enjoyed 5 ____ very much. Are your courses available all year round or only in the summer? Is it true that all your teachers are well qualified? Are 6 the teachers experienced? What facilities do you have at your school? I am a teacher 7 ____ and am therefore very interested in your facilities and courses.

I would be grateful if you could send 8 ____ a brochure about your courses and fees.

I look forward to hearing from 9 ____.

Yours sincerely

Yolanda Perez

She 1 .... 2 .... 3 .... 4 .... 5 ....

6 .... 7 .... 8 .... 9 ....

Exercise 3 Guess the object

What do you think is being described in the 'Guess the object' party game below? Fill in the gaps in the description with a suitable pronoun.

I am going to describe something of 1 .... which is very dear to 2 .... 3 .... was my grandmother's and 4 .... came from Turkey where 5 .... lived in the 1920s. It's not particularly valuable, and 6 .... see a lot of 7 .... around these days, but what makes this one so special is its history. My grandmother worked as a nurse and often visited villages in the mountains. One of the women 8 .... treated gave 9 .... this present to thank 10 .... Her mother had made it 11 .... when 12 .... was a child, and it must have been on the floor of her house for 20 or 30 years before it came into our family. What do you think it is?

Exercise 4 Personalisation

Fill in the gaps in the questions with a pronoun. Then answer the questions.

Do *you* do the cooking in your home? If not, who does? — *No, I don't. My sister does it.*

1 Someone in the street asks you for money. Do you give it to .... ? ....

2 When are .... allowed to vote in your country? ....

3 Did you buy this copy of *Developing Grammar in Context* .... ? ....

4 .... say that too much exercise can be bad for you. What do you think? ....

5 If people talk about you behind your back, does .... upset you? ....

6 In a British home, the host might say 'Help .... to biscuits'. Does the same happen in your country? ....

Classwork

1 **Think of an object that you own – if possible something that is special to you in some way, perhaps because someone gave it to you, or because it has been in your family for a long time.**

2 **Work in groups of three or four. Take it in turns to talk about your object, but don't say what it is. Use pronouns to describe the object, and to say how you got it. (Look back at Exercise 3 on page 192 for help.) Can the others guess what it is?**

Example:

A: *It's quite small, and fairly valuable. I wear it every day. In fact, most people wear theirs every day. Mine is quite old, and my father gave it to me.*

B: *Is it your watch?*

A: *Yes, it is.*

Unit

33 Possessives and demonstratives

Getting started

1 **Read the text about a five-year-old's misunderstanding and answer the question.**

What was his mistake? ....

Twin Troubles

My five-year-old son, David, had just started school. His classroom was up some steps, and each day another mother left her twin babies in their pram at the bottom of the steps, while she took her child into the classroom. After a week of this David said, 'It's sad those babies have been forgotten. They've been left there since I started school.' He felt much better when I explained they were only there for a few minutes each day and hadn't been there for the whole week.

2 **Underline any possessives (*my, your, his, her, its, their, our*) in the text. Double underline any demonstratives (*this, that, these, those*).**

3 **Look at the text again. Who do the words in bold refer to? Fill in the gaps.**

His classroom David's classroom

a) *her twin babies* .... babies

b) *their pram* .... pram

c) *her child* .... child

4 **'... a week of this ...' What does *this* refer to?** ....

Why do you think David says 'those babies', not 'these babies'?

....

Looking at language

Possessives

Use

Possessives (*my, your, his, her, its, our, your, their, David's, whose*) tell us who or what something belongs to.

- They are followed by a noun or noun phrase:
  ***His** classroom was up some steps.*
- We use *whose* to make questions about possession:
  ***Whose** classroom is up a flight of stairs?*
  ***David's** is.*
- To make a noun possessive, we use an apostrophe. With **singular** nouns we use *'s*:
  ***David's** classroom was up some steps.*
  *The **woman's** babies were in a large pram.*
  With names ending in s we can write ***Chris'** book* or ***Chris's** book.*

With **plural** nouns we use *s'*:
*She left the twin **babies'** pram at the bottom.*
*The **girls'** school wasn't far from the **boys'** school.*
With irregular plurals we use *'s:*
*The **children's** mother was with them.*

1 **What possessives could replace the underlined words?**

1 <u>My sister's</u> party was really good. ....
2 I didn't realise it was <u>the boy's</u> pen. ....
3 <u>The men's</u> changing room was very small. ....
4 <u>Nicky and Simon's</u> new house needs a lot of work. ....
5 <u>The frying pan's</u> handle was broken. ....

Other points

- We don't use an article with a possessive:
  *I went back to **my house**.*
  We don't say: ~~*I went back to the my house*~~.
- We use possessives to talk about parts of the body. We say: *I've broken **my** arm.* We don't say: ~~*I've broken the arm*~~.
- *It's* is a contraction of *it is* or *it has*:
  It's nearly six o'clock.
  Its is a possessive:
  *I took the TV back to the shop because **its** remote control didn't work.*

Demonstratives (*this, these, that, those*)

Use

These words give information about where something is. Things can be **near** (*this, these*) or **distant** (*that, those*) in terms of time and space:

Time	*Space*
***This** story will make you laugh. Listen.* ***That** story you told us yesterday was really interesting.*	*Do you want **these** books here?* *No, **those** ones on the other table.*

- *This, that, these* and *those* are not always followed by a noun or noun phrase:
  *Do you want **these**?* (these things I'm holding)
- *This* and *that* are often used to point back to whole sentences or ideas:
  He was terrified of flying. This / That was why he'd never been abroad.
- Often there is little difference in meaning between *this* or *that* in **backward**-pointing reference, although we prefer *that* to point back to something that is now finished and past:
  ***That** was an interesting story.*
- Usually we use only *this* and *these* for **forward**-pointing reference:
  *Watch! **This** is the way to turn on the oven.*

2 Answer the questions about the <u>underlined</u> demonstratives.

1. <u>This</u> book is really good. Do you want to borrow it?
   Is *This* used to refer to nearness of time or space? ....
2. Peter didn't agree with them. <u>This</u> made the decision more difficult.
   Does *This* point back to a single thing or a whole sentence? ....
3. Peter didn't agree with them. <u>This</u> made the decision more difficult.
   Can *This* be replaced with *That*? ....
4. <u>This</u> / <u>That</u> took a lot or work, but I'm glad it's over now.
   Which is better, *This* or *That*? ....
5. I've got some great new CDs. Listen to <u>these</u>.
   Is *these* used for forward- or backward-pointing reference? ....

Other points

- We often use *this / these / that / those + one(s)* to avoid repeating nouns:
  *Which colour do you like? **That one**.* (that colour)
- We say *these days* to talk about the present, but *in those days* to talk about the past:
  *People don't seem so polite **these days**.*
  *I was brought up in the 1970s. **In those days** nobody had CD players.*

Getting it right

▶ Exercise 1 Recognising meaning

Say what or who the underlined possessives refer to.

Within two months a two-year-old girl, Robin Hawkins of Grand Rapids, Michigan, has destroyed her family's television, dishwasher and refrigerator, flushed the cat down the toilet and managed to start **1** their car, making it crash into a tree and causing over $1,000-worth of damages. Among **2** her other acts are painting the walls with nail varnish, and drilling 50 holes in them.

A resident of Oak Harbor, Washington, reported **3** his neighbour to the police for putting **4** his dog on the bonnet of **5** his car and driving along at 70 mph. The owner said the dog loved it.

Patrick M. O'Connor, 21, was arrested when he tried to rob a grocery-store in Calgary, Canada. He failed because of two things: **6** his only weapon was an ordinary can opener, which did not scare the shop assistant, and he was with **7** his girlfriend's 16-month-old baby, who kept falling out of **8** its pushchair while O'Connor was trying to get away.

Robin Hawkins......

1 ....
2 ....
3 ....
4 ....
5 ....
6 ....
7 ....
8 ....

▷ Exercise 2 Learning from learners

Look at Extracts a)–h) from learners' writing and speaking, including possessives and demonstratives. Correct nine more mistakes after the example. There may be more than one mistake in each extract.

a) Then my aunt come round and asked me to go shopping with her to buy something for my sister wedding.

b) I don't like this exercises. Can I do a different one?

c) In the my country we drink tea with sugar and milk.

d) These are the things I don't like much about that country. I'm looking forward to leaving and going home to some good food.

e) My friend class does more fun things. We always study those grammar exercises.

f) My sister was getting married soon. His idea was to have a really big party and invite everyone she knew.

g) José isn't here. He told me he's broken the arm. He'll try and come on Thursday.

h) My parents had booked the biggest hotel in town for the party because his reputation was good. It was one of that places that really knew how to organise a successful wedding.

Which extracts are about:

i) a wedding .... ii) food and drink .... iii) a learner's class .... ?

Exercise 3 Putting back possessives

Fill in the gaps in the conversation with *its*, *my*, *our*, *your* or *their*. You can use a word more than once.

After just two singles, people are describing The Toys as the next big rock'n'roll band. Paul Gray talks to John Rogers in the *Evening Sun*.

John: Do you think you'll still be successful in ten years' time?

Paul: Probably. Our latest recording is the best yet and 1 .... music makes people get up and dance.

John: What do you think when people criticise 2 .... image?

Paul: We don't care about image much. When I get up in the morning I'm not thinking about whether someone might take 3 .... photograph today.

John: How do you feel about 4 .... sudden rise to fame?

Paul: I don't mind being famous, but I don't like it when a journalist tells lies just to try to sell 5 .... papers. I mean, that happened last month, when a newspaper said we were going to break up. 6 .... fans were upset but it was total rubbish. In fact 7 .... editor later apologised to us, which was great!

Exercise 4 Rewriting a letter

In the letter below to a bank, put sections a)–e) in the correct order.

1 c) 2 ..... 3 ..... 4 ..... 5 .....

a) This
Paying back the money will not be possible for the following reasons:

b) I suggest you check your records, and I imagine that your records will show serious errors on your part.

c) I am writing with reference to the letter from you of 14 July. The letter requested that I repay the bank the sum of £1,000 by the coming Thursday.

d) 1 I do not have £1,000.
2 I did not borrow £1,000 from the bank in which you work.
3 I am not, and have never been, a customer of your bank. I bank with the bank opposite you, and the service of this bank is always excellent.
4 You addressed the letter to 'Mr Andrew Rogers'. Mr Andrew Rogers is not my name. My name is Roger Andrews.

e) Should you wish to discuss the matters mentioned above further, the address of my solicitor is reproduced below.

Now replace each of the underlined words or phrases with a word or phrase from the box. There are more answers than you need.

its service	it's service	my solicitor's address	my solicitors' address	That	the one
these	these	these matters	~~This~~	This	this	this sum	this sum of money
those matters	your	your bank	your letter		

Classwork

1 **To play the board game below you will need a dice, and coins as your counters. Work in groups of three or four. The first player throws the dice and talks about the subject they land on.**

Example:
My best friend's house. My best friend is Jane. Her house is near here. It's modern and nicely furnished. There are three bedrooms and it's got a small garden too.

2 **If you land on a *this*, *that*, *these* or *those* square, talk about something you can see around you in the classroom or out of the window.**

Example:
I don't like these chairs. I find them uncomfortable during long lessons.

3 **If you land on a square with a picture in it, you can ask someone else any question you like.**

Example:
Jean Luc, where do you live?

4 **The first player to reach the end is the winner.**

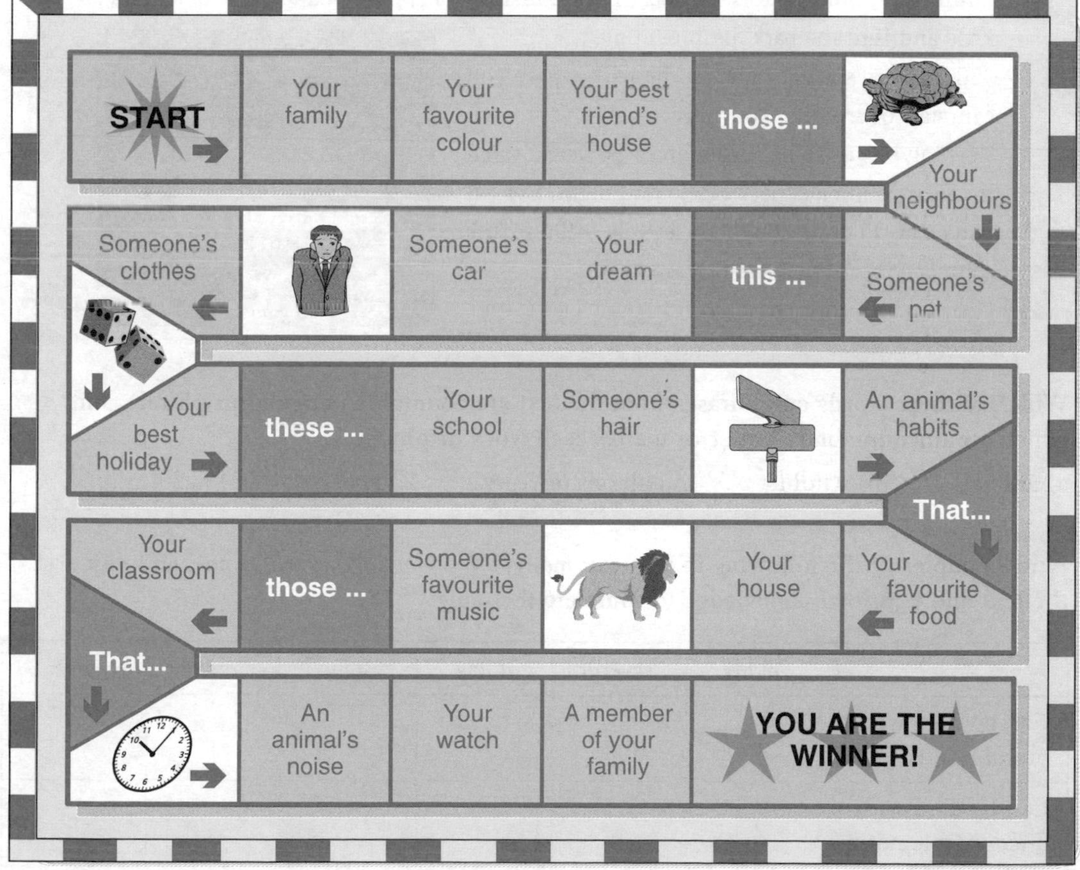

Unit 34 Countable and uncountable nouns and expressions of quantity

Getting started

1 Read the text about Malaysia's rainforests and answer the questions.

a) Why do people visit the national park in the text? ....

b) Why do they need a torch? ....

Malaysia has some of the most ancient rainforests in the world, which have remained unchanged for many millions of years. Mammals in these forests include elephants, rhinos (very rare now), tigers, leopards, several kinds of deer, various gibbons and monkeys and porcupines to name a few.

Malaysia's great national park, Taman Negara, covers 4,343 square kilometres of rainforest. Some visitors see lots of wildlife and come away happy, others see very little and find the park disappointing.

There are several hides in the park where you can stay overnight. You need to take your own sleeping bag or some sheets, and a powerful torch to see any animals that come out at night. Even if you're not lucky enough to see any wildlife, the sounds of the jungle are fantastic.

a gibbon

2 Which of these words and phrases from the text are countable (singular or plural), and which are uncountable? Write *c* or *u* after each word or phrase.

a) animals ..... b) wildlife ..... c) millions of years ..... d) sheets ..... e) hides .....

3 Find examples of the following in the text: *many*, *a few*, *lots of*, *several*, *some*, and *any*. Use the text and your own knowledge to complete the table.

	many	*several*	*a few*	*some*	*lots of*	*any*
Can be used with plural nouns	✓					
Can be used with uncountable nouns	✗					

Looking at language

Countable and uncountable nouns

Nouns can be **countable** or **uncountable**.
Countable nouns have a singular and plural form. They are things which occur in individual units or parts of a whole thing; *bottle, bottles.*
Uncountable nouns usually have only one form (without an s on the end). They are often words to describe materials, substances or abstract things: *wood, air, love.*

Some nouns can be countable and uncountable, with slightly different meanings. Compare:
Can you switch on the ***lights****?* (countable – electric lights)
There isn't much ***light*** *in here.* (uncountable – a 'substance')

Many foods are countable when you're referring to a whole thing and uncountable when referring to a smaller part for serving:
I bought ***two chickens*** *at the market for the party.* (countable)
There's ***some chicken*** *in the fridge if you'd like it.* (uncountable)

We use singular verb forms and pronouns with uncountable nouns:
The food ***is*** *ready. Get* ***it*** *while* ***it's*** *hot.*

1 Are these nouns usually countable (c) or uncountable (u)? Which can be either (e)?

1 information .... 2 furniture .... 3 country .... 4 luggage ....
5 hair .... 6 watch .... 7 news .... 8 computer .... 9 advice ....
10 equipment .... 11 chocolate .... 12 noise ....

Expressions of quantity

- We can use exact quantities to talk about the quantity of things:
  I need ***two*** *pineapples and* ***half a kilo of*** *rice.*
- Or we can use words to describe inexact quantities. With uncountable nouns these are:
  some, any, (not) much, a little, little, lots / a lot (of), plenty (of), a bit (of), most.
  With plural countable nouns they are:
  some, any, (not) many, a few, few, lots / a lot (of), plenty (of), several, most.
- We can use these expressions with a noun to talk generally:
  Most people *like chocolate.*
  A little money *is better than no money.*
  We can use them without a noun if the meaning is clear:
  Of 100 people questioned, ***most*** *said they liked chocolate.*
- We use them with *of the* + noun to be specific:
  Most of the people *in the room were Swiss.*
  I used ***a little of the money*** *to buy the drinks.*

Some and any

Some and *any* come before plural and uncountable nouns.

- *Some* means 'a number of'. Compare:
  I saw ***some*** *monkeys.* (a number of monkeys)
  There are monkeys in most parts of India. (no article: the monkeys are impossible to count).
- *Some* is typically used in statements and questions:
  I drove into town, and noticed there were ***some*** *new traffic lights.*
  Have you got ***some*** *letters for me?*
- *Any* is typically used in questions and negatives (including *never*):
  Were there ***any*** *people?* *Is there* ***any*** *more?* *There weren't* ***any*** *other cars.* *I* ***never*** *eat* ***any*** *breakfast.*
- In questions and offers we use *some* /səm/ when we expect the answer to be 'yes', and *any* when there is a possibility that the answer will be 'no'. Compare:
  Would you like ***some*** *biscuits?* (I expect you to say 'yes')
  Are there ***any*** *biscuits*? (perhaps there aren't any)
- Stressed *some* /sʌm/ means 'not all':
  I like ***some*** *jazz music.* (not all jazz music)
- Stressed *any* can mean 'it doesn't matter which':
  You can put ***any*** *vegetables in this dish.*

Much, many and lots of / a lot of

Much and *many* are usually used in questions and negative sentences. We use *much* with uncountable nouns and *many* with plural countable nouns:

How ***much time*** *have we got?*
There aren't ***many people*** *here, are there?*

We use *lots of* (in spoken English) and *a lot of* (in spoken and written English), with plural **and** uncountable nouns. They can be in positive and negative sentences and questions:

He's had ***a lot of*** *accidents.*
There's ***lots of*** *coffee left.*
We haven't got ***a lot of*** *time.*
Are there ***lots of*** *people in your class?*

(a) few and (a) little

We use *(a) few* with plural countable nouns, and *(a) little* with uncountable nouns.

A few and *a little* mean a small amount. *Few* and *little* are similar in meaning to *not many* and *not much* and usually suggest that the small amount is some kind of problem. Compare:

He explained the situation, and ***a few*** *people understood it.* (neutral)
He explained the situation, but ***few*** *people understood it.* (it was a problem)

Only a little / few also have negative meanings:

Is there any milk left? ***Only a little.***

2 Underline the best quantifier in the sentences below.

1 Can I have *some / any* biscuits, please?
2 Not *lots of / many* people were injured in the crash.
3 *A few / A little* trains were running late.
4 Beth's had *little / few* news of her sister since she left.
5 *How much / How many* sheep are in the field?
6 My cousin likes *some / any* Indian food, but not the really spicy dishes.

Getting it right

Exercise 1 Checking meaning

Read the conversation between three friends and decide if statements 1–10 are true or false.

Sarah: Would you like *any* more?
Fiona: No thanks. It was delicious.
Sarah: Would you like **1** *coffee* then?
Fiona: Yes, that would be nice.
Sarah: Fiona, do you want **2** *some milk*?
Fiona: Just **3** *a little*, thanks, and **4** *lots of* sugar!
Sarah: What about you, William?
William: Oh, milk please, yes, but **5** *not much*. And no sugar. I meant to ask you, Sarah, did you see that programme the other night about the lost city under the sea near Japan?
Sarah: No, but I read about it. Was it interesting?
William: Yes, it was amazing actually. There are **6** *some* incredible ruins. At least they think they're ruins.
Sarah: Yes, the article I read thought it was **7** *a lot of* rubbish and that there were **8** *few* scientific facts to support the idea.
William: Well, on the programme there were **9** *some* facts, such as several stone bowls they've found nearby.
Sarah: Well, I don't know what I think but they'll probably have some definite proof one day soon. **10** *Some more coffee*, Fiona?

Any could be replaced by *some*. *true*

1 *Any* or *some* could be added here. ....
2 *Some* could be replaced by *any* here. ....
3 We use *a little* because *milk* is countable. ....
4 *Lots of* could be replaced by *much* here. ....
5 We use *not much* because *milk* is uncountable. ....
6 *Some* could be replaced by *any* here. ....
7 *A lot of* can **only** be used with uncountable nouns like *rubbish*. ....
8 *Few* could be replaced by *not many* here. ....
9 *Some* is pronounced /sʌm/ here. ....
10 *Some* is only used with uncountable nouns like *coffee*. ....

Exercise 2 Choosing the best form

Read the introduction to a cookery book, *Round the World in Recipes*, and underline the correct expressions of quantity.

Some / *any* recipes in the book are quick and easy. But it's an insult to people's intelligence to suggest they should never do anything which takes more than *a little* / *a few* minutes. **1** *Some* / *any* recipes are long, slow and economical (beans, for example). **2** *Some* / *any* require **3** *little* / *a little* skill but **4** *some* / *any* patience like sourdough bread. **5** *Most* / *much* have ingredients which are easily available. Only **6** *a few* / *few* have unusual spices such as the Thai *kaffir* lime leaves or the Indonesian shrimp paste, *baluchan*, and **7** *some* / *any* cook will know how to adapt the recipes. The traditional fat in the countries of origin is given in the recipes because it can contribute to a special flavour. But beware – **8** *some* / *any* cooks believe that if **9** *a few* / *a little* oil does you good, then **10** *a lot* / *much* must be better. If only this was true!

Exercise 3 Learning from learners

Read the learners' reports below about a survey of people's eating habits in their school. Correct any mistakes in the underlined words and phrases or tick (✓) correct examples.

Report A

> We discovered that <u>a little</u> (a few) people don't have breakfast at all, but that most do. Of those who do have breakfast, 1 <u>not much</u> have a cooked breakfast, 2 <u>most</u> have some cereal or toast, and 3 <u>many</u> have tea and coffee.

Report B

> We wanted to find out how often people ate out and how often they stayed at home. We got interesting results. 4 <u>Several of</u> people have a lot of meals out, three or four a week, especially at the weekend, but one person never has any meals out. 5 <u>Only a few</u> people said they enjoyed cooking at home – 6 <u>most of</u> people had meals out to avoid cooking.

Report C

> We looked at lunches on school days. 7 <u>Lots</u> people pay for school canteen lunches, but 8 <u>most</u> don't think the food is very good! 9 <u>No many</u> people bring their own food, but those that do bring sandwiches and salads. 10 <u>A few</u> people buy takeaway food from outside school.

Find one place where *some* could be added to make the sentence sound better.

Exercise 4 Remembering forms and writing

For each expression of quantity, 1–8, note the types of nouns which can follow. Then include the expression in a sentence about your country.

Quantifier	*Followed by*	*Sentence*
Example: a few	*plural*	*There are a few areas with high mountains.*
1 not many	....	....
2 most of	....	....
3 plenty of	....	....
4 several	....	....
5 some	....	....
6 not much	....	....
7 few	....	....
8 lots of	....	....

Classwork

1 **Divide into two groups: the Noughts, who can write 0s, and the Crosses, who can write Xs. Then divide into small teams in these groups. Rewrite the sentence in each square, using the word(s) in bold under each sentence.**

Example: *Have you got many suitcases?*
luggage
Have you got much luggage?

2 **With another team, take turns to choose a square and read out your new sentence. If it is correct, put your 0 or X in that square on the grid. If it is not correct, you've lost your turn. The winning team is the first to get a line of three 0s or Xs horizontally, vertically or diagonally.**

How many minutes does the cake need? **time**	The equipment we need is pretty expensive. **skis and ski-boots**	She gave me a really good idea. **advice**
Are there any places left on the bus? **room**	I've only got a few coins left in my pocket. **money**	The latest reports from the capital are disturbing. **news**
There isn't much healthy food in the house. **vegetables**	There are lots of boys in my class. **girls**	I had a bit of experience working as a journalist. **years**

Unit

35 Adjectives and adverbs

Getting started

1 **Read the article about tips for shopping in the sales. There is one piece of advice that came from another text. Which one?**

....

Experts' advice –

discount shopping tips from the *Marie Claire* fashion team

- Never feel you have to buy something just because it's very cheap.
- Before going shopping, have a good idea of what you really want.
- Walk around the shop once, and if nothing seems right, simply leave.
- Always, always try things on.
- Choose neutral colours as these will go well with the clothes you already have.
- Check clothes thoroughly for marks or holes. Remember, you can rarely return discounted goods.
- Remember to wash the material before you start to make your clothes.
- Buying something that you can have altered to fit you perfectly is a good idea, but only if you really will do it. Major alterations are not a good idea. Shoulder pads, for example, cannot be removed very successfully. Shortening an item can work well.
- Try to remember what clothes you already have. Do you really need another pair of black trousers?

2 **Look at these sentences from the article.**

Never feel you have to buy something just because it's very cheap.

Check clothes thoroughly for marks or holes.

***Cheap* is an adjective, and *thoroughly* is an adverb. Find more examples of adverbs and adjectives in the article, and write *adjectives*, *adverbs* or *very* in the gaps in the rules below.**

a) .... are usually used with nouns.

b) .... are usually used with verbs.

c) .... can give more information about adverbs and adjectives.

d) .... are often formed by adding *-ly* to the ....

Looking at language

Adjectives

Adjectives are used to describe nouns. They can come:

- **before** nouns:

  *What a **lovely colour**!* *He's a **kind man**.*
- **after** these verbs: *be, become, get, seem, appear, look, feel, sound, taste, smell:*

  *Jane **is tall** for her age.* *She's **become difficult** to talk to.* *Lunch **smells good**.*
- **after** *get / make / keep / find* + object:

  *She **got the room ready** for the guests.*

  *They **made their house bigger** by building an extension.*

See Unit 36 for the order of two or more adjectives. See Units 43 and 44 for comparative and superlative adjectives.

Adverbs

Here are some groups of adverbs and adverb phrases:

- **'Manner' adverbs** tell us **how** something is done or happens. They usually come after the verb and object:

  *Check garments **thoroughly** for marks and holes.*

  *I bought it **quickly**.*
- **'Place' adverbs** tell us **where** something is done. They usually come after the verb:

  *We went shopping **there** last week.* *She went **outside**.*
- **'Time' adverbs** tell us **when** or **how often** something is done. Time adverbs often come before the verb, but adverb phrases can come at the beginning or end of a sentence:

  *Try to remember what clothes you **already** have.* *I bought it **this morning**.*
- **'Intensifying' adverbs** such as *very, really* and *absolutely* change the strength of adjectives and adverbs: *very cheap / very successfully.*

  We use *absolutely* with adjectives that are already very strong.

  We say: *It was absolutely fantastic.* We don't say: ~~*It was absolutely good*~~.

  We use *very* with other adjectives:

  *It was **very** good.*

  We use *really* with both types of adjective, and before *very*:

  ***really** good / **really very** good / **really** fantastic.*

  Intensifying adverbs are often stressed in spoken English:

  *Did you see the match? It was **really** close, wasn't it?*

Note that adverbs nearly always come after *be* and **auxiliary verbs**:

*I'm **never** happy with anything I buy.* *We've **already** seen her.*

If there are two or more adverbs at the end of a clause, the order can vary, but it is usually best to put a time adverb at the end:

manner place time

*They played happily in the snow **all day**.*

See Unit 42 for adverbs of frequency (*never, always, sometimes*).

Form

The form of many adverbs is **adjective +ly**:

rare → *rarely*, *successful* → *successfully*, *perfect* → *perfectly*

Sometimes there are spelling changes:

tragic → *tragically*, *happy* → *happily*.

Some adverbs have the same form as the adjective:

hard → *hard*, *fast* → *fast*, *late* → *late*, *straight* → *straight*

Be careful – some adjectives look like adverbs: *lovely, silly, lonely, friendly*. Use a phrase to form the adverb, such as:

He looked at me ***in a friendly way***.

Some adverbs do not have an adjective form: *already, ever, never, still, there, yet*.

1 Underline the best form, adjective or adverb.

1 The room wasn't very *quiet / quietly*.
2 The dessert tasted *strange / strangely*.
3 He ran home as *quick / quickly* as he could.
4 She put the phone down *sad / sadly*.
5 The business was *successful / successfully* in its first year.

Other points

- Adjectives meaning 'easy' or 'difficult' are often followed by *to* + **infinitive**:
  It's ***hard to understand*** *his behaviour. Some people are just* ***impossible to live with***.
- *Good / well*: *good* is an adjective:
  It was a ***good*** *match*.
  Well can be an adjective:
  I don't feel ***well***;
  or an adverb:
  You played really ***well***.
- *Hard / hardly / hardly ever*: *Hard* is an adjective or an adverb:
  It was a ***hard*** *exam. I tried* ***hard***. *Hardly* is an adverb meaning 'very little':
  I've hardly done any work today.
  Hardly ever means almost never:
  He's always out. We ***hardly ever*** *see him.*
- The verbs *appear, look, feel, sound, taste* and *smell* can be used with adjectives and adverbs, but with a different meaning. Compare:
  With adjective: *He* ***appeared*** *tired.* (seemed)
  With adverb: *He suddenly* ***appeared*** *with a bunch of flowers.* (arrived)

2 Which of these words are adjectives (adj), adverbs (adv) or either (e)?

1 friendly .... 2 fast .... 3 completely .... 4 yet ....
5 nice .... 6 lovely .... 7 softly .... 8 grammatically ....
9 well .... 10 easy .... 11 here .... 12 dead ....

Getting it right

Exercise 1 Word choice and order

In each sentence 1–10, fill in one gap with a word or phrase from the box, and put a cross (✗) in the gap you don't need. Underline *adjective* or *adverb* to show which type of word you've used.

absolutely	angrily	fast	happy	hard	interested	late	next week	really	~~red~~	very

Example: There were hundreds of red flowers ✗ in the field. *adjective / adverb*

1 Jack .... shouted .... at the other driver for being so stupid. *adjective / adverb*

2 He was .... very .... pleasant despite what people say. *adjective / adverb*

3 When we went to Spain, the weather was beautiful although it was .... hot .... at times. *adjective / adverb*

4 I was terrified on the way here because my taxi driver .... drove so .... *adjective / adverb*

5 Many people seem to .... be .... in doing this course. *adjective / adverb*

6 He didn't look .... very .... when I saw him. *adjective / adverb*

7 I got to work .... on Thursday .... and my boss was angry. *adjective / adverb*

8 My new course .... is .... , but I'm really enjoying it. *adjective / adverb*

9 My father is .... coming to stay .... *adjective / adverb*

10 Did you try the chicken? It .... was .... wonderful. *adjective / adverb*

Exercise 2 Matching and linking

Match the sentence beginnings, 1–10, to the endings, a)–k), and add a suitable adjective or adverb in the gaps.

Example: I'm going to take some aspirin because I've got a terrible d).

1 See Samantha over there. She looks ....

2 I want to run the marathon, but I'll have to train ....

3 I'm proud of Maud. She's done really ....

4 I'm worried about the weather for our holiday. They say it's going to be ....

5 He's so lazy. He's ....

6 It's a bad phone line. It's ....

7 Never buy something unless you ....

8 The camera instructions were ....

9 My dog appeared ....

10 Despite my lack of confidence about the answer, my teacher appeared ....

a) wet and cold.

b) wonderful in that dress.

c) like it.

~~d) headache.~~

e) hard.

f) to understand, but it still didn't work.

g) from under a bush with a bone.

h) done anything this morning.

i) to hear what you're saying.

j) with what I said.

k) in her exams.

Exercise 3 Learning from learners

Look at the extracts from learners' writing. There are eight mistakes with adjectives and adverbs. Find and underline them and write the correction.

The kidnappers had taken his daughter. Mr Tasher didn't know what to do. He wasn't a rich man. They must have made a <u>badly</u> mistake and kidnapped the wrong person. When he received the ransom demand, he near died of shock. But that afternoon, imagine his surprise when he heard a car drive quick up to his house and saw his daughter get out. He was very delighted to see she was OK, and he hadn't paid any money.

(three mistakes)

bad

1 ....

2 ....

3 ....

We chatted excited over breakfast about the day out. Lucky, the weather was good. We packed up the car with our food and equipment and set off at 10.00. When we got to the beach we went for a swim while my parents got ready the food. We came back and started to eat hungryly. Everything tasted wonderfully, of course. It was only after lunch that the problems began.

(five mistakes)

4 ....

5 ....

6 ....

7 ....

8 ....

Exercise 4 A treasure hunt

Look at the map and write detailed instructions for the route to the treasure on a piece of paper. Use the words in the box. They are not in the right order.

carefully	hungry	inside	long	old	quickly	quietly	sleeping	~~small~~

Example: First go right, past the small castle.

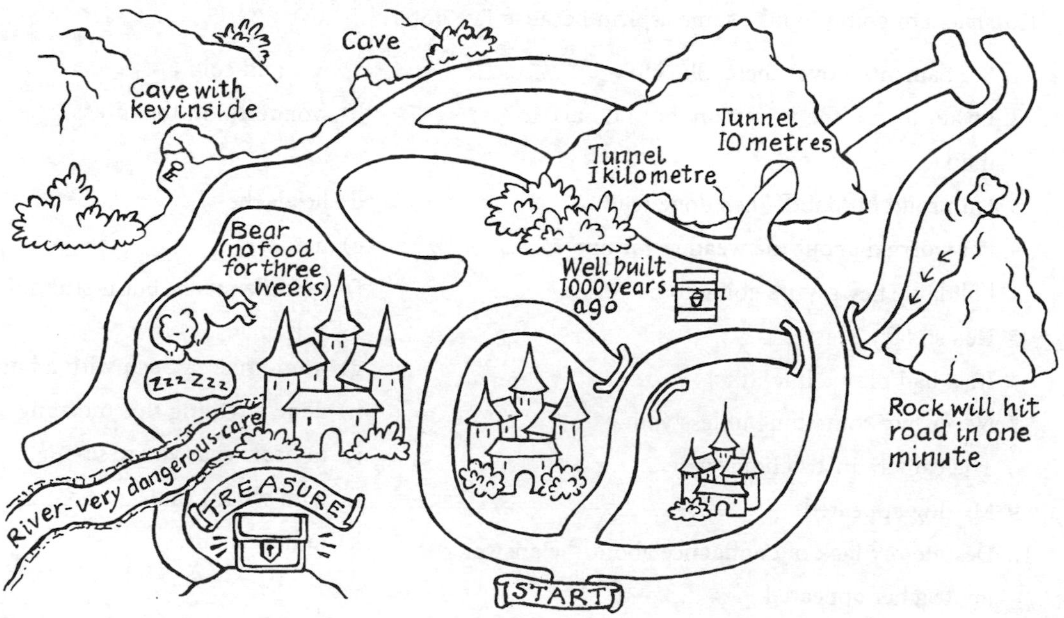

Classwork

Work in small groups. Answer the following questions as quickly as possible. Each question depends on the previous answer, so you must answer in order. The first group to get all the answers correct is the winner.

Questions

1 What object do we use to keep dry in the rain? ....

2 What adjective begins with the last two letters of the answer to number 1 and is the opposite of *small*? ....

3 What adjective begins with the last two letters of the answer to number 2 and means *very kind*? ....

4 Delete the first two letters of the answer to number 3, and add one letter in the middle to make an adjective. What is the adverb form? ....

5 Make an adjective about age starting with the last letter of the answer to number 4. ....

6 The past participle of *hang* rhymes with (sounds the same as) the answer to number 5. Add four letters at the end to make an adverb.

7 What adjective begins with the first two letters of the answer to number 6, and means *enormous*? ....

8 Which adjective and adverb (with the same spelling) has the same number of letters, and begins with the same letter, as the answer to number 7? ....

9 Which meal begins with the last letter of the answer to number 8? ....

10 What rhymes with the answer to number 9 and describes your group if you have finished first? ....

Unit

36 The order of adjectives

Getting started

1 Here is a list of things for sale on a website. Match them to the categories in the box below.

a) A pretty, antique, pine kitchen table ....

b) Japanese hand-painted tea cups ....

c) An ancient Roman oil-lamp ....

d) An outstanding mountain scene ....

e) A set of small blue bowls ....

f) Two beautiful two-seater sofas ....

g) Two large luxury bath towels ....

antiques	ceramics	furniture	paintings	small items for the home

2 Find and underline examples of two or more adjectives, or words used as adjectives, before a noun.

3 Which come first:

- adjectives of **size** or adjectives of **colour**? ....
- adjectives that give **opinion or feelings** about something (e.g. *beautiful*) or adjectives that describe **physical characteristics** (e.g. *ancient*)? ....

4 Which of these adjectives, or nouns used as adjectives, can have *very* in front of them?

a) .... large b) .... Japanese c) .... kitchen

d) .... small e) .... beautiful

Looking at language

Adjectives and nouns can **modify** (change the meaning of) other nouns:

adj noun — *I bought a lovely painting.*

adj adj noun noun — *Two large luxury bath towels.*

There are two types of words which can modify nouns:

- **classifiers** are nouns or adjectives which tell us what **type** something is:
  *a **kitchen** table* *two-**seater** sofas*
- **describers** are adjectives which tell us about the **quality** of the final noun or the speaker / writer's **attitude** to it:
  *a **large** towel* *a **nice** sofa*

There are some rules about the order of describers and classifiers:

- Describers come before classifiers:

We say:	We don't say:
*a **large wooden** table*	~~*a wooden large table*~~
*a pair of **cheap leather** boots*	~~*a pair of leather cheap boots*~~
*a **small sports** car*	~~*a sports small car*~~

- Describers often follow this order:
  opinion before **size** before **age** before **shape** before **colour**:
  *an **interesting old** film* *a **big yellow** truck* *a **small round yellow** clock*
  In general, subjective (feeling and opinion) describers come before objective (factual characteristics) describers.
- Classifiers often follow this order:
  nationality before **material** before **type**:
  *an **Italian leather motorcycle** jacket* *an **English wooden coffee** table*

We don't often use more than two or three adjectives at once, but it is possible:

describers: opinion → size   classifiers: nationality → material

I found a lovely little Swiss gold watch, but it was too expensive.

1 Put these adjectives and nouns in order.

1 a belt leather new wonderful ....

2 a German fascinating movie old ....

3 an intelligent legal new secretary ....

Other points

- In written English, we sometimes break the 'rules' above, and put commas (,) between adjectives:
  It was an old, interesting film. *A round, small clock.*
- Use *and* between two colours:
  *a red **and** yellow dress*
- If there is more than one adjective **after** a noun, use *and* between the last two:
  *Her watch was new **and** expensive.* *The house was large, old **and** cold.*

Getting it right

Exercise 1 Noticing adjective order

Find one example of each adjective pattern, 1–8, from sentences a)–i).

Example: opinion, opinion ..f)..

1 colour, nationality ....
2 colour, colour ....
3 opinion, age ....
4 material, type ....
5 opinion, size ....
6 age, material ....
7 size, shape ....
8 age, type ....

a) My friend's got a *lovely young* son who smiles all the time.
b) I liked the *blue American* car best. What about you?
c) I'm selling my *wooden coffee* table if you're interested?
d) What did that *silly little* boy say?
e) She wore a *red and gold* wedding dress.
f) ~~Frances wanted to meet him because he sounded such a *charming polite* man.~~
g) Shall we throw away those *old coffee* cups?
h) Susan's the one with the *large round* face.
i) Jackie found an *antique silver* bracelet on the beach.

Exercise 2 Learning from learners

In the extracts from learners' descriptive writing below there are some mistakes with the order of adjectives. Correct the mistakes, or tick (✓) the order if it is correct.

A LUCKY ESCAPE

My aunt was a overweight plain woman, with 1 grey short hair and a pair of 2 brown sparkling eyes. I loved her very much. She lived alone with her cats. One of her cats, Farid, who was a 3 ginger very small cat, always liked to sit on me when I visited. One day when I visited my aunt, I knocked on the door but there was no answer. Suddenly I heard a 4 horrible loud scream from inside the house. I found that the door was open. I went inside and up the stairs. In the bedroom I found Farid making the terrible noise sitting next to my aunt. She was unconscious and lying on the 5 wooden dark floor. I managed to phone for an ambulance and get her to hospital. She recovered, but if I hadn't heard the cat I wouldn't have gone into the house.

plain overweight

1 ....
2 ....
3 ....
4 ....
5 ....

A CHILDHOOD MEMORY

It was a 6 bright Sunday beautiful morning. Birds were singing and dogs were barking. It was the day of my first picnic on the beach. As soon as we parked the car, I ran down to the 7 lovely golden long beach. I could feel the 8 refreshing gentle breeze on my skin. My family found a tree to sit under for our picnic, and my mother unpacked all the 9 fresh delicious food she had prepared. I played in the sand for a while. I built a sandcastle, but unfortunately a 10 little nasty girl came and walked on it. This upset me, but I decided to build another one after lunch.

6 ....

7 ....

8 ....

9 ....

10 ....

Exercise 3 Completing conversations

Choose adjectives from each box to complete each conversation. More than one answer may be possible.

Example: | ~~leather~~ ~~small~~ |

A: Judy found a small leather purse. Is it yours?
B: Oh, thanks. I've been looking for that everywhere.

| Italian leather leather lovely low modern Turkish wooden |

A: I'm looking for some 1 .... trousers. Have you got any?
B: Italian? I've got some very nice 2 .... trousers, but they've got a 3 .... design. You'll find them on the 4 .... shelves at the other end of the shop.

| French funny new old shiny |

A: Have you seen James and Alice recently? There's a 5 .... car sitting outside their house!
B: Really? I rather liked that 6 .... one they had, but they needed something newer.

| cotton dark white woollen |

A: Can you pass me my hat?
B: There's a 7 .... hat here.
A: No, not that one. It's much too warm. The 8 .... one, please, if you can find it.

▶ Exercise 4 Spot the difference

Look at the two similar pictures. There are eight differences between them. Write a sentence for each difference using the language you have learnt in this unit.

Example: In picture 1 there's a shiny sports car, but in picture 2 there's a dirty saloon car.

1

2

1 In picture 1 there's a ...., but in picture 2 .... (house)

2 In picture 1 there's a ...., but in picture 2 .... (man)

3 In picture 1 ...., but in picture 2 .... (tie)

4 In picture 1 ...., but in picture 2 .... (fence)

5 ...., but in picture 2 .... (woman)

6 ...., but in picture 2 .... (dog)

7 ...., but in picture 2 .... (bag)

8 .... , but in picture 2 .... (trees)

Classwork

1 Make nine pieces of paper by tearing up an A4 sheet:

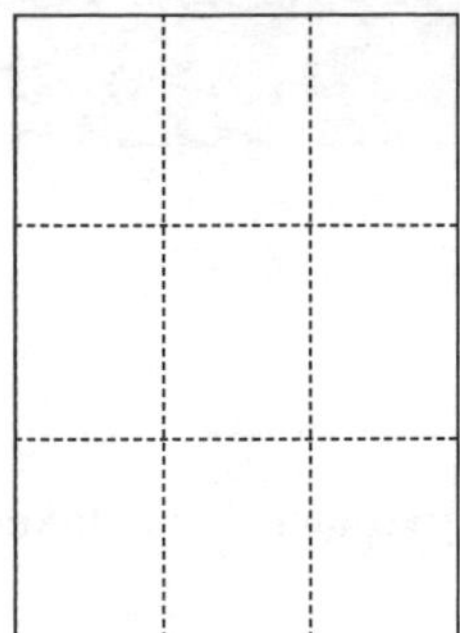

2 On six of the pieces, write a different adjective: 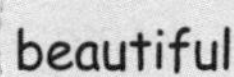

hot large etc.

On the other three pieces of paper write three different nouns: garden piano etc.

3 Work in groups of three or four. You will have 27 or 36 pieces of paper. Mix them together. Add one more piece of paper with a picture of a donkey on it. Deal the pieces out between you.

4 Look at your cards, but don't let anyone else see them. Make as many combinations of adjective + adjective + noun as you can, and put them down on the table in front of you.

beautiful large garden

5 Hold your remaining cards up, but don't let the other players see what they are. Now Player 1 takes a card from the player on their left (Player 2) and tries to make a new combination.

6 Put any new combinations down in front of you.

7 Player 2 now takes a card from Player 3 and so on. Continue until no one has any cards left. The winner is the player with the most combinations of cards on the table. The loser is the player left with the donkey card.

Unit 37 -ed and -ing adjectives

Getting started

1 **The article below is about a little girl who got lost. Read it and correct two factual mistakes in these notes.**

> *Emily Waterhouse – three years old – walked one and a half miles – missing two hours – found by parents – safe and well*
>
> ....

Lost girl takes a tough walk through field and forest

WHEN little Emily Waterhouse left her home, she went on an amazing mile-and-a-half walk through the winter countryside The lost two-year-old made her way across thick woodland, pools of water, and rough tracks. Finally, after she had been missing for two hours, a police helicopter spotted her among the trees.

Emily set out on her journey as she was playing in the back garden of the family's seven-bedroomed home.

'It's amazing that a girl of her age and size managed to get so far. It is difficult for adults to walk there, never mind a small child,' said her mother Henrietta.

PC Shaun Laverty spotted her as he hovered in a helicopter. 'We were all pretty amazed by how far she had got. It is rough ground and there are no paths, so it was quite remarkable.'

Mrs Waterhouse said, 'I was astounded that she wasn't hurt. But Emily didn't seem upset by it all. She was just disappointed she could not ride back in the helicopter.'

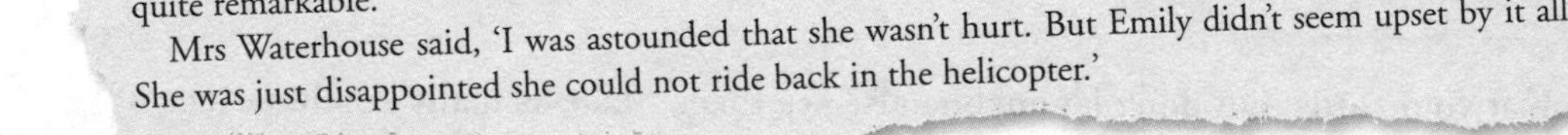

2 **Look at these sentences from the text:**

… *she went on an* *__amazing__* *mile-and-a-half walk through the winter countryside.*

We were all pretty *__amazed__* *by how far she had got.*

Some adjectives have an -ing and an -ed form. Which of these statements is / are true about them?

a) They are formed from verbs. ....

b) They often describe feelings. ....

c) *-ed* adjectives refer to the past. ....

Are there any others in the text?

....

Looking at language

-ed and *-ing* adjectives

Adjectives which come from verbs (**participles**) can have two forms:

Verb	*Adjective 1: present participle*	*Adjective 2: past participle*
disappoint	disappoint**ing**	disappoint**ed**
amaze	amaz**ing**	amaz**ed**
fall	fall**ing**	fall**en**

The *-ed* participle describes a feeling caused by something or somebody else:

We were all pretty amazed by how far she had got ... (our feeling was caused by how far she had got)

The *-ing* participle describes something or somebody that causes a feeling:

In an amazing mile-and-a-half walk ... (the walk causes the feeling)

We use the *-ing* participle with *It* ... :

*I didn't enjoy myself at the party last night. **It** was **disappointing**.*

1 **Fill in the gaps with *-ed* or *-ing*.**

1 Maudie gave me an amaz............ present for my birthday.
2 My teacher was really pleas............ with our exam results.
3 The new musical is quite bor............ actually.
4 She seemed interest............ in our ideas.

Here are some more present and past participle adjectives:

Verb	*Present participle -ing*	*Past participle -ed*
amuse	amusing	amused
annoy	annoying	annoyed
bore	boring	bored
depress	depressing	depressed
embarrass	embarrassing	embarrassed
excite	exciting	excited
frighten	frightening	frightened
interest	interesting	interested
please	pleasing	pleased

Verb	*Present participle -ing*	*Past participle -ed*
satisfy	satisfying	satisfied
shock	shocking	shocked
surprise	surprising	surprised
worry	worrying	worried
Irregular		
delight	delightful	delighted
hurt	hurtful	hurt
impress	impressive	impressed
scare	scary	scared

Occasionally the difference is **time**:

*They ran from the **falling** tree.* (**Present participle** to describe an unfinished action.)

*They walked past a **fallen** tree.* (**Past participle** to describe a finished action.)

Only verbs that describe an action that has a beginning and an end can form these adjectives. They often describe natural processes:

*They stood and watched the **burning** car.* *Burnt sugar is delicious.*

Other examples are: *boiled / boiling; closed / closing; cooled / cooling; dead* (not died) */ dying; fallen / falling; grown / growing; melted / melting; increased / increasing*

2 Fill in the gaps with the correct adjective form.

1 You make tea with boil............ water, but for coffee you need to let it cool a bit.

2 Heat it slowly and when it is totally liquid pour the melt............ chocolate over your ice cream.

3 There was no air in the house because the windows were all tightly clos............ .

Getting it right

Exercise 1 Who had the feeling?

In each sentence, write *f* above the person who had the feeling expressed by the adjective. Write *c* above the cause of the feeling.

Examples: He (*c*) was so *amusing*. We (*f*) laughed at his jokes for hours.

We (*f*) were very *impressed* by your work (*c*).

1 She was *amazed* when I told her about the accident.

2 It was a *delightful* meal. I enjoyed the first course most.

3 I've had enough of him. His behaviour has been really *hurtful*.

4 We didn't tell you about this *amazing* castle we visited the other day, did we?

5 I was so *bored* by that stupid man. He just talked and talked and talked.

6 It was a *depressing* day for everyone when the company closed. No one knew what to say.

7 You've been to Kuala Lumpur? Did you see the Twin Towers? I know Joe was really *impressed*.

8 She was rather *shocking*, really, wearing clothes like that. I didn't like it at all.

Exercise 2 Learning from learners

Write ✗ if the underlined adjective is the wrong participle.

I'm very satisfying with everything in the school.

I am so **1** *boring with my lessons. I've done eveything before*

We had a wonderful time and saw 'The Lion King' at the theatre which was really **2** *amazing. My sister was really* **3** *exciting to be in London. It was her first time.*

I'm not very **4** *pleased with this bike. I think I'll take it back tomorrow.*

I'm really enjoying my class, but I'd find it a bit more **6** *stimulating if the other students took it more seriously. They're always mucking around.*

I was quite **5** *embarrassing by the other students. They were talking all through the lesson. I think that's rude.*

I thought it was quite **7** *disappointed, actually. I'd expected lots of beautiful historical buildings, but my memory of it is dirty buildings, and* **8** *appalling traffic jams.*

I know it's much cheaper, especially if you do it by the month, but I think it's a **9** *frightened thought to be doing it on such busy streets, so I'm going to stick to the bus.*

It was an incredibly **10** *interested museum, with all those things you can touch and experiment with.*

	✗	i)
1	.....	.....
2	.....	.....
3	.....	.....
4	.....	.....
5	.....	.....
6	.....	.....
7	.....	.....
8	.....	.....
9	.....	.....
10	.....	.....

Label each extract a), b) or c) depending on whether it is from a conversation: a) with a teacher; b) about hiring a bicycle, or c) about a trip to London.

Exercise 3 Choosing the right form

An interviewer (I) is talking to a politician (P). Fill in the gaps in their conversation, using the verb in brackets to form a suitable present or past participle adjective. Use the chart in *Looking at language* if you need to.

I: It's *interesting* (*interest*) that after so many years of high tax rates, you're talking about lower taxes. Why?

P: You shouldn't be **1** .... (*surprise*). We have always kept tax as low as possible, and now with **2** .... (*increase*) numbers of new jobs, and a **3** .... (*fall*) rate of inflation, people will be **4** .... (*please*) with our plans to lower tax rates still further.

I: Yes, but there is a **5** .... (*worry*) trend towards spending less on public services. The statistics on hospitals can only be described as **6** .... (*shock*) – six 7............... (*close*) hospitals last year alone. Surely that is pretty **8** .... (*embarrass*) for your government?

P: Any hospital closures are simply due to the **9** .... (*impress*) number of large hospitals. Most people will be **10** .... (*delight*) with what we're doing.

Exercise 4 Writing responses

Write a suitable response for each of the comments or questions below. Include a participle adjective each time.

Example: I didn't laugh at his comments very much. What about you?

Oh, *I thought he was quite amusing.*

1 How did you feel about your exam result?

....

2 Her dress cost nearly $3,000!

Really? ....

3 I don't enjoy talking about politics.

Don't you? I ....

4 Have you seen the results of the questionnaire? They're not at all what I was expecting.

Yes, I agree. ....

5 I thought that some of his comments were rude and insensitive.

Yes. ....

6 How was the holiday?

Oh, ...

Classwork

1 **Work in pairs. Make two copies of the grid below on a piece of paper. Put six adjectives (some *-ed*, some *-ing*) from the chart in *Looking at language* anywhere in one grid. Do not show your partner your grid. (Use the other grid to keep a record of your partner's grid.)**

	1	2	3	4
A				
B				
C				
D				

2 **Take turns to call out a grid square. If your partner has an adjective in the square, she / he tells you the adjective. Make a sentence (of at least six words) including the word.**

Example:

A: *B3.*

B: *Excited.*

A: *We were so excited about going to the cinema that we forgot our tickets.*

If your sentence is correct, your partner says 'Hit!' and crosses out the word like this: ~~excited~~. If there is no word in the square, your partner says 'Missed!'

3 **It's now your partner's turn to call a grid reference. The winner is the first to 'hit' all six of their partner's adjectives.**

Unit 38

Too, (not) very, (not) enough, so *and* such

Getting started

1 **Look at the cartoon. Cuthbert is the cleverest boy in the class. He has just invented a cloning machine (for copying people exactly). Why does the teacher's dream turn into a nightmare?**

....

2 **Look at these extracts from the cartoon:**

(There are) <u>Too many clever pupils</u> for him to handle!
These are far <u>too easy</u>!

Put ticks (✓) and crosses (✗) in the chart to show the rules for the use of *too* and *too many*.

	Used before an adjective	*Used before a noun or noun phrase*
too		
too many / too much		

3 Read the information about two other clever children, and look back at the cartoon. Decide if statements a)–e) are true or false.

Ruth Lawrence

In 1985, Ruth Lawrence became Oxford University's youngest graduate at the age of 13. As a small girl Ruth was so good at maths that her father decided to teach her himself. Her teachers agreed that they were not experienced enough to teach a small child about high level mathematics. Now 25, Ruth is assistant professor of mathematics at the University of Michigan, USA.

Luke McShane

In April 1997, at the age of 13, Luke McShane became the UK international chess champion. No other British chess player has become champion at such a young age. However, it may not be very easy for Luke to hold on to his record. There are several young players showing signs of great chess talent at the moment. With so much talent around, a new, younger chess champion is possible in the next few years.

a) *So* and *such* are used to emphasise something. ....

b) *So* is used before nouns. ....

c) *Too* usually means that there is some kind of a problem. ....

d) *Not very easy* = difficult. ....

e) *Not enough* is only used with nouns. ....

Looking at language

The words and expressions in this unit affect the meaning of nouns, adjectives and adverbs.

So and *such*

To emphasise an **adjective** or **adverb** we use:

- ***so*** **+ adjective / adverb:**
  *It's **so beautiful** here. They always talk **so loudly**.*
- ***such a / an*** **(+ adjective) + singular noun:**
  *That was **such a wonderful film**.*
- ***such*** **(+ adjective) + plural or uncountable noun:**
  *They're **such clever children**. He's **such a professional**.*

We can also use *very* for emphasis, but *so* and *such* are stronger.

To emphasise **quantity** we use: ***so much*** **+ uncountable noun**, ***so many*** **+ countable noun** or ***such a lot of*** **+ noun:**

*I've never seen **so much mess**. There are **so many people** here.*
*I've eaten **such a lot of junk food** recently.*

So and *such* are often followed by a *that* clause showing the **effect** of the adjective:

cause / effect
Ruth was so good at maths | *that her father decided to teach her himself.*

So and *such* are usually stressed in spoken English.

Too and *(not) ... enough*

These suggest a **problem** or **difficulty**. Compare:

*It's **very expensive**, but it's good quality. I'll buy it.*	*It's **too expensive**. I can't afford it.*
*There are **a lot of people** here. How exciting!*	*There are **too many** people here. There's no room to move.*

- ***too* + adjective / adverb:**
  The camera's too expensive. You're speaking too quickly.
- ***too many* + countable noun / *too much* + uncountable noun:**
  *There are **too many** students here.* *There is **too much** food.*
- *Too* ... and *not* ... *enough* can mean the same when used with adjectives of opposite meaning:
  *This classroom's **too small** for our class. (This classroom **isn't big enough** for our class.)*
- Sometimes you have to choose more carefully:
  We say: *This coffee's **too hot.*** We don't say: ~~*This coffee isn't cold enough*~~. (coffee should be **hot**)
  We say: *I've lost weight. These trousers are **too big***. We don't say: ~~*These trousers aren't small enough*~~. (I've got smaller; the trousers haven't)
- *Enough* goes **before** nouns:
  *We had just **enough time**.*
  and **after** adjectives / adverbs:
  *Their new house is **big enough** for all of us.*

  To give extra information about the difficulty, we use *to* ... or *for* ... after *too* and the adjective and adverb:
  *This is **too hot to drink**.* *These trousers are **too big for me**.*

1 **In this text about another clever child, the words *so*, *such*, and *very* have been removed. Put them back in the most suitable place.**

Sarah Chang

Sarah was only four when she first started to play the violin. At the age of eight, Chang played for the conductor Zubin Mehta who was **1** .... impressed that he invited her to be a surprise guest soloist with the New York Orchestra two days later. Her performance was **2** .... successful and she has since become a star. In 1982, at the age of 12, she was awarded the Avery Fisher Career Grant, the first time this award has been given to **3** .... a young person.

Not very

Not very good means the same as *bad*. However, when we have to say something **negative**, we prefer to use **positive** language, and ***not very* + adjective / adverb** helps us to do this.
We say: *She isn't very friendly, is she?* We don't say: ~~*She's unfriendly, isn't she?*~~
This is also common when a speaker wants to be modest:
A: *This painting I've done **isn't very good**, is it?*
B: *Yes, it is. It's wonderful!*

Getting it right

▶ Exercise 1 Choosing the best meaning

In 1–8 below, look at the speaker's thoughts. What did they say? Choose a) or b).

Example:

I wanted the questions to make me think.

a) I thought question 6 in that exercise wasn't difficult enough. ..✓..
b) I thought question 6 in that exercise was too difficult. .....

1 I want to emphasise how nice he is as much as I can.

a) He's such a nice man. Have you met him? .....
b) He's a very nice man. Have you met him? .....

2 I probably won't buy the dress because of the price.

a) That dress I want is so expensive. .....
b) That dress I want is too expensive. .....

3 I'll say a fact about that part of Australia.

a) It's too hot in that part of Australia. .....
b) It's very hot in that part of Australia. .....

4 I don't think I like their garden.

a) They've got so many trees in that garden. .....
b) They've got too many trees in that garden. .....

5 I can't go to university because of my exam results.

a) My exam results weren't good enough. .....
b) My exam results weren't very good. .....

6 I think we should give him the job.

a) I'm sure he's got enough experience. .....
b) He hasn't got very much experience. .....

7 I didn't like the ending of the film.

a) The film seemed to finish too quickly. .....
b) The film seemed to finish very quickly. .....

8 I want to make it very clear how busy I am.

a) I've got such a lot to do. .....
b) I've got a lot to do. .....

Exercise 2 Replacing missing words

In the interview below from a plane passenger who had a lucky escape, the last letters of each line have not been printed. Use language from this unit, and any other language necessary, to complete the lines.

PILOT'S ACTION SAVES LIVES

It was terrible. If it hadn't been for the pilot's quick thinking w.e'd.
probably all be dead now. I can't explain my feelings. It was **1** s...............
scary. I heard this bang and looked out of the window and saw a **2** fir...............
on the wing. My life didn't flash before my eyes. There wasn't **3** en...............
time for that. I remember thinking 'Help! I don't want to die. **4** I'm t...............
young to die.' I suppose everybody thinks that. There were too **5** m...............
things I still wanted to do. Anyway, we're all very lucky, we **6** kn...............
that for sure. And you know what the captain said? Honestly, **7** he's s...............
modest! He said he was only doing his job, but he made the **8** decisi...............
to ignore the rule book and make an immediate crash **9** landi ....
Apparently, a fire on the wing isn't supposed to be serious enough **10** t...............
cause us to turn back, but in fact, if we'd carried on we **11** prob...............
would have crashed into houses and we'd all have died. He's **12** s ....
a hero!

Exercise 3 Learning from learners

Correct the mistakes (both grammar and style) in extracts 1–6 from learners' speech.

Example: A: Welcome back! Did you have a good holiday?

B: Wonderful! The time seemed to go ~~too much quickly~~ much too quickly

1 A: Have you heard about Karin's new job?
B: Yes. I saw her yesterday. It's so good news. It's just what she was looking for.

2 A: Did you enjoy the film?
B: Not really. It was very long for me and I was bored in the last half hour.

3 A: I'm so glad to have finished this term's work, aren't you?
B: Yes, but I feel sorry for Fabienne. They said her project was bad. She'll have to do it again.

4 A: Did you see the football?
B: Of course. Don't I always? Not very good, though, was it?
A: No. The problem is the forwards – they're just not enough fast.

5 A: Everything is so much expensive in this country. I don't know how you can afford it.
B: We can't – or at least I can't most of the time.

6 A: Did you buy anything?
B: I got these shoes, but I'll have to take them back. They're not small enough.

Exercise 4 Rebuilding a text

Put phrases a)–f) in spaces 1–5 in the newspaper article. Join them with one word from the language in this unit.

a) … time to study them properly
b) … impressive they may help in the design of robots
c) … huge weights with so little effort
d) ~~… strong it would make a weightlifter look weak~~
e) … long
f) … strong

Beetle weight lifters

It's only three inches long but this beetle has incredible strength. In fact, the insect is so d) . Researchers have discovered that it can carry one hundred times its own body weight. The results of their study were **1** .... A big mystery was how the beetles managed to move **2** ....

Research leader Rodger Kram said last night, 'It is a mystery why they are **3** .... It shook us. But we will have to wait until August to do any more research. This year we didn't have **4** .... The beetles come out in August and don't live **5** .... – only a few weeks.'

Classwork

1 **Work in groups. You need at least three groups in the class.**

2 **Write any three words or phrases on a piece of paper (try to make them unusual and unrelated) and give it to another group.**

a very long time   sailing boat   chocolate bar

3 **Write a short story including the words on the piece of paper you receive and any three phrases from the box below.**

too much work	so unpleasant	not very interesting
very pleased	such a wonderful place	not (-n't) enough people

4 **Read your story to the class. Can the other groups (not the group who gave you the words) guess which words were on the piece of paper?**

eview unit 4

Units 30–38 Naming and describing

Exercise 1 Determiners Units 30–34

Read the text about a very large family. In 1–13 underline the correct determiner. Choose – if you think no word is needed.

It's Sunday teatime in the Turners' house, and 14 people are about to sit down around <u>*the*</u> / *its* table. But **1** *this* / *these* isn't a party or a special get-together. In fact, I am **2** – / *the* only visitor. All the other 13 diners are Turners: Mike, Rowena and **3** *their* / *theirs* 11 children. Even around their big table it's a bit of a squeeze, but the Turners try to eat together **4** *the most* / *most* evenings. Today tea is **5** *a* / – baked potatoes, a giant bowl of **6** *a* / – cheese, and **7** *a* / *the* mountain of bread – one of **8** *the* / *this* ten loaves a week eaten by the family. The Turners' children range in age from 20 years to three months, and they don't appear to have **9** *any* / *some* plans to stop there. John, who at 16 is the third eldest, is **10** *most* / *the most* talkative. Yes, he agrees, when you see the family all together it can be **11** *a bit* / *bit* of a surprise. At **12** *the school* / *school* people joke about it all the time. 'When the pictures of my school came out, someone said it was a snap of the Turner family,' he says. 'There are **13** *thousand* / *a thousand* people in my school.'

Exercise 2 Adjectives and adverbs Units 35–38

In 1–10 put a tick (✓) if you think the underlined word or phrase is correct, or write a correction if you think it is wrong.

There's a <u>black big</u> cloud coming this way .... *big black*

A: That smells **1** <u>well</u>. What's cooking? ....

B: Nothing very **2** <u>exciting</u>, I'm afraid. It's just soup, that's all. ....

A: Oh, that'll be fine. I'm not very hungry anyway.

I saw a job ad that looked **3** <u>perfectly</u> for me, but I'm **4** <u>not old enough</u> for it. They want someone over 21. ....

....

A: It's a very 5 impressive painting, isn't it? ....
B: Hmm. The colours are 6 very wonderful. I like it. ....
A: Yes, but it seems 7 sadly to me, somehow, as well. ....

Jane wants to go to Corsica for a holiday this year, but I 8 already have been there. ....

A: Why did you come home early?
B: Oh, the party was 9 bored. I found it 10 difficult to enjoy myself, so I left. ....
....

Exercise 3 Mixed structures **Units 30, 34 and 38**

Read the stories about Hodja and fill in gaps 1–19 with a word from the box. Write – if no word is possible. You can use words from the box more than once.

a an enough little so such the too

One day Hodja was very hungry. 'If I just had ..a.. nice hot bowl of soup,' he thought, 'I would be 1 .... happy.' Just then someone knocked at 2 .... door. He opened it and there stood 3 .... young boy with 4 .... empty bowl in his hands. 5 .... boy said, 'My mother is not feeling well. Can you please give her a 6 .... hot soup?'

'Oh, no!' exclaimed Hodja. 'Not even my thoughts are my own. I only have to think of 7 .... soup and my neighbours can smell it!'

A farmer once brought Hodja 8 .... letter and asked him to read it to him. '9 .... handwriting is 10 .... bad that I can't read it,' Hodja said. 11 .... farmer became angry and said 'You wear 12 .... turban of a learned man and you're not even clever 13 .... to read a letter!' Hodja took off his turban and placed it in front of him. 'If you think that everyone who wears 14 .... turban is a learned man, then you put it on and see if you can read it.'

One summer day it was 15 .... hot to travel, so Hodja got off his donkey and lay down under the shade of a nut tree near where watermelons were growing. He thought for a while and said, 'How strange it is that God created 16 .... watermelons to grow on 17 .... a tiny stalk while these little nuts grow on 18 .... a large tree.' Just then 19 .... nut fell from the tree and hit Hodja on the head. Hodja rubbed his head and said, 'God knows best! If watermelons grew on trees my head would have been seriously injured.'

Exercise 4 Pronouns and *this, that, these, those* Units 32–33

Look at sentences 1–10 and say if the statements on the right are true or false.

Example:

I had expected a red T-shirt for my birthday, so I was quite disappointed when I opened the present and *it* was green.	*It* refers to the T-shirt. true
1 The weather was terrible, with heavy rain and a cold wind, but *this* didn't stop us from setting off for our picnic as planned.	*This* refers to 'a cold wind'. .....
2 I don't like tomatoes but *they* now say they help prevent cancer.	*They* refers to tomatoes. .....
3 *You* can't get such delicious chocolate in my country.	*You* means 'everybody'. .....
4 *You* know about computers, don't you?	*You* means 'everybody'. .....
5 Someone phoned for you, Mike, but *they* didn't want to leave a message.	*They* refers to more than one person. .....
6 At first Joe hated his new job but he decided to give *himself* a few months to see if it got any better.	*Himself* is necessary because the subject and object are the same. .....
7 As I was walking along I heard *these* strange noises and I got pretty scared.	We use *these* here to make the story more dramatic. .....
8 Once everything had gone quiet again I looked out of the window and saw that all the *cars'* windows were broken.	The windows of one car were broken. .....
9 I made the dress *myself*, what do you think?	*Myself* is used to emphasise the subject. .....
10 *That* was an excellent meal. Thank you.	*That* is used because they are still eating the meal. .....

Exercise 5 Countable and uncountable nouns Unit 34

Put the correct form of *be* (*is* or *are*) in the gaps in the following pairs of similar sentences, and underline a word when you have a choice in *italics*.

Examples: There are too *much* / <u>*many*</u> people here. I can't find anywhere to sit.

There isn't <u>*much*</u> / many space here. I can't find anywhere to sit.

1 The information you need .... in this file, and I hope *it* / *they* .... useful.

2 The facts you need .... in this file, and I hope *it* / *they* .... useful.

3 The chairs in the room next door .... over 100 years old, and *it* / *they* still *look* / *looks* wonderful.

4 The furniture in this room .... over 100 years old, and *it* / *they* still *look* / *looks* wonderful.

5 Can you open the curtains? There .... n't enough light in here.

6 It always seems dark in here. There .... n't enough lights.

7 There .... a hair on the sleeve of your jacket.

8 Her hair .... darker than mine.

9 My suitcases .... still in Chicago. *It / They* got left behind, and I hope I get *it / them* back.

10 My luggage .... still in Chicago. *It / They* got left behind, and I hope I get *it / them* back.

11 Love ....n't everything.

12 Friends .... just as important.

Exercise 6 Order of adverbs and adjectives **Units 35–36**

Put these jumbled sentences in order.

Example:

with	and	children	white	The	were	playing	ball	large	a	blue

The children were playing with a large blue and white ball.

1

a	was	He	velvet	wearing	black	jacket

....

2

never	classical	has	She	liked	music

....

3

little	It	just	mistake	was	a	stupid

....

4

nice	coffee	like	a	cup	of	I'd	hot

....

5

before	been	here	I've

....

6

Chinese	in	She	food	bowl	the	served	a	beautiful

....

Unit 39

Requests, permission and offers

Getting started

1 **In the conversation below, two guests are visiting friends at their house. Read the conversation and answer questions a), b) and c).**

a) There are four speakers, A, B, C and D. Which ones live at the house, and which ones are visitors?

....

b) Does everyone know everyone else? How do you know?

....

c) A says, 'Shall I just put these upstairs?' What do you think *these* are?

....

A: Actually, I wonder if they're in.
Oh, they are in.
B: They obviously are.
C: Hello.
A: Hello.
C: Come in.
B: I'm Mike.
C: How are you?
B: Fine.
A: Shall I just put these upstairs?
C: Well, yeah. Can you put them in our room, please?
A: Sure.
C: How were the roads?
A: Oh, fine. No problem.
B: No problems. No.
A: Are you in there, Alison? Mmmm.
Hello there.
D: Hello.
A: Do you mind if I put my bag here?
D: Oh, go ahead. Want a cup of tea?
A: Yeah.

2 **Match these questions from the conversation to their functions.**

a) *Shall I just put these upstairs?* .....
b) *Can you put them in our room, please?* .....
c) *Do you mind if I put my bag here?* .....

i) a request
ii) asking for permission
iii) an offer

3 **Which words are missing from this offer from the text?**

.... *Want a cup of tea?*

4 **Without looking back at the conversation, can you remember how the phrases in Exercise 2 were answered?**

....

Looking at language

The way we make a request, ask for permission or make an offer depends on:
- the relationship between the people involved, and
- how likely it is that we will get a positive answer.

Requests

A **request** is when we ask someone to do something:
William, ***would you make*** *me a cup of coffee?*

We use the modal verbs *can, could, will* or *would* in requests:
Can *you put them in our room, please?*
Could *I have my glasses, please?*
Would *you pass me my glasses?*
Would you mind *phoning the doctor for me?*
Will *you come with me to the dentist, please?*

In informal, spoken English we sometimes make requests using *Do you want to …* or *Would you like to …*:
A: ***Do you want to*** *get me a glass of water?* B: *Yes, OK.*

We often add *just* in spoken English:
Would you like to just open a window for me?

Sometimes we use *Can / Could I have …* with the meaning *Can you get it for me?*:
Can I have *my suitcase?* (Can you get my suitcase for me?)

Requests are often longer when the situation is more formal, and / or there's a strong possibility of a negative response. Compare:
Can you *give me your pencil for a minute?* (informal, likely to get a positive response)
This is a huge favour, but ***I was wondering if you could*** *lend me your music system for the party?* (more formal, less likely to get a positive response)

Here are some other expressions to make requests longer and more polite:
Would it be possible to *borrow your car tonight?*
Do you think you could *help me?*

1 Which one of these requests is made to someone in a formal situation?

a) Would you like to make some coffee for everyone? .....

b) Do you think you could work late for the next couple of nights so we can get this finished? .....

c) Could you pass me a piece of paper? .....

Responses to requests

✓ Positive responses:
We use expressions such as: *Yes, of course. Sure. Yeah. OK. No problem.*

✗ Negative responses:
If you **can't** do something, apologise and give an excuse:
Can you pick me up from the station? ***Oh, I'm so sorry, but I can't. Our car is at the garage.***

Asking for and giving permission

We use *Can / Could / May I* ... to ask if it is all right to do something:

A: ***Can / Could / May I*** *give my homework in late?* B: *Well, all right, since you've been unwell.*

We can also use other more formal expressions:

Would you mind if I / Would it be all right if I *went out tonight?*

Do you mind if I / Is it all right if I *go out tonight?*

We use *can* to **give** permission:

You ***can*** *borrow the car whenever you want to.*

Offers

We use these expressions to say we will do something for someone:

Can I *help you?*

Shall I *open the door for you?*

I'll *post those letters for you.*

Would you like me to *speak to him on your behalf?*

Other points

- The request phrase *I would be grateful if you could* ... is useful in formal letters:
  Following our telephone conversation, ***I would be grateful if you could*** *send me a copy of your latest catalogue.*
- Ellipsis is common in very informal offers:
  Want a cup of coffee? (Do you want ...)
  Like me to give you a lift home? (Would you like me ...)

Pronunciation

Would you and *Could you* are pronounced with a /dʒ/ sound:

Could you *pass me that newspaper?*

/kudʒuː/

Intonation: if we begin a request with a high intonation it sounds more polite.

2 Match sentences a)–c) to the responses, i)–iii).

a) Shall I carry those bags for you? .....

b) Could you type a few letters for me? .....

c) Would it be at all possible for my brother to borrow your beach house at the weekend? .....

i) Oh, thank you. That's very kind.

ii) Oh, I'm sorry. I think it's already booked for the next few weeks.

iii) Yes, OK, but I can't do them until later this afternoon.

Getting it right

▶ Exercise 1 Recognising function

Decide if questions 1–10 are a request (r), offer (o) or asking for permission (p).

Example: Can I look at the newspaper a minute? ..r..

1 You don't look too good. Shall I call a doctor for you? .....
2 I'm sorry to be a nuisance, but would it be all right if I spread these papers on the table here? It'll only take a couple of minutes. .....
3 This train's running rather late. Would you like me to go and ask what's happening? .....
4 Would you post these letters for me on your way to work? .....
5 I know you hate giving bad news. I'll tell him if you like. .....
6 Would you mind being a bit quieter, only I've got a headache? .....
7 Could I use your phone for a minute? .....
8 Would you mind if I had a quick look at your newspaper? .....
9 Can you pick up some milk for me when you go out? .....
10 Do you want to lay the table for me? .....

Which extracts sound like people who know each other well? ....

▶ Exercise 2 Making offers, requests and asking for permission

Use situations and instructions 1–8 to make offers and requests and ask for permission.

Example: The phone is ringing. Offer to answer it.

Would you like me to answer the phone?

1 Someone is carrying heavy bags. Offer to help.

....

2 You're writing a letter to a travel company. Request their brochure.

....

3 You're in a friend's house. It's hot. Ask permission to open the window.

....

4 Your friend needs to go to the airport. Offer to drive him / her there.

....

5 You're at a restaurant table with friends. Request the salt.

....

6 You need a day off work. Ask your boss for permission.

....

7 Your brother has a broken arm. Offer to tie his shoelaces.

....

8 Your new neighbour is playing loud music late at night. Ask her to turn it down.

....

▶ Exercise 3 Preparing for a holiday

A couple are preparing for their holiday. Fill in the gaps in their requests and offers using words and expressions from this unit.

A: Just two days to go. ...Can... you switch the TV off?

B: Why?

A: Well, I was **1** .... if we could spend a few minutes thinking about what we need to do before we go.

B: Oh, yes. OK. Would you like **2** .... to collect the tickets in the morning?

A: Yes, please. And do you **3** .... you could go to a bank and get some money?

B: Oh, sorry, I **4** .... The bank's too far from the office. I can't get there in my coffee break.

A: OK, **5** .... go to the bank. **6** .... you stop at a shop on your way home and get some first aid supplies? You know, plasters, sun cream, insect repellent – that sort of thing.

B: No **7** .... **8** .... you check and see if we've got aspirin and travel sickness pills?

A: Sure. **9** .... I phone to check the airport terminal?

B: Thanks, yes. And **10** .... get the suitcases out.

A: Oh, good. I can never remember where you keep them.

Exercise 4 Responses

Think of a suitable negative response to the requests and requests for permission (1–8).

Example: I'd like to borrow your minidisc player if it's not too much trouble.

Oh, I'm sorry. I'll be using it this weekend.

1 I need some fresh air. Is it OK if I open the window?

....

2 Oh, I've just remembered. I need to call Jan. I don't suppose it would be possible to use your mobile for a few minutes?

....

3 You're going out, are you? Do you think you could post these letters for me?

....

4 Will you take these chairs and move them into the other room?

....

5 Can you give me a hand getting the food ready tomorrow night? I've got a lot of people coming for dinner.

....

6 Do you mind if we eat out tonight? I don't feel like cooking.

....

7 You couldn't help me with this DVD player, could you? I don't understand the instructions.

....

8 Can I have some more apple juice? I'm still thirsty.

....

Classwork

1 **You are going to plan a class newspaper. Work in groups of four to eight, and choose an 'editor' to lead your group. As a whole class, think of all the parts of a typical newspaper, and make a 'contents' list.**

Examples:
News articles
A travel section – a description of an interesting place to visit

2 **Look at your contents list, and hold a meeting to decide who will write what. You can offer to write something, or the editor may make a request for you to write something.**

Example:
I'll do the travel bit, if you like. I've just come back from Sri Lanka.

3 **If you have time, produce your class newspaper. You'll need to write the articles, add headlines, and give the paper a name. You may want to wordprocess the articles and find pictures. Display the newspaper in the classroom for other groups to read.**

Unit

40 Suggestions and advice

Getting started

1 **Look at the cartoon. What are the family talking about? (Frinton is a seaside town in England.)**

....

2 **Answer the questions.**

a) How many suggestions are made? ....

b) Who doesn't make a suggestion? ....

3 **Here are some examples of suggestions. Use the cartoon to help you fill in the gaps.**

Making suggestions:

a) *Why* .... *we* + infinitive (without *to*) or

b) *We* .... + infinitive (without *to*)

Replying to suggestions:

c) .... + an alternative suggestion

d) *I don't* .... + question word (*where*, *what*, *how* etc.)

Looking at language

Suggestions and advice

Use

Suggestions are ideas for someone else to think about. **Advice** is stronger, and means telling someone what you think they should do.

Forms

Asking for suggestions	*Making suggestions*	*Responding to suggestions*
What shall I / we do? *Has anybody got any ideas?*	To others, or ourselves and others: ***Why don't you / we** etc. **go** to the cinema?* ***You could** (always) **go** to the cinema.* ***How about** / **What about** going to the cinema?* To ourselves and others: ***Let's go** to the cinema.* ***Shall we go** to the cinema?* ***Let's go** to the cinema, **shall we?***	Accepting: ***That's a good idea.*** ***That sounds like a good idea.*** ***Yes, let's.*** ***Yes, OK.*** Refusing: ***Good idea, but I'm busy** this evening.* ***Hmm, I think I'd prefer to** stay in tonight.* ***Couldn't we** stay in tonight?*
Asking for advice	*Giving advice*	*Responding to advice*
What shall I do? ***What do you think I should do?*** ***What would you do if you were me?***	***I think you should*** / ***If I were you I'd*** / ***You'd (had) better*** *change jobs.*	Accepting: ***That's a good idea.*** ***That sounds like a good idea.*** ***Yes, I'll do that.*** ***Yes, I could / should.*** Rejecting: ***That's a good idea but*** / ***Yes I could / should but*** / ***I know, but*** *I can't.*

1 Are the following comments suggestions (s) or advice (a)?

1 Why don't you tell him you don't want to see him again? .....

2 Let's not go out tonight after all. .....

3 If I were you I'd stop taking that medicine. .....

4 I think you should buy yourself a nice new dress for the party. .....

5 Why don't we get married? .....

6 Shall we cancel the holiday? .....

Other points

- Imperatives (see Unit 14) are often used to give advice, especially when we are sure our advice is right:
  Don't leave the TV plugged in while you're away.
- In spoken English we can use *let's* to mean 'let me'. It is a request or an offer (see Unit 39), not a suggestion:
  Let's have a look. (give it to me to see)

Getting it right

Exercise 1 Thinking about function

Match the suggestions / advice in 1–8 to the responses, a)–i).

Example: You should try doing more exercise. .b).

1 Why don't we go to Hawaii this year? .....
2 You shouldn't work such long hours. .....
3 Don't think about her. .....
4 We could get her a new pen. .....
5 Shall we go out tonight? .....
6 Why don't you ask her to meet you? .....
7 Let's go for a walk, shall we? .....
8 You could always put the decision off a little bit longer. .....

a) That's a good idea. She's always losing hers.
b) ~~Yes, you're right. It would do me good.~~
c) Yes, or we could go somewhere cheaper.
d) We could, but I think I'd prefer to watch TV.
e) That's sensible advice, but I can't forget her.
f) I know, but I've got a lot to do.
g) Do you think so? If I leave it much longer I might miss my chance.
h) Hmm. I'm too shy to do that.
i) Yes, good idea. I need some fresh air.

Exercise 2 Getting the forms right

Use the verbs in brackets, and the instructions to complete the conversation.

Ask for advice	A:	What do you think I should do?
Give advice	B:	It's a difficult situation, but if I were you I'd think *(think)* about it.
	A:	I have, and I just don't know what to do. That's why I'm asking you.
Give advice	B:	Well, 1 you .... always .... *(accept)* both jobs now.
Reject advice	A:	2 .... that's just delaying the decision.
Make a suggestion	B:	Well then, perhaps you 3 .... *(write)* a list for each job with advantages and disadvantages.
Accept a suggestion, make a suggestion	A:	That's a 4 .... 5 .... we .... *(do)* it now?
Accept a suggestion, make a suggestion	B:	Yeah, OK. 6 .... *(start)* with the local job, and then do the overseas one, 7 .... ?
Refuse a suggestion	A:	Yes, or we 8 .... *(do)* each one together, comparing the positive and negative points as we do it.

What is A's problem? ....

Exercise 3 Learning from learners

A learner wrote this reply to a letter asking for advice. Underline six more mistakes and write the corrections. Does the letter reply to Extract A, B or C below? .....

Dear Unhappy
Your letter was very interesting, and you are certainly in a difficult situation. I think the first thing you do is arrange a meeting with your daughter. Then, if I were you I tell her exactly how I felt about her husband's behaviour. She might get angry at first, but hopefully she will listen and understand your situation. You could trying asking her to speak to her husband. She should to talk to him and find out why he's always rude to you. If she still doesn't understand your problem, perhaps you should to try to talk to your son-in-law yourself. And finally, why you don't stop worrying too much. You should being happy that your daughter is such a good friend!

Fabienne

you should do ....

1 ....

2 ....

3 ....

4 ....

5 ....

6 ....

A	B	C
He drinks too much and never gets home until very late at night.	She always agrees with him and is never friendly to me any more.	He is always rude to me and seems to disagree with everything I do.

Extension

Write your own reply to one of the other two problems.

Exercise 4 Completing conversations

Add the missing line in conversations 1–8 below.

Example: A: I'm fed up.
B: Well, perhaps that's your fault. You never do anything.
A: OK then. *Let's go out for a meal and then on to a club tonight.*
B: Great idea. You sound more positive already.

1 A: Have you told anyone else about this problem?
B: No, I'm not sure who to talk to.
A: ....

2 A: It's Rory's birthday next week. Any ideas for a present?
B: No, I'm useless at presents. Why don't you think of something?
A: Well, I had one idea. ....

3 A: Sandra, you know about these things. I've won some money, and I'm not sure what to do with it.
B: Why don't you open an Internet-only savings account? They give very good rates.
A: ....

4 A: What are you doing tomorrow night?
B: Nothing. Why?
A: Do you fancy going out somewhere?
B: Definitely. ....

5 A: I'm cold. Are you?
B: A little bit. It would be nice to get a hot drink somewhere, wouldn't it?
A: Yes. ....

6 A: What do you think Simon and Nicky should do about living in that tiny flat now that they're having a baby?
B: ....

7 A: I can't sleep at night these days.
B: Really? Do you know why?
A: No. I just lie there with thoughts going round and round in my head.
B: ....

8 A: Jake keeps asking for a pet, you know. Do you think we should get him one?
B: Oh, dear. I'm not too keen. It's a huge responsibility. And anyway, I don't like cats or dogs much. I suppose something small and easy to look after would be OK.
A: ....

Classwork

1 **Work with a partner. Together think of a real or imaginary problem.**

Example:
I want to speak good English, but I'm shy speaking to strangers. What shall I do?

2 **Now divide into two groups, with one from each pair in each group. Ask each student in your new group for advice about your problem, and give them advice about theirs.**

3 **Go back to your partner and compare the advice you have been given. Decide who gave the best advice.**

Unit 41

Talking about ability

Getting started

1 The four extracts below all talk about different abilities. Match Extracts 1–4 with topics a)–d).

a) animal intelligence .....

b) using a part of the body, in an unusual way, to do a job .....

c) learning a new dance .....

d) using a part of the body for an unusual task ....

Which extract is from spoken English? .....

1 An 11-year-old girl is to appear on a TV show tonight – as a human juicer. Sally Harmer, of Darlington, can squeeze juice from an orange between her shoulder blades.

2 In the 1980s, Alex, the talking parrot of Purdue University, Indiana, was famous because he could name more than 40 objects, recognise five colours and four shapes and name them correctly.

3 Bob has a long moustache. It has been growing since 1986 and last Friday reached 299 centimetres. Thanks to his moustache, Bob is able to help aeroplanes park without using hand signals. That's why Bob has recently been promoted to Senior Parking Instructor at Inverness Airport.

4 Four or five of them made it look so easy. And I followed this young man, and he'd got the jeans and the shirt on and the right kind of boots, and he could do it perfectly. And he said to me, 'When the music's really quick like this', he said, 'do the steps a bit smaller.' When I came out of there, I managed to get a lift home from somebody who didn't live far from me, and they brought me all the way home. And coming in, I found muscles I never knew I had. Well, on Monday morning I couldn't get out of bed.

2 Which of the underlined phrases in the extracts:

- express ability (or inability):
  - a) in the present? ....
  - b) in the past? ....
- are about ability (or inability):
  - c) to do something at any time? ....
  - d) to do something on one occasion? ....

Looking at language

Ability

Expressing present ability

We use *can / cannot / can't*:

Sally Harmer, of Darlington, ***can*** *squeeze juice from an orange between her shoulder blades.*

Be able to is also possible:

Bob ***is able to*** *help aeroplanes park without using hand signals.*

Expressing ability in the future

We use *will be able to* to make predictions:

By 2050 people will ***be able to*** *learn a language by taking a pill.*

Expressing ability with perfect forms

We use *be able to*:

He's ***been able to*** *speak fluent French since he was a child.* (present perfect)

If she'd ***been able to*** *type she might have got the job.* (past perfect)

Expressing past ability

We use different verbs for **general** and **specific** past ability:

- to describe ability at any time in the past (general ability) we use *could, couldn't* or *(not) be able to:*

  Alex the parrot ***could / was able to*** *name more than 40 objects.*

  I ***couldn't / wasn't able to*** *dance until I met you.*

- to describe ability on one occasion only in the past (specific ability) we use *couldn't* (but not *could*), *(not) be able to, (not) manage to:*

  I ***wasn't able to*** *phone her last night.*

  I ***managed to*** *get a lift home after the party.*

  I ***didn't manage to*** *phone him yesterday.*

  I ***couldn't*** *get out of bed on Monday morning.*

General ability	*Specific ability*
could, couldn't, be able to	couldn't, be able to, manage to

Manage to means you are able to do something, but only with difficulty:

I ***managed to*** *start the car, but only after ten minutes of trying.*

Notice the different negatives of *manage to*:

I ***didn't*** *manage to get out.* (I wanted to get out but I couldn't)

I managed ***not*** *to see him.* (I tried not to see him and I succeeded)

1 **Can the verbs of ability be replaced by *could(n't)* in the following sentences? Write *yes* or *no*.**

1 He was able to type 80 words a minute. ....

2 I managed to escape from the crowd. ....

3 The hotel was terrible, but Belinda was still able to enjoy her holiday. ....

4 Although it was hot, they didn't manage to get a suntan. ....

Form

	Statement	*Negative*	*Question*
can	She **can** swim.	She **can't** swim.	**Can** she swim?
could	She **could** swim.	She **couldn't** swim.	**Could** she swim?
be able to	She**'s able to** swim.	She **isn't able to** swim. She's **unable to** swim.	**Is** she **able to** swim?
manage to	I **managed to** swim.	I **didn't manage to** swim. I **managed not to** drown.	**Did** he **manage to** swim?

Pronunciation

Can is pronounced /kaen/ when it is stressed, usually in short answers:
A: *Can you come?* B: *Yes, I can.*
Can is pronounced /kən/ when it is unstressed, usually in statements:
I can speak Greek.
Can't is usually stressed, and pronounced /kɑːnt/:
I can't swim.

Other points

- With the sense verbs *see, hear, smell, feel, taste* we often use *can* instead of the continuous form to express a sensation happening at the time of speaking:
  *I **can** smell something cooking. Can you?*
  We don't say: ~~*I'm smelling something cooking. Are you?*~~ (See Unit 3.)
- With the verbs *remember, understand, speak, play* (an instrument), we can leave out *can* with little change in meaning. Compare:
  *I **can** remember seeing that film at university.* *I **remember** seeing that film at university.*
- In conditional sentences *would be able to* can be replaced by *could*:
  *If I had more time to practise I **could** play football really well.*

Getting it right

Exercise 1 Recognising meaning

In sentences 1–10, do the underlined verbs and expressions refer to the past, present or future or are they a perfect form? Do they talk about general (g) or specific (s) ability?

Sentence	*Tense*	*General ability (g) or specific ability (s)*
Example: When I was a child I was able to stand on my head easily.	*past*	*g*
1 I managed to get a doctor's appointment yesterday.	....	.....
2 New research suggests that people will soon be able to lose weight by taking pills.	....	.....
3 People are able to do all sorts of things today that were impossible only 30 years ago.	....	.....
4 My uncle can't hear very well.	....	.....
5 Sue was unable to understand why I wanted to keep that old chair.	....	.....
6 I didn't manage to phone my sister last night.	....	.....
7 I haven't been able to run since I broke my leg last year.	....	.....
8 Tyrannosaurus Rex was able to bite with the force of a lorry on each tooth.	....	.....
9 I'm not able to do the tango. It's really difficult.	....	.....
10 My friend Alice lost her house keys yesterday, but she was able to climb in through the bathroom window.	....	.....

Extension

In three sentences the verb or expression of ability can be replaced with *could* or *couldn't*.

Which three sentences? ....

Exercise 2 Choosing the best form

Underline the correct verb or verb phrase. (Sometimes both are possible.)

Example: Animals can / *manage to* communicate with each other.

1 I *managed to* / *could* persuade him to come to the restaurant with us.
2 She *managed to* / *could* persuade anybody to do anything.
3 I *couldn't* / *didn't manage to* understand the instructions for the game.
4 Pierre *wasn't able to* / *couldn't* wash the car because he had to leave early.
5 '*I can smell* / *I'm smelling* something burning,' said Natasha.
6 To be an airline pilot you must *be able to* / *can* react quickly in difficult situations.
7 Rebecca *won't be able to* / *can't* come at the weekend after all.
8 I*'ve been able to* / *can* drive since I was 17.

Exercise 3 Solving puzzles

Read puzzles A–E below. Then put phrases 1–5 back in a suitable place, either in a puzzle or as a solution to a puzzle. You can use more than one phrase in a puzzle.

A In a hotel two businessmen stay in rooms next to each other. The first businessman sleeps very well *example*. He phones the other and falls asleep immediately after the call. Why can he now fall asleep?

Solution: ....

B Every morning a man gets into the lift on the fourteenth floor, and goes down to the ground floor. Every evening when he gets home from work he gets out of the lift on the seventh floor, and walks up to the fourteenth floor. Why?

Solution: ....

C One day a father and son were badly injured in an accident and taken to hospital. The son was taken to the operating theatre. The surgeon said, 'He's my son.' How is this true?

Solution: ....

D Mrs Jones wanted a new house. She liked to see the sun shining into a room, so she asked the builder to build a house with all four walls facing south. How?

Solution: ....

E A taxi driver picked up a talkative passenger. The driver was tired and didn't want to talk. At the end of the journey, he pointed to the meter to show the passenger how much to pay. She walked away from the taxi. How did she realise the truth?

Solution: ....

Example: , but the second cannot sleep

1 , so he pretended not to be able to hear or speak
2 He isn't very tall, and he can't reach the button.
3 I can't operate on him.
4 Suddenly she realised that he had been able to hear.
5 After much thought, he managed to do it.

Can you think of solutions to the remaining puzzles?

Exercise 4 Completing a text

Fill in each gap in the sentences below with a verb of ability. (More than one is possible for most of the gaps.)

- Monkeys ..*can*.. count up to nine, and **1** .... recognise which groups of objects are larger than others. Scientists have shown that animals **2** .... think, even though they **3** .... talk.

  Humans **4** .... look at groups of four or fewer objects and know how many things are in the group without having to count. Researchers found that the monkeys **5** .... count to four, so they were then tested on five to nine objects. They did just as well. They **6** .... do this, the researchers say, because they had learnt some rules about numbers and counting.

- Some years ago in Atlanta, Georgia, a bonobo chimpanzee called Kanzi **7** .... slice his food by breaking a rock into small pieces and using a sharp part to cut with.

- British experimenters tested sheep's abilities by showing them photographs of each other. Now we know that sheep **8** .... recognise each other from photographs.

Classwork

1 **Complete as many of the sentences in the grid below as you can. Write about yourself. You have just three minutes.**

	A	B	C
1	I could … when I was younger, but I can't now.	I managed to … but I'd never expected to.	I couldn't … when I was younger.
2	I can't	I hope one day I might be able to …	I can remember …
3	I've never been able to …	I could … if I had more time.	I can …

2 **Work in pairs. Take turns to say the names of a square from the grid. Your partner reads out their sentence from that square, and has to explain it in more detail. If your partner is able to do this, she / he gets one point. If they wrote nothing, you get a point.**

Example:

Player 1: *Square 2B.*

Player 2: *I hope one day I might be able to play a musical instrument. I'm too busy learning English and studying for exams at the moment.*

3 **Continue until all the squares have been called. The winner has the most points.**

Unit

42 Frequency expressions and tend to

Getting started

1 **Read the article about a 90-year-old woman. What makes her unusual for her age?**

....

Miriam, 90, puts her feet up for yoga

A 90-year-old woman is so good at yoga that she can do it standing on her head. Grandmother Miriam Horton has been practising yoga for the last 16 years, and her favourite position is the yogic headstand.

Miriam, who celebrated her 90th birthday on Sunday, first started the eastern meditation technique when she was 74. She said, 'I didn't think the teacher would accept me because I was 74, but luckily she decided she would.'

Now Miriam practises yoga every morning and evening, and talks enthusiastically about the benefits. 'I feel much better for it,' she said. 'I do ache a bit the next day, but I feel so good, it's worth it.'

In fact, Miriam does more than just yoga. 'I go swimming twice a week, and like to do lots of gardening as well,' she said.

And she has no intention of slowing down. 'I shall keep coming to my yoga classes until they throw me out,' she said.

2 **Underline these expressions in the article: *every morning and evening / twice a week*. Then put these questions in the right order.**

a) A: do How practise often yoga you ? B: Every morning and evening.

....

b) A: often go do How swimming you ? B: Twice a week.

....

3 **What other expressions can you make with *every* and *twice*?**

every *morning, evening*, ...

twice a *week*, ...

Looking at language

Frequency expressions

This unit looks at language that tells us **how often** something happens.

- We use these expressions to talk about **definite frequency** (real time):

once, twice, three times a(n) *second, minute, hour, day, week, month, year*	***every*** *minute, hour, morning* etc., *day, week, month, season, year* / ***every two weeks*** etc.	*hourly, daily, weekly, monthly, quarterly, yearly* (as adjectives or adverbs)
I go swimming ***twice a week. Two or three times a year*** *I see my cousins.*	***Every morning and evening*** *Miriam practises yoga. She goes to a yoga class* ***every two weeks.***	*The society produces a* ***quarterly*** *newsletter. It meets* ***weekly****, on a Thursday.*
These expressions can begin or end sentences and clauses.		Adjectives come before the noun, and adverbs come after the verb.

- We use these adverbs and adverbial expressions to talk about **indefinite frequency**: *always, ever, frequently, from time to time, generally, hardly ever, never, now and then, occasionally, (quite) often, once in a while, rarely, regularly, sometimes, usually.*

  A: *Do you ever see Miriam?* B: *Yes,* ***from time to time****. We* ***usually*** *stop for a chat.*

1 **Put these expressions of frequency in order from *never* to *always*.**

usually   occasionally   often   sometimes   hardly ever

never .... ***always***

Word order

Adverbs of indefinite frequency come after *be* and auxiliary verbs, and before other verbs:

She's ***often*** *late.*   *They've* ***often*** *talked about you.*   *I* ***often*** *see Miriam when I'm in town.*

Questions: *Is she* ***often*** *late?*   *Do you* ***often*** *see Miriam?*

You can also put most of these expressions (but **not** *never* and *always*) at the start or end of a sentence or clause:

Once in a while *I like to watch a really romantic film.*
Occasionally *I eat something really naughty, like a large chocolate cake.*
She's rather unfriendly ***sometimes****.*

Questions

You can use these questions to ask about frequency of activities:

A: ***How often*** *do you see James?* B: *Just occasionally.* A: *Oh, I thought it was more.*
A: ***Do you*** *go out* ***much*** *in the week?* B: *No. Not often.* A: *No, me neither.*

Tend to

Tend to **+ infinitive** is very common in English to describe regular actions, events and habits:

*People **tend to think** big shopping centres are cheaper, but it isn't always true.*

*I **tend not to enjoy** dinner parties. I **tend to prefer** a night out in a club.*

*We **tend to go out** on a Friday evening, and spend Saturday at home.*

Other points

- We can use the modal verb *can* to tell us about frequency:
  It can get quite hot here in July and August. (it sometimes gets hot)
- *Per* is more formal than *a / an* in expressions with *once a*:
  *I have meetings three or four times **per** week.*
- We say: *once a week / month / year.* We don't say: ~~*once in a week / month / year*~~.

Getting it right

Exercise 1 Word order

Look at the groups of three sentences. Underline the frequency expression. Tick (✓) the sentences which have acceptable word order, and cross (✗) any sentences which do not.

Example: Often I feel like going for long walks by myself. ..✓..

I often feel like going for long walks by myself. ..✓..

I feel often like going for long walks by myself. ..✗..

1 a) Never he gets here before 9.00 in the morning. .....
b) He never gets here before 9.00 in the morning. .....
c) He gets here before 9.00 in the morning never. .....

2 a) We're sometimes surprised by his attitudes. .....
b) Sometimes we're surprised by his attitudes. .....
c) We sometimes are surprised by his attitudes. .....

3 I tried calling Joanne but she wasn't there. It's funny –
a) she's usually in at this time of day. .....
b) usually she's in at this time of day. .....
c) she's in at this time of day usually. .....

4 a) I've thought about that holiday we had quite often. .....
b) I've quite often thought about that holiday we had. .....
c) I quite often have thought about that holiday we had. .....

5 a) She from time to time is really amusing. .....
   b) From time to time she's really amusing. .....
   c) She's really amusing from time to time. .....

6 a) Twice a day I have to take one of these orange pills. .....
   b) I have to take twice a day one of these orange pills. .....
   c) I have to take one of these orange pills twice a day. .....

Exercise 2 Similar meanings

Rewrite sentences 1–8 using a different frequency expression with similar meaning. (The meaning does not have to be exactly the same.)

Example:

I generally visit my parents about twice a month. ... *I generally visit my parents every two weeks.*

1 We try to hold a meeting four times a year. ....
2 I go to an English class every Thursday. ....
3 He seems to work seven days a week. ....
4 Do you travel abroad much? ....
5 She has to spend a week in Paris every month. ....
6 Once in a while the whole family gets together. ....
7 I try to exercise daily. ....
8 It can get cold high up in the hills. ....

Exercise 3 *Tend to* in spoken English

In conversations 1–5 below, examples of *tend to* have been removed. Put them back in the most appropriate place. You may need to change the form of *tend to*, or of other verbs.

Example: It's boredom, I suppose. I ^*tend to* eat too much if I spend a morning in the house.

1 A: What's the matter?
B: I've got a headache. I get them if I sit in front of a computer screen for too long.

2 A: What are your best-selling lines?
B: T-shirts, shorts, beachwear. We sell a lot of them in summer, obviously, though you'd be surprised what people will buy at Christmas.

3 A: Are there any types of clothes you don't sell?
B: Yes, more formal work clothes. They don't fit in with our younger ranges.

4 A: I'd just like more variety around here. I get bored doing one thing all the time.
B: Yeah, so do I. Last week wasn't too bad though, was it?

5 A: Careful – Sian's around again. She wants to talk when she's out of her office and you can never get anything done.
B: Thanks for warning me!

Which two conversations are with the owner of a boutique, and which three come from a chat between two colleagues in an office?

Exercise 4 About yourself – sentence completion

Complete sentences 1–8 by choosing and underlining a suitable expression of frequency and finishing the sentence about yourself.

Example: I often / *never* forget my brothers' birthdays.

1 I *usually / always* wear .... when I see friends.
2 I *tend to / tend not to* listen to .... music when I'm in a good mood.
3 *Occasionally / Quite often* I eat ....
4 I go .... about *once a week / twice a month.*
5 I *hardly ever / sometimes* see ....
6 I think about .... *every minute / every day.*
7 I *can be / tend to be* quite .... when I need to.
8 *From time to time / Now and then* I enjoy ....

Classwork

1 **Work with a partner. Write ten expressions of frequency on separate pieces of paper. Mix them up and put them upside down in a pile.**
Examples:

sometimes | every day | once a week

2 **Take turns with your partner to turn up an expression of frequency. Make a sentence about yourself or someone in your family using the expression. The sentence can be true or false.**
Example:
Sometimes I don't have any breakfast.

3 **Your partner has to decide if the sentence is true or false. If your partner guesses correctly he / she keeps the piece of paper, but if he / she is wrong you keep it. The winner is the player with the most pieces of paper at the end.**

Unit 43

Ways of comparing 1

Getting started

1 **The text and picture below describe a Japanese idea for transport between cities in the future. Read the text and answer the questions.**

a) Would you like to travel this way?

....

b) Why is the 'flying train' better than present transport systems?

....

Leading Japanese scientists and a building company are working together to create what they hope will be the ideal mode of transport between big cities in the 21st century. It is a vehicle that will be faster, cheaper, more reliable and more environmentally friendly than existing systems: it is the flying train.

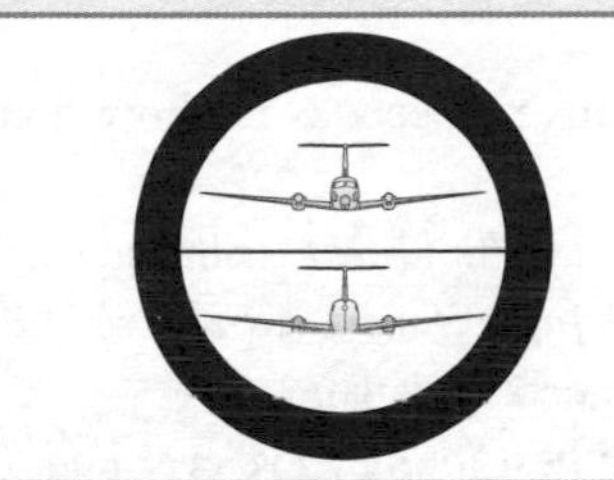

The idea is to build a large tunnel into which they will put a type of aircraft capable of flying about one metre above the ground at speeds of 650 kilometres an hour.

2 **Look at this sentence from the text:**

It is a vehicle that will be faster, cheaper, more reliable and more environmentally friendly than existing systems: it is the flying train.

The underlined words are comparative adjectives. How much do you know about comparatives and superlatives? Fill in gaps 1–4 in the chart below.

	Adjective	*Comparative*	*Superlative*
Short adjectives	1	faster	the fastest
	cheap	2	the cheapest
3 .... *adjectives*	reliable	more reliable	the 4 .... reliable

Looking at language

Comparative adjectives

We use comparative adjectives to:

- compare two things:
  *The flying train is lighter **than** a jet.*
- or compare the same thing at different times:
  *Train tickets are **more expensive** now, aren't they?*

Comparatives are often followed by a *than* ... clause, especially in written English.

To give more information about a comparison, we can add a word or phrase before the comparative:

*The flying train is **a lot / far** safer than a plane, but it's **a bit** slower. It can take you **much** nearer to a city centre, and it's **a little** quieter than road traffic.*

We can emphasise comparatives with *even*:

*It was cold yesterday, but it's **even** colder today.*

Superlative adjectives

We use superlative adjectives to show that something is different from all the others it is compared to:

*They're building **the fastest** jet in the world.* (it is faster than all other jets)
*The tunnel is **Japan's most expensive** building project.* (It is more expensive than all other building projects in Japan.)
*That was **the best** journey I've ever had.* (it was better than all other journeys)

We usually put *the* or a possessive (*my, your, her, Japan's* etc.) before a superlative.

We can also use *one of the / some of the* + **superlative + plural**:

*This is **one of the most exciting** modern transport **developments**, and it will have **one of the world's longest** tunnels.*
*Japan has **some of the fastest** trains in the world.*

We often use **in + place** and ***of* + period of time** with superlatives:

*It's **the tallest building in the world**.*
*Yesterday was **the hottest day of the year**.*

Comparing quantities

Plural nouns		*Uncountable nouns*	
more / the most	clothes, people, cars	more / the most	information, cheese
fewer / the fewest	fish, women, men	less / the least	luggage, fuel

For example:

*The flying train will carry **more people** than a jet, but **fewer** (people) than a ship. It will use **the least fuel** of any fast transport.*

Many native English speakers now use *less* with plural nouns: ***less** clothes, **less** people.*

Forms

	Adjective	*Comparative*	*Superlative*
Most one-syllable words: *+er, +est*	fast cheap	faster cheaper	the fastest the cheapest
One-syllable words ending in -e: +r, +st	large nice	larger nicer	the largest the nicest
One-syllable words ending in consonant, vowel, consonant: double the last consonant	hot thin	hotter thinner	the hottest the thinnest
Two-syllable words ending in y: ~~y~~ +ier, +iest	heavy dirty	heavier dirtier	the heaviest the dirtiest
Two or more syllables: more, the most …, less, the least …	modern expensive reliable	**more** modern **more** expensive **less** reliable	**the most** modern **the most** expensive **the least** reliable
Irregular	good bad far	**better** **worse** **further (or farther)**	**the best** **the worst** **the furthest (or farthest)**

1 **The text below compares the flying train to a present-day jet plane. Look at the text and the table of statistics. Underline the mistake in the text.**

Better than a jet?

At just over half a kilometre long, the flying train carries 400 passengers into city centres without the need for a runway. Wind, snow and fog are not a problem, and nor is noise pollution. The flying train would be lighter and faster and carry more people than a jet, and the designers say it would use a quarter of the fuel of a jet.

Flying train	Jet
45 tons 400 people 650 km/h 1,000 litres fuel	80 tons 236 people 880 km/h 4,000 litres fuel

Other points

You can use *the* + **comparative**, *the* + **comparative** to link two things that change:

*The **faster** the journey, the **happier** I am.*

Pronunciation

Than is unstressed in comparative expressions and pronounced /ðən/:

*The flying train is lighter **than** a jet.*

See Unit 44 for more ways of comparing in English.

Getting it right

Exercise 1 Choosing the best form

In the conversation below, two friends are talking about a train journey. In numbers 1–8, underline the best phrase in *italics*.

A: Why are you going by train?

B: Because it's much *cheaper / more cheaper* than the plane.

A: But aren't they both **1** *the most expensive / more expensive* than the coach?

B: Yes, but the coach is **2** *less comfortable / least comfortable*, and **3** *much / more* slower. And it's **4** *more easy / easier* to read on a train if I want to. All in all the train is **5** *the best / the good* choice for me.

A: How long does the train journey take?

B: About five hours. But I think it's one of the most beautiful **6** *trip / trips* you can do. You go very near the country's **7** *highest / the highest* mountains. Even the food's **8** *the best / better* these days!

Extension

Think of a journey that you make regularly, perhaps to work or school. Write a few sentences comparing different forms of transport that are possible for that journey.

Exercise 2 Learning from learners

A learner wrote the composition below, which compares her home city and her capital city. Underline eight more mistakes in it and write the corrections.

If you want to visit my country, you should try to visit my city and the capital, but there are some differences. My city is much more far north, so it gets colder in the rainy season, but you can sunbathe and swim in the sea in summer. It's more beautiful than the capital, too, because it's by the sea, and it has more hill, park and garden. It's bit more difficult to visit my city than the capital because we don't have an international airport, but there are the best train and coach services than there used to be. One of the most interesting thing you can do near my city is take a tour into the jungle, and we also have some of the oldest buildings in the country. The capital is more modern, of course, so the buildings are more taller, and it has much more exciting nightlife. It's also hoter in the dry season. But I think the people of my city are friendlier – maybe friendliest in the world! So do come and visit. The sooner you visit, happier I'll be.

much further ....

1 ....

2 ....

3 ....

4 ....

5 ....

6 ....

7 ....

8 ....

Exercise 3 Comparatives in spoken extracts

Five sports stars are talking about how their performance has changed in the last year. Read their descriptions and fill in the gaps with the comparative or superlative form of an adjective from the box. Which sport do you think each person is talking about?

confident	difficult	easy	fast	fit	good	happy	old	~~strong~~	tall	tired

I feel much *stronger* now than last year. I've lifted 180 kg this year for the first time. **Sport:** *weightlifting*

Yes, my game has improved a lot. I've done a lot of training, so I'm much **1** .... than before, and I'm scoring more goals. The whole team is a lot **2** .... to beat now! **Sport:** ....

This car is **3** .... on the circuit. With the changes, everybody is much **4** .... about the engine and gears, and it's a bit **5** .... to drive than it was. **Sport:** ....

Well, I'm a little **6** .... every year, and I get **7** .... after a race these days. But I feel **8** .... with every race, and if my legs are strong enough, I'm sure I can win again! **Sport:** ....

Oh, my game's much **9** .... now. I've grown a bit **10** .... , which helps my serve, and I'm winning more often. I still prefer playing doubles, though. **Sport:** ....

Exercise 4 Comparatives and superlatives in written extracts

The health facts and tips below are unfinished. For each gap, 1–8, choose a word from Box A and a phrase from Box B to complete the extract.

A

better	bigger	cheaper	~~far~~	less	more	older	the	warmest

B

... happier	... dirty than	... ~~more effective~~	... the person	... relaxed you are
... to keep	... place in the house	... the ears	... pets	

When it comes to pain relief, some painkillers seem to work differently for women and men. Researchers found that some painkillers were *far more effective* in women.

If you want to know someone's real age, look at their ears. According to some doctors, the ears are the only part of the body which keep growing, so the **1** .... , the **2** ....

One thing you can do to avoid getting a cold is to calm down and avoid stress. 3 .... and the 4 .... , the stronger your body will be for fighting illness.

Snakes make 5 .... than cats and dogs because they are good for your health. Touching them can calm you down. Derek Grove keeps his in the bedroom because it's the 6 .... Snakes are 7 .... dogs or cats, and after paying for the cage are 8 ....

Classwork

1 **Work in groups of three to five. Describe an advertisement you have seen or heard to the other people in your group. Have they also seen or heard it?**

2 **Choose a product, perhaps something that one of you has bought recently. What adjectives could you use to describe it?**

Examples:
computer game: exciting, difficult, fast
leather jacket: fashionable, comfortable

3 **What name will you give your product?**

4 **Prepare a television advertisement for your product. You can:**

- compare your product with others using comparatives.

Example:
Triton shampoo makes your hair shinier and cleaner than any other shampoo.

- show that your product is better than all others using superlatives.

Example:
Santando – the most exciting computer game you've ever played.

- show that your product has improved using comparatives.

Example:
The new camera from Ashiba is smaller and easier to use than ever before.

5 **Perform your advertisement to the class. Who has the most interesting and effective advertisement?**

Unit 44

Ways of comparing 2

Getting started

1 How much do you pay for a pair of jeans? Read the text about antique jeans and answer the questions.

a) What product is worth: i) £500 ....

ii) £5,000? ....

b) Why are these jeans so valuable?

....

At £5,000 a pair, the jeans worth inheriting

If your favourite pair of jeans dates back to before 1971, they could be valuable.

Collectors are prepared to pay up to £5,000 for denim jackets and jeans more than a few decades old. 'Jeans have become the classic thing of our century and people want the earlier examples,' says antiques expert Madeleine Marsh.

Levi's number one jackets – made around a hundred years ago – and Big E Levi's – which have a capital 'E' on the label – are the most wanted. 'They are as rare as a Ming vase,' says Miss Marsh.

'Until quite recently, jeans were just work clothes. People didn't save them,' Patricia Penrose, owner of a clothing shop, said. 'Good, original examples can be as hard to find as the most precious antiques.'

Levi's says jeans become valuable before 1971, the year the company began to use a small 'e', rather than capital 'E' on its label. A pair of 1950s Levi's can be worth up to £500 while a pair of 501s from the 1930s sell for up to £5,000.

2 Look at these sentences from the text. Tick (✓) the true statement i), ii), or iii).

a) '*They are as rare as a Ming vase.*'

i) The jeans are rarer than a Ming vase. .....

ii) Ming vases are rarer than the jeans. .....

iii) Jeans and Ming vases are equally rare. .....

b) '*Good, original examples can be as hard to find as the most precious antiques.*'

i) Original examples are harder to find than precious antiques. .....

ii) Original examples and precious antiques are equally hard to find. .....

iii) Precious antiques are harder to find than original examples. .....

3 In this sentence, what other words could replace *while*?

A pair of 1950s Levi's can be worth up to £500 while a pair of 501s from the 1930s sell for up to £5,000. ....

Looking at language

Ways of comparing

In Unit 43 you studied some ways of comparing. This unit looks at more ways.

Saying things are different	*Saying things are the same*
Comparative adjective (+ *than* ...) *Jake's shoes are* **nicer than** *mine.* See Unit 43 for adjective + *er*.	***the same as / the same*** *Those jeans are* **the same** *price* **as** *mine.* *The cost of living is* **the same** *here* **as** *in my country.* *Our mobile phones are* **the same**.
not as ... as = less than *Most jeans aren't* **as expensive as** *Levi's.* (most jeans are cheaper than Levi's) We can also say *not so ... as*: *It's* **not so** *hot* **as** *I thought it would be.* (it's cooler than I thought it would be) We don't always need to say what we are comparing something with: *We're* **not as** *happy here (as we were in London).*	***as ... as*** with adjectives or adverbs *Old Levi's are* **as** *rare* **as** *a Ming vase.* (they are equally rare) *I like shopping here* **as much as in the market**. (I like both places equally) *She runs* **as** *fast* **as** *I do.* (we run at the same speed) See Units 45 and 46 for more ways of describing similarities.
different from *Gina's school is completely* ***different from*** *mine.*	
compared with / to *I think trousers are comfortable* **compared to / with** *skirts.* (trousers are more comfortable)	

Conjunctions

These link two clauses to show a contrast. *And* and *but* usually come **between** two clauses:

John's British, **but Mike** *isn't.* *Josh likes playing the piano* **and I** *play the flute.*

(Al)though, while and *whereas* can be **between** two clauses or at the **beginning** of the first:

I want to go to university **(al)though** *my sister doesn't.*

While / Whereas *this pair of jeans cost £20, these cost over £100.*

Comparison of adverbs

We can use **adverbs +** ***more*** or ***most*** to compare **actions:**

My secretary types much **more quickly** *than me.* *I can read* **more easily** *now I have glasses.*

But there are some exceptions:

- adverbs that have the same form as the adjective (*fast, hard, straight*), add *-er*:
  My secretary types much **faster** *than me.*
- irregular adverbs (e.g. *well, better, best, far, further, furthest, badly, worse, worst*):
  She speaks English **better** *than me.*

1 **Are these sentences saying things are different (d) or the same (s)?**

1 This year's holiday wasn't as good as last year's. .....

2 We seem to like the same things. .....

3 Pierre always speaks French in the break, but I never do. .....

4 I've never met anyone as tall as me before. .....

5 You're very shy compared with your brother. .....

Other points

- In **spoken** English we often use *quicker / slower* instead of *more quickly / slowly*:
  *She always finishes the exercises **quicker** than me.*
- Note these ways of comparing quantities:
  *These jeans cost **twice as much as** yours (or **three times as much, four times** etc.).*
  *My salad is **half the size of** yours, but is **twice the price**!*

Getting it right

Exercise 1 Checking meaning

For sentences 1–8, tick (✓) the sentence, a) or b), with the closest meaning. Once, you will need to tick both a) and b).

Example: My father isn't as tall as my brother.
a) My brother's taller than my father. ..✓..
b) My father's tall, but my brother's even taller. .....

1 This perfume's not as nice as the one I had before.
a) The perfume I had before was nicer than this one. .....
b) This perfume is not nice. .....

2 Their house is big compared with ours.
a) Their house isn't as small as I thought it would be. .....
b) Their house is bigger than ours. .....

3 I don't know anyone who speaks as fast as him.
a) He's the fastest speaker I know. .....
b) He speaks faster than anyone else I know. .....

4 The test wasn't as easy as I'd hoped.
a) The test was quite difficult. .....
b) The test was easier than I'd expected. .....

5 My father's as old as the President.
a) My father's older than the President. .....
b) My father and the President are the same age. .....

6 My boyfriend can't cook very well, but I can.

a) Although I can cook quite well, my boyfriend can't. .....

b) My boyfriend can't cook very well and I can't cook very well. .....

7 We've just moved to a new house and it's not as far from work as the old place.

a) The old house was nearer work than the new one. .....

b) The new place is nearer work than the old one. .....

8 You're a really good cook, whereas I can't even make a simple cake.

a) Our cooking is equally good. .....

b) Your cooking is better than mine. .....

Exercise 2 Learning from learners

A teacher has underlined some mistakes in the learner's text below. Write the corrections. There is one mistake with language from Unit 43.

Learning English at home and abroad

Although I stayed with a British family when I studied in Britain, but when I was in my own country I lived at home. Also I studied more hours in the UK than at home. My course 1 wasn't so much intensive at home. I think I did about six hours a week only, whereas in Britain my course was every day. The teaching methods were 2 same in my country as in Britain, but you learn 3 more quick in Britain because you have to speak English to the other people in the class. It's 4 not the same like learning English at home, because the students come from all over the world and we have to speak English. I liked that, but sometimes I wished there was someone else from my country. 5 One of the best thing about studying in Britain was that I also learnt English outside the classroom. At home you speak 6 as much you can but after the lesson you can't really practise your English. But in Britain I practised my English all the time. I definitely think it's worth spending the money to go abroad. You learn 7 much quicker 8 compared studying at home.

Example: I stayed with a British family when I studied in Britain, but ....

1 ....

2 ....

3 ....

4 ....

5 ....

6 ....

7 ....

8 ....

Which mistake is acceptable in spoken English? .....

Exercise 3 Completing a text

In the text about fakes (copies of real products), fill in gaps 1–11 with suitable language of comparison from this unit and Unit 43.

Fakes are everywhere, especially perfume, watches and clothing. However, fakes are never exactly the same as the real product. The price of a product is *as* good a place to start *as* any. If a famous product seems much **1** .... than you expected, it's probably a fake. Other signs help you to know if you are buying the real product or not.

First, you need to check the labels on clothes carefully. Fake labels are usually **2** .... detailed **3** .... labels on the real thing. Sometimes the colour of fake perfume boxes is strange. Look at perfume boxes **4** .... carefully **5** .... usual to see if the colour is right. With jeans, especially Levi's, colour is again a clue. Very pale but thick material is probably a fake. The light-coloured authentic jeans are made of a **6** .... material. With watches it's **7** .... to tell if they are copies or not unless you can look inside! However there are still some things you can do. Look at the strap. Is it real leather? If not, you've probably got a fake. Fake gold watches often look extremely shiny **8** .... to the real thing because they are not real gold. Look for signs of paint coming off. Fakes are painted with gold (or silver) paint **9** .... the real thing will be made of the solid metal. Remember, you get what you pay for. If you don't want to pay much, maybe a fake is **10** .... close to the real thing **11** .... you are likely to get.

Exercise 4 Making comparisons with other people

Write sentences comparing yourself and your life with people in your family and other people in your class. Use each of the ways of comparing in the box once.

... compared to ...	... different from ...	not as ... as ...	as ... as ...	although ...
... while ...	... the same as ...	... more + adverb ...		

Example: *Carmen's house is completely different from mine.*

1 ....

2 ....

3 ....

4 ....

5 ....

6 ....

7 ....

8 ....

Classwork

1 **Work in pairs. Are the sentences true or false?**

1 Moscow to Paris isn't as far as Rio de Janeiro to New York. ....
2 The Eiffel Tower in Paris is the same height as the Empire State Building in New York. ....
3 Spoken Japanese and Chinese are completely different from each other. ....
4 *Antidisestablishmentarianism* is the longest word in the English language. ....
5 Cheetahs run faster than horses. ....
6 Humans don't usually live as long as tortoises. ....
7 Summer in Ireland is hot compared with summer in Florida. ....
8 The Pyramids are as old as Stonehenge. ....

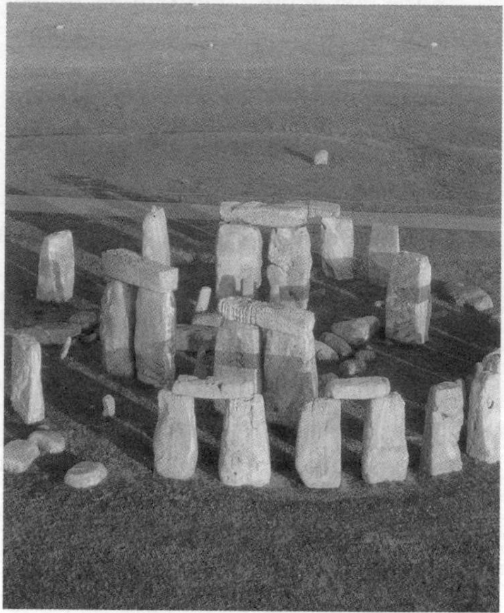

Stonehenge

2 **Join up with another pair and check the answers on page 326 if you have the Answer Key. Which pair got the most right?**

3 **Winners: choose your prize from the winners' list below.**
Others: choose from the non-winners' list.
There is only one prize for each pair, so you need to agree which prize you want. Come to agreement by discussing why you want the prize you want and using the language of comparison that you have studied in this unit.

WINNERS' PRIZES	NON-WINNERS' PRIZES
A new car	A personal computer
A two-week holiday in Hawaii for two	A digital camera
£2,000 to spend on clothes	A motorbike
A year of evening English lessons at a school of your choice	A designer watch
£2,000 to spend on music	A weekend in Paris for two
£2,000 of gold jewellery of your choice	A mobile phone for a year

Unit

45 *Describing with* look *and* like

Getting started

1 **Read the extract from a radio interview with a woman called Jayne. What do you think a 'lookalike' is?**

....

Liz Hurley

I was modelling for television, and the photographer took some photos and he said, 'You know, you really look like Liz Hurley* in these photos', and another man said 'You can make a lot of money doing this. Why don't you send the photos to a lookalike agency?' And as a sort of joke I said, 'Well, OK,' and the next week they wrote back saying 'Oh, yes. We'd like you to work as a lookalike.'

In my first job as a lookalike, I walked into the room and there were Richard Gere, Joan Collins and Joanna Lumley*, and they looked so realistic, I had to look twice!

Jayne

*Liz Hurley, Richard Gere, Joan Collins and Joanna Lumley are famous actors

2 **Underline any examples of the verb *look* in the extracts.**

3 **Match the questions about Jayne, a)–e), to the correct answers, i)–v).**

a) Who does she look like? .....
b) What's she like? .....
c) What does she like doing? .....
d) What does she look like? .....
e) What's she looking at? .....

i) She's tall, with a round face.
ii) The camera.
iii) She looks like Liz Hurley.
iv) Reading, travelling and eating good food.
v) She's a lovely woman, always friendly and pleased to see you.

Looking at language

Look and *like*

The diagram below shows the main forms and uses of *look like* and *be like* for comparing and for describing.

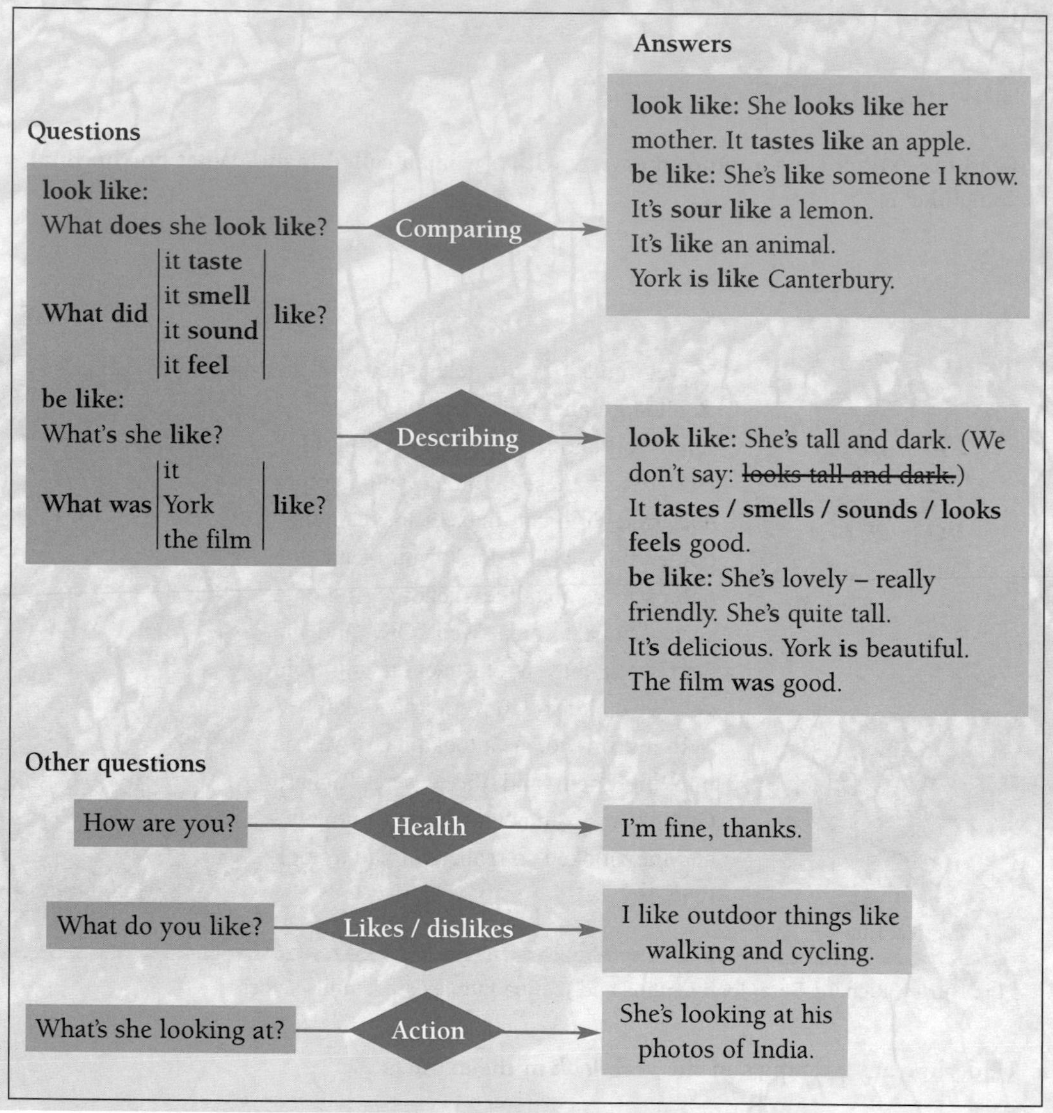

Answers
look like: She looks like her mother. It tastes like an apple.
be like: She's like someone I know. It's sour like a lemon. It's like an animal. York is like Canterbury.
Questions
look like:
What does she look like?
What did it taste / it smell / it sound / it feel like?
be like:
What's she like?
What was it / York / the film like?
Comparing
Describing
look like: She's tall and dark. (We don't say: ~~looks tall and dark.~~)
It tastes / smells / sounds / looks feels good.
be like: She's lovely – really friendly. She's quite tall.
It's delicious. York is beautiful.
The film was good.
Other questions
How are you?
Health
I'm fine, thanks.
What do you like?
Likes / dislikes
I like outdoor things like walking and cycling.
What's she looking at?
Action
She's looking at his photos of India.

1 In this extract, Jayne, the 'lookalike', talks about what she's doing at the moment. Fill in the missing words. (Sigourney Weaver is a famous American actress.)

Actually, I'm doing some acting. I'm going to do a student film next week – *Alien 3* – because they thought I **1** .... a bit **2** .... Sigourney Weaver. You can really **3** .... anyone!

Other points

- *Look (taste / smell / sound / feel) like* is often used with these expressions to say **how much** someone looks like someone else:

	a bit	
She looks	*a lot / very*	*like me.*
	just / exactly	

- We use *look* + **adjective of character** to comment on people:
  She looks nice. *He looks friendly.*
- We **cannot** use the preposition *like* with *how*. We say: ***What was the film like?*** We don't say: ~~How was the film like?~~

2 **Which of the answers to the questions are correct (✓), and which are incorrect (✗)?**

1 A: What does she look like? B: She looks like pretty with large blue eyes. .....

2 A: Does it taste nice? B: Yes. It tastes a bit like chicken. .....

3 A: What's your new teacher like? B: He likes reading and playing basketball. .....

4 A: Who does your daughter look like? B: She exactly looks like her father. .....

Getting it right

Exercise 1 Thinking about meaning

Look at the picture of a party, and answer questions 1–8.

Example: Find someone who likes dancing. Serena

1 Who is looking at Serena? ....

2 Find someone who likes Cola. ....

3 Miguel's shy. Who's like him? ....

4 Who thinks the food tastes good? ....

5 Find two people who look like each other. ....

6 Who looks tired? ....

Exercise 2 Learning from learners

Two learners in an English class, Marco and Maria, are finding out about each other's family. Decide if sentences and questions 1–8 are right (✓) or wrong (✗), and correct any that are wrong.

Marco: So, can you tell me about your family, Maria? What does your father like?

Maria: Well, people often say he looks bad-tempered, but they don't know him well enough. He's quite shy, but friendly when you get to know him.

Marco: 1 What's he look like?

Maria: 2 He certainly doesn't look like me! He's quite short, grey haired, and doesn't have a beard or moustache. 3 I'm look much more like my mother. 4 She still looks like great, even at 60.

Marco: 5 What she like? 6 Is she like you?

Maria: In some ways. 7 We both like arguing, and I've got her love of music. 8 She's like my sister as well.

Examples: ✗ *What's your father like?*

✓ ....

1 ....

2 ....

3 ....

4 ....

5 ....

6 ....

7 ....

8 ....

Extension

Put someone in your family (father, sister) in the gap and answer the questions.

1 What is your .... like?

....

2 What does she / he look like?

....

3 Do you look like him / her?

....

4 What does she / he like?

....

Exercise 3 Spoken extracts

In Extracts A, B and C below, someone describes a fruit or vegetable to a friend from another country. Fill in gaps 1–10 with one word from this unit, and decide which fruit or vegetable is being described.

A Well, it's ..like.. a lemon, but it's smaller. It doesn't 1 .... like a lemon because it's green, not yellow, but you can use it in the same way. It's sour 2 .... a lemon, but drinks 3 .... good when you add a slice.

Fruit or vegetable: ....

B It looks a bit 4 .... a cauliflower, but it's green, not white. It 5 .... strange when you touch it, and a lot of children don't 6 .... it.

Fruit or vegetable: ....

C The inside is orange 7 .... a peach, but the outside is green. When it 8 .... soft it's ready to eat. Nearly everyone 9 .... it because it 10 .... so sweet.

Fruit or vegetable: ....

Exercise 4 Matching and writing

Match the sentence beginnings, 1–8, to the endings, a)–i), and then write an alternative answer.

Example: What was the party like? ..c)

1 What does she look like? .....
2 What was the concert like? .....
3 What's Cambridge like? .....
4 How is your sister? .....
5 What are you looking at? .....
6 What does it taste like? .....
7 What does it feel like to be a new parent? .....
8 What are your neighbours like? .....

a) They seem really nice.
....
b) She's young-looking, with lovely, long, blond hair.
....
c) ~~It wasn't very good really. I didn't know many people.~~
It was great. I had a wonderful time.......................................
d) It was wonderful. The orchestra was great.
....
e) It's an old city with lots of beautiful buildings.
....
f) A bit strange. I never thought I would be one, you see.
....
g) Oh, nothing. I just thought I saw someone I knew.
....
h) It tastes a bit like an apple.
....
i) Oh, she's much better now, thank you.
....

Classwork

1 **Take a piece of paper and fill in information about yourself following the instructions below.**
In the top left corner, write the name of somebody in your family.
In the top right corner, write the name of your favourite place.
In the bottom left corner, write the name of something you don't like.
In the bottom right corner, write the name of your favourite actor or other famous person.
In the middle, write the name of your favourite meal.

Example:

Simon (brother)		Florence, Italy
	Paella	
Mobile phones		Tom Cruise

2 **Now go round the class with the piece of paper. Practise comparing and describing with *look* and *like* by asking other students about what they have written.**

Examples:
What does Simon look like?
What's Florence like?
Why don't you like mobile phones?

3 **Who in the class has the most similar family, likes and dislikes to yours?**

Unit 46

Similarities and differences: so and neither

Getting started

1 **Read the article about two married couples with a lot of similarities. How many similarities do they share?** ....

Sunshine seekers meet their shadows

TWO COUPLES who met when they shared a table at a holiday hotel found that they also shared first names and much more.

Albert and Betty Cheetham and Albert and Betty Rivers arrived and departed for their holidays in Tunisia on the same days. During their holiday they realised that both had celebrated 55 years of marriage and the date and time of their weddings were the same: 2.00 p.m. on August 15, 1942.

Mr Cheetham, 77, and his wife, 78, have two sons born in 1943 and 1945, as have the Rivers. Both couples have five grandchildren.

Mr Cheetham said yesterday, 'It was absolutely unbelievable. At first we were laughing. Then it got quite strange. The coincidences just kept coming.'

Both Bettys had worked in post offices in their home towns. Both Alberts had been workers in railway workshops at the same time. Neither Betty could show the other her engagement ring as both had lost them. But they did have identical watches, which had had the same parts broken and repaired.

2 **Underline examples of *both* and *neither* in the article.**

3 **Put *both* and *neither* in the correct box in the chart.**

	Betty Rivers	*Betty Cheetham*	*Both or neither?*
Worked in the post office	✓	✓	....
Could show engagement ring	✗	✗	....

Looking at language

Both, neither, all and *none*

Both and *neither* are used to talk about two things that are the same:

__Both Bettys__ had worked in post offices in their home towns. (**both + plural**; one and the other)

__Neither Betty__ could show the other her engagement ring. (**neither + singular**; not one and not the other)

All means 'every member of a group':

***All** visitors* (everyone who is a visitor) *should report to Reception.*

We can use *both, neither* and *all* before a **noun**: ***both** Bettys* / ***neither** girl* / ***all** visitors*
or with *of* + **noun phrase / object pronoun**: ***both of** the women* / ***neither of** the girls* / ***all of** us.*

We can use *both* and *all* after *we* and *they*:

*We **both** speak French.* *They **all** had colds.*

We can use *both* and *neither* as pronouns:

*I've got two brothers. **Both** are older than me, but **neither** is taller.*

We do not use **both + negative**; We use ***neither***
We don't say: ~~*Both Bettys couldn't …*~~ we say: ***Neither** Betty could …*

Both and *all* can go before nouns, before main verbs, or after *to be*:

***Both** Bettys had worked in post offices.*
*The two Bettys had **both** worked in post offices.*
*They are **both** retired.*

None means 'not any' (of a group of more than two) and is used with *of* + **noun / object pronoun**:

***None of the coincidences** was easy to explain.* ***None of us** wanted to go home.*

So and *neither*

When we want to answer someone by saying that something is similar, we use:
so / neither **+ auxiliary verb /** ***be*** **+ pronoun / noun / possessive.**
To show differences, we use **pronoun / noun / possessive + auxiliary /** ***be***.

	Examples	*Similarities*	*Differences*
Positive	*We **went** to Tunisia last year.* *My name's Alfred.* *My mobile's been stolen.*	*Really? **So did we.*** ***So is mine!*** ***So has Lucy's.***	*Really? **We didn't.*** ***Mine isn't.*** ***Mine hasn't.***
Negative	*We **didn't** go out at all at the weekend.* *I **can't** understand this exercise.* *I **haven't** seen Jane this morning.*	***Neither did we.*** ***Neither can I.*** ***Neither have I.***	*Oh, **we did!*** *It's OK. **I can.*** *I **have**. She's outside.*

Other points

Me too, me neither and *as well* also express similarities in spoken English:

A: *I'll come back later.* B: ***Me too.*** (So will I.)

A: *I don't like this weather.* B: ***Me neither.*** (Neither do I.)

A: *I saw Elaine earlier.* B: *Oh, I did **as well**.* (So did I.)

1 Add the correct auxiliary.

1 A: I won't see her tomorrow.
B: Neither .... I.

2 A: I don't understand this.
B: Neither .... I.

3 A: We didn't stay long.
B: Neither .... we.

4 A: I haven't been here long.
B: Neither .... we.

Getting it right

Exercise 1 Recognising meaning

In 1–8 below, look at the sentences and the pictures. Tick (✓) them if the meanings match the pictures, and put a cross (✗) if they do not.

Example: Neither of them have beards. ✗

1 None of them have beards. .....

2 A: Sue's hair is really short.
B: Oh, so is Anna's. .....

3 A: Have you seen Mike recently? He's really tall now.
B: Oh, Dennis isn't. .....

4 Both of us like watching football. .....

5 A: I didn't pass my driving test first time.
B: No, neither did I. .....

6 They all wear jeans all the time. .....

7 A: I don't like getting up early.
B: Me neither. .....

8 A: I haven't brought my camera.
B: Oh, I have. .....

Exercise 2 Learning from learners

A teacher has asked two learners in a new class to talk to each other and find things they have in common. Tick (✓) the underlined phrases or correct them if they are wrong.

A: OK, I'm from Rome, and I live with my family.
B: So do I, but I'm from Caracas. I have just one younger sister. ✓ ....
A: I'm not. I've got three brothers. I'm finishing high school this year. I'm 18. ✗ *I haven't.* ....
B: 1 So me. Do you play any sports? 1 ....
A: Volleyball, and I swim a lot too. 2 ....
B: I don't play volleyball, but 2 I swim quite often as well. I haven't got a boyfriend at the moment. 3 ....
A: 3 So don't have I. I play the guitar, but I'm not very good at it. 4 ....
B: Well, I don't play any musical instruments, but I listen to a lot of music. 5 ....
A: Yeah, 4 so listen I. What sort of music? 6 ....
B: Lots, but I'm listening to a lot of reggae just now. 7 ....
A: So, what have we got in common? 5 We live both at home, 6 both of us like swimming ... 8 ....
B: ... yes, and 7 we're both 18 and like music. Oh, and 8 none of us has a boyfriend at the moment.

Exercise 3 Completing a conversation

Fill in the gaps, using a *so* ... or *neither* ... phrase, in this conversation between the two couples you read about in *Getting started*.

A: My name's Alfred.

B: How funny! *So is mine* !

A: Isn't that strange, that we've got the same names! If you don't mind me asking, how long have you been married, then?

B: We've been married, well, 55 years this year.

A: Really? 1 .... ! Since 1942?

C: That's right. We got married on August 15, 1942.

D: You didn't? That's extraordinary! **2** .... – at two o'clock.

C: And two o'clock for us, too. How incredible.

D: It was a lovely day. Unfortunately I haven't got my engagement ring any more.

C: **3** .... I lost mine.

D: **4** .... Years ago. Have you got any children or grandchildren?

C: Yes – two sons and five grandchildren.

B: This is getting really strange. **5** .... When were your sons born?

A: 1943 and 1945. And yours?

B: The same again. What did you do before you retired?

A: Oh, I worked in a railway workshop …

B: No! **6** .... !

A: … and Betty in a local post office.

B: You can't have done! **7** .... !

Exercise 4 Summarising an article

Use your memory of the article about the two couples to complete the summary of it.

The two couples who met on holiday had the same names, Albert and Betty, and they all arrived and left on the same day. Both couples ....

....

....

....

....

Classwork

1 **Work in groups of three. Two of you have three minutes to find as many things in common with each other as possible, while the third member of the group listens and takes notes. Things you could compare:**

age family travel languages occupation interests likes / dislikes

Example:
A: *I'm 22.*
B: *I'm not. I'm 20. I've got a brother and a sister.*

2 **The listener from each group reports any similarities to the class.**

Example:
They're different ages, but ***both of them*** *have a brother and sister.*

Unit

47 Possibility in the present

Getting started

1 **Read the two stories about monsters that people believe they have seen in lakes and answer the questions.**

a) Where are the lakes in each story?

....

b) Which story says it is definitely **not** a monster? .....

Story 1

A 15-second video clip taken by a Japanese film crew <u>may</u> show a present-day dinosaur swimming in Lake Tele, in central Africa.

The film shows something large moving across the lake a few hundred metres from land. Looking closer, it seems to show a flat shape with two tall, thin shapes rising from it – <u>maybe</u> a neck and a hump. The object also dived under water suggesting it is an animal, according to expert Karl Shuker. 'You could see it as a dinosaur if you wanted to, but it <u>could</u> be one of the big turtles that live in the lake.'

Story 2

CAMERON TURNER, 27, discovered six bones 60 ft (18 m) down at Loch Morar, a 310 metre-deep lake in Scotland, during a diving expedition. It was suggested they <u>might</u> be the bones of Morag, the monster, first seen in 1895, that some people believe lives in the loch; but they were later identified as deer bones.

2 **Tick (✓) the statements which are true about the <u>underlined</u> words in the texts.**

a) They are all modal verbs. .....

b) They all show some kind of possibility. .....

c) They are all followed by an infinitive. .....

d) They suggest that we do not **know** the facts for certain. .....

Looking at language

We can talk about possibility in the future, present or past.

Expressing possibility in the present

The modal verbs *must*, *may*, *might*, *could* and *can't*, and adverbs such as *certainly*, *probably* and *possibly* are used to express the speaker's view of how certain something is:

Speaker's view	*Positive*		*Negative*	
	Verbs	*Adverbs*	*Verbs*	*Adverbs*
more certain	must	certainly	can't / couldn't	certainly not
↓		probably		probably not
	may	maybe / perhaps	may not	
less certain	might / could	possibly	might not	possibly not

For example:

*That **must** be a fish, not a dinosaur.* (I'm certain it's a fish)
*They **can't** be dinosaur bones.* (I'm certain they are not dinosaur bones)
*We **may** have the game you want. I'll look at the back of the shop.*
*They **may not** be ready to leave. They're still talking.*
*She **might** be home by now. Let's phone her and see.*

- There is only a small difference in meaning between *may*, *could* and *might*.
- *Must not* is not used for possibility.
- *Couldn't* is the same as *can't*, not *mightn't*.

1 The modal verbs *can't*, *could*, *might* and *must* have been removed from the text below. Put them back in the right places.

Scientists have never found the death worm of the Gobi Desert. People who live there believe it is real. A local man told researchers that a death worm once killed a boy and his parents instantly when they tried to remove it from the child's toy box. An American also died when he touched a worm.

The incredible conclusion that **1** .... be drawn is that the worm can kill by using electricity. This amazing animal **2** .... even be able to pass electricity across a small space, which **3** .... explain the belief among the Gobi people that it can kill from a distance.

But does the worm exist? The answer **4** .... be far off, surely, with all those scientists looking for it.

Form

Modal verb + infinitive without *to*:
*He **must be** happy now he's married.*
*He **might visit** her every Saturday. I can't remember.*

or **modal verb + *be* + *-ing* form:**
*She isn't at home. She **must be** visiting her sister.*

Questions often have the form *Do you think* + modal (**not** *may*):
*Do you think she **might** be at home at the moment?*

Adverbs of possibility – word order

Perhaps and ***maybe*** often start a sentence:
***Perhaps** she's at home. **Maybe** she's getting lunch ready.*
Certainly, ***probably*** and ***possibly*** can come:
after an auxiliary / *to be*: *She's **certainly** at home.*
before main verbs and negatives: *She **certainly** likes cooking.*

Other points

- *Can* can have the same meaning as 'sometimes':
  *It **can** rain a lot round here in early summer.* (it sometimes rains ...)
  *She **can** be very determined if she doesn't get what she wants.* (she is sometimes very determined)
- We often say ***You must be joking!*** to respond to unbelievable news or impossible requests:
  A: *Can you come to work on Sunday? We've got lots to do.*
  B: ***You must be joking!** I need the break.*

Getting it right

Exercise 1 Thinking about meaning

In comments 1–8 below, tick (✓) the beginning, a) or b), which best matches the continuation on the right.

Example: a) He can't be the murderer. ..✓.. — His feet look bigger than the footprints found at the scene of the crime.
b) He isn't the murderer. .....

1 a) That might be someone swimming out there. ..... — Who knows?
b) That's someone swimming out there. .....

2 a) Maybe he's unhappy at work. ..... — It's just an idea.
b) He's unhappy at work. .....

3 a) Shhh! Someone must be listening! ..... — I'm sure I heard someone in the next room.
b) Shhh! Someone may be listening! .....

4 a) He could be the one for the job. .....
b) He must be the one for the job. .....

I don't think we even need to interview him.

5 a) You can get a sore wrist from using the computer. .....
b) You can't have a sore wrist from using the computer. .....

You only use it for a few minutes each day.

6 a) It must be hard working at night all the time. .....
b) It's hard working at night all the time. .....

I don't know why I do it.

7 a) He must like Beethoven. Look at all his CDs. .....
b) He likes Beethoven. Look at all his CDs. .....

He belongs to a Beethoven society too.

8 a) She might not be home yet. .....
b) She can't be home yet. .....

I think she sometimes works late on Tuesdays.

Exercise 2 Learning from learners

What do you think the small parts of pictures below are? Some learners discussed the pictures. Find four mistakes in their discussions and correct them using modal verbs.

Example: It ~~is~~ ^could be^ a tyre, but I'm not sure.

A: It can be some kind of fence, or maybe a gate.

B: I don't think it's a gate, but it could be a boat.

A: It mustn't be a boat. The water would get in.

A: Perhaps it's a modern carpet with a simple design.

B: Or it might be road markings of some sort.
No, wait a minute. Aren't those lines, painted on the ground?
It must a tennis court or football pitch or something like that.

A: I have no idea! Is it food of some kind? Do you think it could be sweets?

B: Yes, or perhaps it's soap. It could be soap before it's wrapped up.

A: Yes, it can be soap.

▷ Exercise 3 Completing a conversation

Fill in the gaps with an appropriate modal verb or another way of expressing possibility.

Deputy Director: Excuse me. Have you seen Bob anywhere? We had a meeting arranged for 10.00 and now it's 10.05.

Receptionist: Er, no. Have you tried the canteen? He *might* be there, I suppose.

Deputy Director: Yes, I've looked there. Do you think he 1 .... be with James?

Receptionist: No, he 2 .... be because James is out this morning. I know – he 3 .... be with Sharon. He's working on a project with her.

Deputy Director: Oh, right.

Receptionist: Oh, hang on. I'm wrong. He 4 .... be there because Sharon's on holiday this week. I forgot. Look, that's his coat, so he 5 .... be somewhere nearby. Are you sure he's not in the design office?

Deputy Director: Yes, positive. I was in there with Jeremy and his desk was empty. 6 .... he's not in today?

Receptionist: No, I'm sure that's his coat.

Use the plan to help you finish this sentence:

Bob must be in the .... because ....

▷ Exercise 4 Phrase writing

Fill in the gaps with a suitable phrase expressing possibility.

Example: A: Let's go and see Louise.

B: No, let's phone first. She *might not be there* and it would be a shame to go all that way and then have to come home again...

1 A: Look at that! There's an animal through those trees. What do you think it is?

B: I don't know, but I suppose it .... because it's big and brown.

2 A: I'm really sorry. I don't have those figures you asked me for.

B: I don't believe it! You .... ! The presentation is this afternoon, and they're the main part of it!

3 In my opinion, football is the only sport worth watching, although baseball .... from time to time.

4 What? You want me to do my job and yours while you're on holiday? You .... ! No way. Sorry.

5 I think we should go to his party. I know the last one was boring, but we know he's put a lot of effort into it. You never know, this one ....

6 A: Come and look at this! Strange, isn't it? Is it some kind of spider?

B: No, it .... It's only got six legs.

7 A: I'm bored. This is much too easy.

B: It .... for **you**, but **I'm** having trouble with it.

8 Oh, look at the view! You're so lucky. It .... to live in such a beautiful spot.

Classwork

The Modals are a pop group. Complete the chart about them using the information below. Work with a partner.

Example:
Alvin, Chas and Elvis can't be the drummer because they are not the youngest in the group.
So, the drummer could either be Damon or Buddy.

The youngest member of the group plays the drums.
The oldest member of the group is ten years older than the youngest.
The members of the group are called Alvin, Buddy, Chas, Damon and Elvis.
Buddy plays the keyboards.
The singer is 27, three years older than the bass player.
Buddy is younger than Alvin, Chas or Elvis.
Alvin is two years older than the singer.
Alvin is the oldest, and doesn't sing or play bass.
Chas can't play any instruments.
One member of the group is 21.

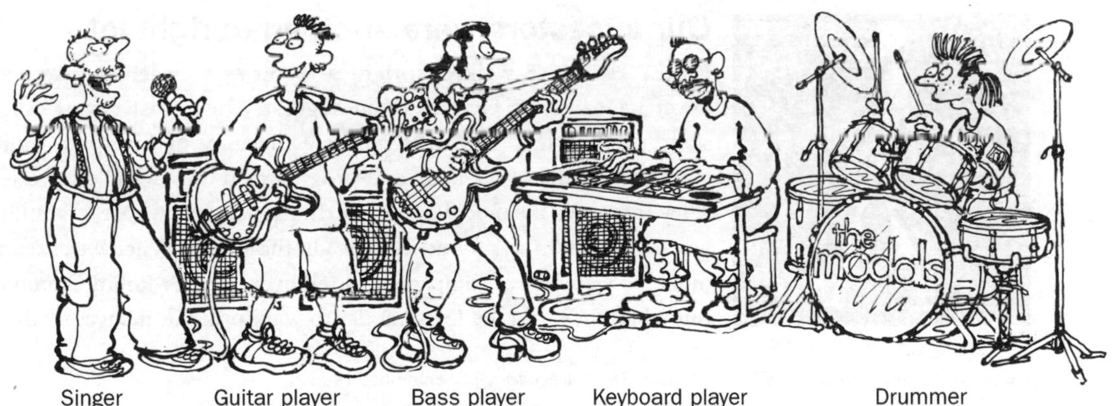

Singer Guitar player Bass player Keyboard player Drummer

Name	Alvin	Buddy	Chas	Damon	Elvis
Position in band	....	keyboard player	singer	....	bass player
Age	....	....	....	....	....

Unit

48 Possibility in the past

Getting started

1 **The articles below are about new ideas about early life on earth. Read them, and answer the questions.**

a) How does the first article suggest the dinosaurs died out?

....

b) How did early humans walk, according to the second article?

....

Killer comet's deadly strike

The first results from a mission to explore the largest crater on Earth are starting to show the size of a disaster which may have led to the death of the dinosaurs. A huge comet or asteroid is believed to have crashed into our planet 65 million years ago. 'We just can't imagine what it must have been like when the asteroid hit,' a researcher from Cambridge University said.

(adapted from *The Cambridge Evening News*, 29 January 1997)

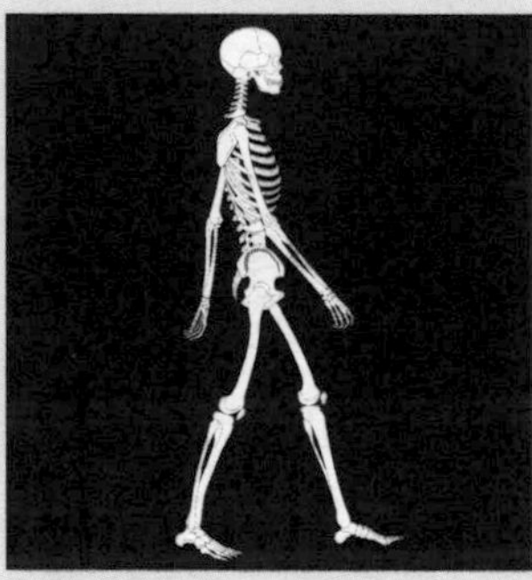

Our ancestors were such an upright lot

EARLY HUMANS walked upright as soon as they left the trees and never bent over as pictures often suggest. They must have learnt to stand on two feet. Scientists at the University of Liverpool built a computer model of the body and programmed it to 'walk' on two legs. They then gave the model the proportions of 'Lucy', whose 3.6 million-year-old skeleton was found in Africa in the 1980s. 'When we asked the model to walk like a chimpanzee, it fell over,' said Dr Robin Crompton. But when they told the Lucy model to walk upright, it succeeded.

(adapted from an article by Charles Arthur, *The Independent*, 11 September 1996)

2 **Look at these phrases from the articles. Which <u>underlined</u> modal verb shows certainty, and which shows uncertainty?**

a) *... a disaster which <u>may have led</u> to the death of the dinosaurs.* ....

b) *They <u>must have learnt</u> to stand on two feet.* ....

3 **Finish this sentence:**

To talk about possibility in the past, we can use a .... verb + *have* + ...

Looking at language

Expressing possibility in the past

To talk about possibility in the past you can use:
- the modal verbs *must, may, might, could, can't / couldn't*
- the adverbs of possibility, *probably* and *perhaps.*

Use

We use this language to make guesses about the past using information we have:

Guess: *Early humans … **must have learnt** to stand on two feet.*

Information we have: Experiments by scientists at the University of Liverpool.

See Unit 47 for the meanings of the different modal verbs.

Probably is stronger than *perhaps*:

***Perhaps** I saw a UFO, but it was **probably** just a plane.*

Form

Modal verb + *have* + past participle:

*They **must have learnt** to stand on two feet.* *It **may have led** to the death of the dinosaurs.*

or **modal verb + *have* + *been* + *-ing* form:**

A: *She looks exhausted.* B: *Yes, she does. She **must have been working** too hard.*

1 **In these crime stories, <u>underline</u> the most appropriate modal phrases.**

Stop, thief! You've dropped your cash

A thief running away after robbing a supermarket couldn't believe his luck when customers raced after him – to help him pick up money falling out of his bag.

Police said: 'Several people stopped to help him pick up the cash. It **1** *might have been / must have been* his lucky day.'

£30,000 dog kidnapped

A £30,000 show dog which disappeared during a walk with its owner **2** *may have been / can't have been* stolen to order. Police fear the animal has been sold on to a breeder and **3** *could have been / must have been* smuggled abroad.

Pronunciation

In spoken English *have* becomes weak:

*She **might've** wanted to see you.* *I **must've left** my wallet in the café.*

Other points

The **modal verb + *have* + past participle** can express the **past simple**:

The dog must have eaten it. (it is probable that the dog **ate** it)

or the **present perfect**:

I might have passed the exam. (it is possible that I **have passed** the exam)

Getting it right

Exercise 1 What would you say?

Read the information on the left, and tick (✓) the most appropriate comment, a) or b), on the right.

Information	**Comment**
Example: You start talking about a news headline. Your friend says, 'Sorry – what are you talking about?'	a) Oh, you can't have heard the news. ..✓. b) Oh, you might not have heard the news. .....
1 You arrive on an empty beach expecting to meet a friend. There are no footprints.	a) He can't have been here. ..... b) He may not have been here. .....
2 You missed the last five minutes of a football match. When you left, the score was United 4, Rangers 1. You arrive home and talk about the final result.	a) United must have won. ..... b) United might have won. .....
3 A student is late for class. She sometimes drives, and sometimes takes the train.	a) She must've missed her train. ..... b) She might've missed the train. .....
4 A famous personality has disappeared while on holiday. No one knows what has happened.	a) He could've drowned, I suppose. ..... b) He must've drowned, I suppose. .....
5 You hear the phone ringing but you don't get to it in time.	a) I wonder who that was. It might've been my mother. ..... b) I wonder who that was. It must've been my mother. .....
6 You're expecting a friend called Peter about now. The doorbell rings.	a) Perhaps that's Peter. ..... b) That's probably Peter. .....

Exercise 2 Completing conversations

Complete the extracts from conversations using a suitable modal verb and the correct form of the verb in brackets.

Example: A: Have you got the car keys?
B: Oh, sorry – I think I *must have left* (*leave*) them in my jacket pocket.

1 A: ... and then this man appeared holding a knife and took my bag!
B: Oh! You .... (*be*) terrified.

2 A: Jane went for an interview yesterday in bright pink tights and those yellow boots of hers!
B: Really? She .... (*not make*) a very good impression.

3 A: I feel terrible. I didn't realise she was in the room when I said those things.

B: Come on, it .... (*be*) worse. You didn't say anything awful.

4 I was on the motorway when this car went past followed by a police car, sirens blaring. They .... (*do*) at least 160 km an hour when they passed me.

5 Do you know, I think I saw Joe this morning. He .... (*see*) me because he walked straight past without stopping.

6 A: Can you tell me what he looked like?

B: Oh, he .... (*be*) about 55, and he was tall with grey hair.

7 A: Have you seen Estelle anywhere?

B: No, but she .... (*go*) home. She said she had a headache.

8 A: David hasn't spoken to me since I got the job we both tried for.

B: Yeah, he's really upset, isn't he? He .... (*want*) it a lot.

Exercise 3 Who killed Henry?

Learners were asked to try to solve a murder mystery using the information in the box. Read some of the things they said and correct the mistakes. One extract has no mistake but the others have one each.

The rich businessman Henry Farringdon was found dead from gunshot wounds in his own home. Shots were heard at 3.00 p.m. and size 44 footprints were found near the body.

Example:

Thomas could ~~be~~ have done it. He wanted his father's money to pay his debts.

1 I think the farmer, Jack, Thomas's friend, can have done it because we know he had a gun. He was in love.

2 No, Jack mustn't have done it. He has an alibi. He was in town.

3 What about Charlotte, Henry's daughter? She could have killed him because Henry hated her.

4 Yeah, but Alice might do it. She hated Henry because he didn't pay her much.

5 Or Edie, his wife – she might wanted to kill him because her marriage was unhappy.

6 No, Edie mustn't have done it. Her feet weren't size 44, surely? That's a man's size.

Who do you think the murderer was? ....

Exercise 4 Writing: unsolved mysteries

Read Stories 1–4 which are real mysteries which have never been solved. Using modals or adverbs of possibility, suggest possible explanations. Try to write at least two sentences for each story.

1

Owen Parfitt was an old man who was unable to walk. He was sitting in the doorway of his cottage, next to a busy road, on a summer evening in 1768. His sister left him alone for a few minutes and when she returned he had disappeared. He was never seen again.

He can't have left by himself because he was unable to walk.

....

2

Many ships and planes have disappeared in the small area known as the Bermuda Triangle. Most of them leave no wreckage or bodies, they simply disappear. Take the example of the British passenger plane, the Star Tiger. The last message heard from the plane was 'Expect to arrive on schedule.' There was no further word. A year later, another plane disappeared in the middle of the Bermuda Triangle, with their last message being that the weather was fine and all was well.

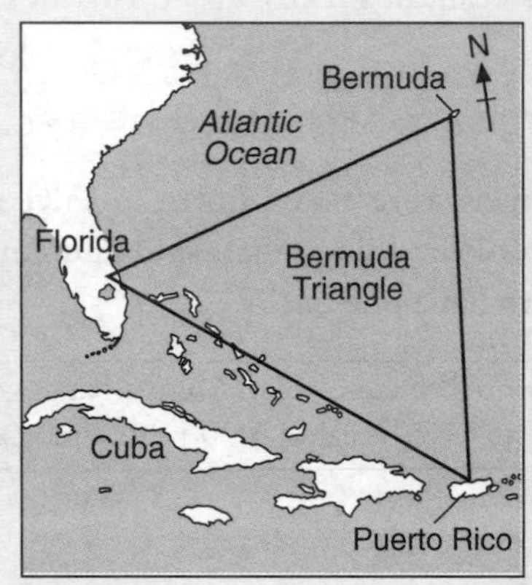

....

....

3

In the nineteenth century, Daniel Dunglas Home demonstrated the ability to handle burning hot coals. He could also pick up a glass lampshade that was hot enough to light a match, and show no burns or injury.

....

....

4

The story of the *Marie Celeste* is a famous unexplained puzzle. In 1872 the ship was discovered floating in the sea with no one on board, alive or dead. The ship was in good condition and there was plenty of food on board. What could have happened to the people, and why did they abandon an undamaged ship?

....

....

Classwork

1 **Have you ever seen or heard anything you could not explain?**

2 **Work in groups of three or four. Tell the group your story. It could be something that happened to you, or to someone you know, or a news story.**

Example:
When I was about seven or eight, I was on holiday with my family in the countryside. At dusk one evening I saw lights, red and white through the trees, moving away, but there was no sound. I still don't know what it was, so it's my UFO story.

3 **The rest of the group should try to explain the story.**

Example:
A: *It might've been a plane or helicopter.*
B: *It can't have been. He didn't hear anything. It was probably just the lights of a car in the distance.*

4 **If there is a particularly interesting story in your group, tell the rest of the class and let them try to explain it.**

Unit 49 Present obligation and necessity

Getting started

1 **Denise Lewis is a British heptathlete (an athlete who competes in seven events). Read the interview with her and answer the questions.**

a) What different things does she do in her training?

....

b) How can we tell this interview took place over the phone?

....

Anna Blundy calls

Denise Lewis

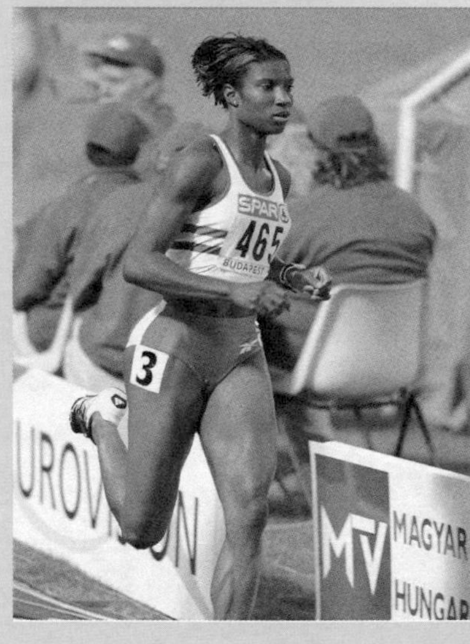

DL: I do about four or five hours' training a day, six days a week.

AB: *How awful. What do you do exactly?*

DL: Oh, it's not too bad really. You get used to it. I do running and aerobic exercise and then high-jump technique, shot put, hurdle, javelin. If you want to achieve, you have to make sacrifices.

AB: *But wouldn't you rather stay in bed?*

DL: Yes, always. I love my sleep. I had to get up at eight o'clock this morning instead of 8.45, and it was awful. It makes a difference, that 45 minutes.

AB: *But you lie in at the weekend?*

DL: Hmmm... Well, I don't really mind getting up early when I don't have to. Hang on! I've got to go through to make-up now. I'll take my mobile with me. ●

(adapted from an article by Anna Bundy, *The Times Magazine*, London, 14 February 1998)

2 **Match the phrases, a)–d), taken from the text, to the descriptions, i)–iv).**

a) *I had to get up at eight o'clock this morning* .....
b) *... when I don't have to.* .....
c) *... you have to make sacrifices.* .....
d) *I've got to go through to make-up now.* .....

i) a present necessity
ii) a past obligation
iii) freedom from obligation or necessity
iv) a present obligation using informal style

Looking at language

Obligation: This is a requirement to do something which comes from the speaker.
Necessity: This is a requirement to do something which comes from external circumstances (for example, rules and customs) or the situation.

Obligation

The verbs *must, have to* and *have got to* can all be used to express **obligation**:

*You **must tell** me. You promised. / You **have to tell** me. You promised.*

The verb *should* is also common to express weaker obligation or advisability. (See Unit 40.)
Note, however:

- *must* is more common than *have to* in conversation to express obligation.
- *have got to* is used especially in spoken English: ***I've got to go now.***
- to express past or future obligation, we use *have to*. (See Unit 50.)

Necessity

The verbs *must, have to / have got to* and *need to* can all be used to express necessity. Note, however:

- when the necessity is due to a rule, *have to* or *need to* is usually used:
  *You **have to wear** a uniform in the army.* ***I need to / have to be** at work by 8.45 every day.*
- *Must* is often used in public notices or signs:
  *Visitors **must report** to reception.* *Guests **must be signed in** at the desk.*

Negatives

We use *mustn't* to express an obligation or necessity **not** to do something:

*You **mustn't talk** about people behind their backs.* (this is a bad thing to do)
*Bananas **mustn't be** kept in the fridge.* (this is not a good thing to do)

- We use *don't have to / haven't got to* when obligation / necessity is **usually** expected, but **not** on this occasion or in this situation:
  *I **don't have to go** to school today. It's a holiday.* (I usually go to school, but today is a holiday)
  *We **don't have to wear** a uniform at my school.* (I can wear my own clothes)
- *Don't need to* is similar to *don't have to* to express freedom from necessity:
  *You **don't need to bring** a sleeping bag. We've got a spare duvet.*
  Need not is also possible:
  *You **needn't** worry.*

Questions

- Questions with *have to* and *have got to* are common:
  ***Do** I **have to go** to school today?* ***Have** I **got to wear** smart clothes?*
- Questions with *must / mustn't* are unusual, but possible:
  ***Must** I **go** to school today?*

1 **Read the text about MI5, Britain's secret service, and answer the questions. Write *yes* or *no*.**

> **Oddjobs for young Bonds**
>
> MI5 is sending out a glossy recruitment brochure to universities to attract students into spying. It says agents need to have imagination and patience, but must 'keep a low profile'. You don't need to be like James Bond to be chosen. In fact you mustn't be too outgoing. They say they are looking for ordinary people who will fit in anywhere.

1 Can you replace *need to* with *must*? ....

2 Can you replace *need to* and *must* with *have to*? ....

3 Can you replace *don't need to* with *don't have to*? ....

4 Can you replace *mustn't* with *don't have to*? ....

Pronunciation

Have to is pronounced /hæftə/ in spoken English. However, in short answers it is pronounced /hæftuː/:

A: *Do you always look smart for work?* B: *Yes, I* ***have to****.*

Other points

- *Need* can be followed with a direct object:
  You ***need*** *a qualification in English to do this job.*
- Words like *just, only, also, always, sometimes* etc. come **before** *have to / have got to / need to* but **after** *must*:
  You only ***have to*** *do it once. You* ***must*** *only do it once.*
- The present perfect form is:
  We've ***had to*** *sell the boat. The restaurant's* ***had to*** *close.*
- Other verbs can express obligation or necessity:
  I insist that you leave now. (obligation) *You* ***are required to*** *leave now.* (necessity)

Getting it right

▶ Exercise 1 Recognising meaning

Match the sentence beginnings, 1–6, to the endings, a)–g), and state if the phrases in *italics* express obligation (o), necessity (n), or freedom from obligation or necessity (f).

Example: I must do something about my cough ..d).. ..o..

1 We *don't have to* go out ....

2 I *have to* wait in a traffic jam ....

3 You *have to* work hard ....

4 They *needn't* wait for an invitation because ....

a) every time I go to our other office.

b) but I hate going so I keep putting it off.

c) if you'd rather stay in.

d) ~~before it gets worse.~~

5 I *need to* go to the dentist, ...

6 He *needs to* be there by 8.00 ....

e) if you want to succeed in this job.

f) or else he'll be in trouble.

g) they are welcome to come any time.

Extension

Write an alternative beginning for five of the endings a)–g), using expressions of obligation or necessity.

Example: I must fix this broken door before it gets worse.

Exercise 2 Learning from learners

Read the descriptions of jobs, A–C, written by learners. Tick (✓) their use of modal verbs of obligation or necessity if they are correct, or use a different verb if they are not.

A I work in the theatre. You mustn't have any formal qualifications, but you have to be trained by an experienced supervisor and you 1 must work long hours.

B In this business you 2 must work long, irregular hours. You 3 have to be prepared to do simple tasks like the washing-up as well as manage your staff. People 4 mustn't be highly qualified; they just 5 must be enthusiastic. I really 6 have to go now and phone some of my staff.

C I have a very ordinary job. You 7 mustn't be anything special; you 8 must like people. Oh, and you 9 must be able to be polite even when you're feeling annoyed with someone. I suppose something else that the bosses consider important is that they 10 must be able to trust you with all that money. I 11 mustn't wear a uniform like they do in some of the other places, but I 12 must look smart.

don't have to

✓

1 ....

2 ....

3 ....

4 ....

5 ....

6 ....

7 ....

8 ....

9 ....

10 ....

11 ....

12 ....

Match the jobs in the box to learners A–C.

banker	wardrobe assistant	catering manager .....

▷ Exercise 3 Choosing the right form

Fill in the gaps 1–8 in the conversations below, using ways of expressing obligation and necessity you have learnt in this unit.

A: Do you fancy going for a pizza?

B: I can't. I*'ve got to* make some phone calls and do some packing. I just haven't got time.

A: Oh, I'm hopeless at this. I'm giving up.

B: Oh, you **1** .... say that! It's just a matter of practice. Everyone finds driving difficult at first.

A: What's the matter? What are you trying to do?

B: It's this word processor. I want to make a table with shaded boxes, but I can't get it to work.

A: Oh, you **can** do it like that, but you **2** .... Just use 'Autoformat'.

A: Any holiday plans?

B: Yes, I've booked a safari in Kenya. You've been, haven't you? What do I **3** .... take?

A: I **4** .... remember to phone Judy later. She's off to the States tomorrow and I want her to get me some bits and pieces.

B: Oh, is she? I'll try and remind you.

A: Here. This is for you.

B: Oh, Joe! It's beautiful, but I can't accept it. You made it, didn't you?

A: Yes, I did, and you **5** .... accept it. I absolutely **6** .... that you do.

A: What **7** .... you .... do in your new job?

B: It's not very different from the old one, but now I have more responsibility, that's all.

A: How is your brother these days?

B: Oh, not very good really. He's **8** .... give up work because of his bad back.

A: Oh, I am sorry to hear that.

▷ Exercise 4 What could we say?

Rewrite each of the written notices 1–6 below, using spoken language. Use the verbs you have studied in this unit. Start each sentence with *You*.

PLEASE SIGN THE VISITORS' BOOK	*You've got to sign the visitors' book.* ....
SHOW YOUR PASSPORT AT RECEPTION	1 ....
Wear rubber gloves when using this product	2 ....

Shake bottle for best results

3 ....

DO NOT LEAVE YOUR BAG UNATTENDED

4 ....

Remember to take all your belongings with you when you leave the aircraft

5 ....

DANGER – DO NOT TOUCH!

6 ....

Classwork

1 Work in groups of three to play *Excuses Excuses*. Player 1 makes a request based on any picture in the chart below. Player 2 makes an excuse using *have to / have got to / need to*, based on a **different** picture.

Example:
A: *Could you take the dog out for a walk?*
B: *Oh, I'm sorry, I can't. I've got to make some urgent phone calls.*

2 Player 3 decides whether the excuse is reasonable or not. If it **is** reasonable, Player 2 scores a point.

3 Take turns, so that in the next round Player 2 makes a request, Player 3 makes an excuse, and Player 1 is the judge. Do not use a picture twice. Continue until you have used all the pictures. Who has the highest number of points?

Unit 50 Past and future obligation and necessity

Getting started

1 **Read the two stories and place Extracts a) and b) in the correct gaps.**

a) … hundreds of birds descended on the field and the game had to be delayed for half an hour while they were removed.

b) … in front of the wrong motorbike.'

Story 1

On driving tests

In London, a man was taking his motorbike driving test. At the test centre they gave him the instructions they always gave: he had to drive a specific route and at some point the hidden examiner would appear and step in front of the motorbike. He had to brake quickly to show how quickly he could stop. The man drove the route but no examiner appeared, so he did it again, and still no examiner appeared. Finally the man stopped at the test centre and asked where the examiner was. 'We're sorry,' he was told. 'He stepped out …..

Story 2

BIRD MAN

This story concerns a student at the Massachusetts Institute of Technology who went to the Harvard football ground every day for an entire summer wearing a black and white striped shirt. He would walk up and down the pitch for 10 to 15 minutes throwing birdseed all around him, blow a whistle and then walk off the field. At the end of the summer, the Harvard football team played its first home match to a huge crowd. When the referee walked on in his black and white shirt and blew his whistle, …..

2 **Compare these two sentences which express past obligation and answer the questions.**

a) *When I was at school we had to wear a horrible uniform.*
b) *The funfair had to close down because it was too dangerous.*

Which sentence suggests action was needed:

- because there was a **rule**? …..
- because of **circumstances**? …..

3 **Find one example of past obligation in each story, and say if the obligation comes from rules (r) or circumstances (c):**

Story 1 …..   Story 2 …..

Looking at language

Past obligation

To talk about past obligation we use ***had to*** **+ verb**. The obligation can come from rules:

*My parents were very strict and I **had to go** to bed at 7.00 every night.*

or from circumstances:

*The game **had to be delayed** for half an hour while they removed the birds.*

Note that *must*, used for present obligation, does not have a past form.

Negatives

We use ***couldn't*** **+ verb** or ***wasn't / weren't allowed to*** **+ verb** to express an obligation **not** to do something in the past:

*We **couldn't wear** rings to school.* *We **weren't allowed to smoke**.*

We use ***didn't have to*** **+ verb** to describe a past situation where obligation is usually expected, but this time there was **no** obligation:

***I didn't have to pay** for parking. This man gave me his ticket as he was leaving.*

***We didn't have to go** to school yesterday. It was a staff training day.*

We can also use ***didn't have to*** **+ verb** to show we had a choice:

***I didn't have to go** to the meeting, but I went because I thought it might be useful.*

Future obligation and necessity

To talk about future obligation and necessity we use ***have got to*** **+ verb** or ***will have to*** **+ verb**:

***I've got to give** a talk next week.* *You**'ll have to train** hard before you go trekking.*

Past necessity

To talk about something that was necessary to do in the past, we use ***needed to*** **+ verb**:

A: *I went to the station on my way home.* B: *Did you? Why?* A: *Oh, I **needed to check** the train times.*

To say that something **did** happen, but now we know that it was unnecessary, we use ***needn't have*** **+ past participle**:

*You **needn't have washed** those socks. I'm throwing them away.* (you **did** wash them, but it wasn't necessary)

When we use ***didn't need to*** **+ verb**, we don't say whether something happened, but we say that it was unnecessary:

*They **didn't need to wash** the car.* (we don't know whether they washed the car, but it was unnecessary)

However, the context often makes it clear whether something happened:

*I didn't need to wear a hat to the ceremony, **but I did because I'd just bought a new one**.*

1 **Fill in the gaps with *had to, didn't have to* or *needn't have* and put the verb in brackets in a suitable form.**

1 Yesterday I .... *(stay)* at work late, so I missed my favourite TV programme.

2 I .... *(go)* to the talk. It didn't tell me anything I didn't already know.

3 It was my choice really. I .... *(go)* but I wanted to.

Other points

Other verbs and expressions can show past obligation or necessity:

*The weather was terrible, so we **were forced to cancel** the festival.*

*The rules changed, and I **was required to work** another four hours a week.*

*School **was** only **compulsory** until you were 14 in those days.*

Pronunciation

We don't contract *had to*. We say: *I had to go to the doctor.* We don't say: ~~*I'd to go to the doctor.*~~

Getting it right

Exercise 1 Thinking about meaning

A *Have to*

Decide if the obligation comes from rules (r) or circumstances (c).

Example: We were lucky, actually. We bought our tickets the day before the price rise so *we didn't have to pay* as much as you. ..c..

1 We locked ourselves out last night and *had to break a window* to get in. .....

2 *Cars didn't have to have seat belts* when I first bought one. .....

3 *We've got to wear* a black skirt and white blouse for graduation. .....

4 When I was at *school we had to have lunch there*, but nowadays children can have packed lunches. .....

5 It rained so hard while I was out yesterday that *I had to buy an umbrella*. .....

6 *I had to wait for ages* at the dentist yesterday. It was really busy. .....

7 Even if I'd had insurance *I would have had to pay for the first £100 of damage*, so it didn't make any difference in this case. .....

8 It's no good. *We'll have to get a new car*. This one is on its last legs. .....

9 *They've got to go to London* to catch a direct Edinburgh train. .....

B *Need to*

Decide whether the action happened (h), didn't happen (dh), or we don't know (dk).

Example: We *didn't need to see Terry*, so we left before he got there. dh

10 Tillie *didn't need to pass her exams* to get into university because they'd already given her an offer of a place. ....

11 You *needn't have done the washing-up*. We've got a dishwasher. ....

12 Luckily *we didn't need to go to the police station* or anything like that. ....

13 I'll tell you why your cake probably didn't rise. *You needed to heat the oven* before you put the cake in. ....

14 We *needed to get someone in* to replace the window the next day. ....

Four of sentences 1–14 come from the same story. Which ones? ....

Exercise 2 Link up

Use a verb from the box to join the sentence beginnings, 1–8, to the endings, a)–i). You may need to change the form of the verb.

book buy buy do the washing up get ~~make~~ talk wear write

Example: When I was a child I had to	make f)	
1 I didn't have anything to wear to the wedding so I had to	....	a) with your right hand until fairly recently.
2 In many schools it was compulsory to	....	b) the table because the restaurant was empty.
3 Although the weather wasn't great we didn't have to	....	c) jumpers or coats at all.
4 Oh, Robert. You didn't need to	....	d) the bus into town.
5 The car wouldn't start so we had to	....	e) to you?
6 We realised we needn't have	....	~~f) my bed every day.~~
7 Sorry about the mess. I'll have to	....	g) me a present, but thanks very much.
8 Where were you when I needed to	....	h) later because I've got to go out now.
		i) a new outfit.

Extension

Write new endings for the sentence beginnings.

Example: When I was a child I had to eat all kinds of things I hated .

Exercise 3 Learning from learners

Read the two extracts from learners studying in the UK describing what they did at the weekend. Improve the extracts by following the instructions.

Gianluca Add two more examples of *had to*, and rewrite a phrase using *needn't have*.

> *had to go*
>
> Orhan and I went to London for the weekend. We couldn't afford the train so we ~~went~~ by bus. Actually it wasn't as bad as we thought it would be and it wasn't necessary to have bought our tickets in advance – there was plenty of room on the bus. The hotel was cheap and quite good, although the rules meant we checked out really early – 9.00 yesterday morning. So we carried our bags around most of yesterday until we got the bus back in the evening.

Kumiko Add four examples of *had to*, one example of *will have to* and rewrite one phrase using *didn't have to*.

> We had a funny weekend. We didn't go anywhere. We just stayed here, but lots happened. The first thing that happened was that I locked myself out of the house and I phoned up my landlord to get him to come and open the door for me. Then when I met Mari in town for lunch she realised she'd lost her purse, so we went to the police station to report it. Just when we sat down to eat in a café she found her purse in her coat pocket, so we went back to the police to tell them. And then in the evening we went to the cinema and I had my purse stolen whilst we were there, so we went back to the police one more time. I'll phone them again later today just to check they haven't found it before I complete my insurance claim. I'm sure 20 years ago it wasn't necessary to be so careful about your bags and purses.

Exercise 4 Text completion

In the two extracts a printer error caused the last few letters of each line to disappear. Write what you think they were. They may be past obligation structures, or other language.

Extract 1 A hairdresser talks about her work

I qualified in June and got work going to other people's houses, which meant I	*had* ....
to do it in the evenings on the nights when Peter wasn't working. Peter h	1 ....
drop me off where I was going because, of course, I can't drive. We even h	2 ....
have the next-door neighbour come and watch the kids for half an hour someti	3 ....
while he came and picked me up. So it became too difficult and I decided to w	4 ....
from home, but people aren't so keen to come to you, so it's not so good. I ha	5 ....
carry on though, because we had to pay the rent somehow.	

Extract 2 A visit to the dentist

I hadn't been for ages and was dreading it. Even if I'd gone years ago I would h 6 ....
had to pay the money because I work, and this is the first time in my life I've h 7 ....
to pay, so it just shows how long it's been. But she was really good. I just w 8 ....
traight in. It didn't use to be like that, but maybe it was because of the p 9 ....
Actually, it probably was because other people had complained they had to w 10 ....
an hour and then pay loads of money for a five-minute appointment.

Classwork

1 **Look at the chart below. In groups of three or four, think of four more sentences like the examples, and write them in the chart.**

Circumstances	*Obligation*
I left home without any money	so I had to go back and get it.
My brother hurt his leg playing football	and he had to go to hospital.
1	....
2	....
3	....
4	....

2 **Groups take turns to read out the circumstances only from a sentence. The other groups write down the possible obligation. The group with the closest idea to the original gets a point.**

Example:

Group 1's circumstances: *I left home without any money.*

Group 2's obligation: *so I had to go to the bank.*

Group 3's obligation: *but it didn't matter because I didn't have to buy anything.*

Group 4's obligation: *and I had to go home again to get it.*

Group 4 has the closest idea (see Group 1's obligation in the chart above) and gets a point.

3 **Continue until all groups have read out all their circumstances. The winning group is the one with the most points.**

Review unit

5 Units 39–50 Functional areas

Exercise 1 Mixed modals and *tend to* Units 39–42 and 47–50

Choose a modal verb from the box for each gap. You can use each verb more than once.

can	could	had to	have to	might	must	shall	should	tend to	~~will~~	would

Example: I'll (will) get the shopping tomorrow if you like.

1 .... you read Japanese? I need some help with this article.

2 A: Well, what do you think? .... I stay or .... I go and live in the States?
B: If I were you, I .... think about it for a few more days. It's a big decision.

3 This fish is rather tasteless. .... you pass me the salt?

4 You look terribly thin. You .... eat more.

5 My parents were very old-fashioned. I ....n't watch television after eight o'clock.

6 A: Oh, these bags are heavy.
B: .... I help you with them?

7 A: We're meeting on Thursday, aren't we?
B: I'm not sure. It .... be Friday.

8 We .... eat out about once a week. Nearly always at the same place, though.

9 I didn't sleep well. There was a lot of noise. It .... have been the traffic.

10 That .... be Peter over there. I don't know anyone else that tall.

Exercise 2 Functions Units 39–42 and 47–50

Look at Exercise 1 again and find examples of the following functions in sentences 1–10. There may be more than one example, and you can use a number more than once.

Ability in the present	....	Obligation in the past	....
Asking for advice	....	Offer	....
Describing regular habit	....	Possibility	....
Giving advice	....	Request	....

Exercise 3 Frequency expressions Unit 42

Put these jumbled sentences in order.

Example: The | hour | bell | rings | an | once

The bell rings once an hour.

1 or | week | other | We | each | a | see | two | three | times

....

2 a | holiday | time | go | for | I | to | abroad | from | time

....

3 a | have | to | meeting | try | We | weekly

....

4 evenings | at | home | I'm | usually | the | in

....

5 a | while | food | once | in | I | Thai | cook

....

6 in | live | house | ever | to | I've | hardly | larger | wanted | a

....

7 see | do | you | often | How | Janice | ?

....

8 you | out | Do | eat | much | ?

....

Exercise 4 Comparing and describing Units 43–46

Fill in the gaps in the extracts below by making a suitable comparative or superlative, using the adjectives in brackets (), or by using words from the box, or both. You can use words from the box more than once.

as … as both both from less like like looks look like ~~more~~ same as sounds whereas

A Yes, the location is great. It's much *more suitable* (*suitable*) for us than the old one. But the view here isn't **1** .... (*beautiful*) the old one. Actually, we **2** .... really miss that view.

B You've grown so much. You **3** .... your mother now. Your eyes and mouth are exactly the **4** .... your mother's. But you're **5** .... (*tall*) than she is. And your hair is completely different **6** .... hers.

C Did you have a good time? What was the place **7** .... ? Did you get on well with your mother for such a long time? I don't think I'd **8** .... to go on holiday with my mother. I'm sure I'd end up **9** .... (*relaxed*) than before, and I'd need another holiday!

D I can't make up my mind about where to go. Greece **10** .... wonderful, but maybe it'll be too hot for me. And Spain has such interesting places to visit as well as some of the **11** .... (*good*) beaches in Europe. They cost about the same, and the accommodation in **12** .... places **13** .... excellent from the pictures in the brochure. At the moment I think I'll choose Greece because it's **14** .... (*easy*) to get there from where I live. You can fly direct from my local airport **15** .... for Spain I have to fly from London. But I'm just not sure.

Extension

Match these titles to Extracts A–D.

Choosing a holiday ..... Like mother like daughter .....
A new home ..... On holiday with mother .....

Exercise 5 Possibility **Units 47–48**

Match a word or phrase from a grey box to a word or phrase from a white box. Make two sentences from them using language of possibility and any other language you need.

August	~~not see the sign~~	looks tired	a cat	board pens
a teacher	light in the window	eat them all	~~driving too fast~~	working late
no answer	on holiday	hairs all over the house	Hungarian	no more apples
new batteries	interesting accent	at home	camera doesn't work	not at home

He was driving too fast. He can't have seen the sign. ....

....

....

....

....

....

....

....

Exercise 6 Obligation Units 49–50

Match the sentence beginnings, 1–9, to the endings, a)–j), to complete the texts about becoming a pilot and taking a driving test. Fill in the gaps with words from the box in an appropriate form (past, present, positive or negative).

be allowed to	have to	must	need	need to

HOW TO BE AN AIRLINE PILOT

Example: If you want to be a pilot you (..e)..)

1 I'm not sure what the maximum age is for starting training, (.....)

2 You .... to be good at (.....)

3 You .... also pass a (.....)

4 When I first started the job you (.....)

5 And most important of all, you .... (.....)

CHANGES IN THE DRIVING TEST

6 When I took my test 20 years ago you only .... do the driving test, and (.....)

7 You .... drive backwards round a corner, (.....)

8 You .... ask the examiner (.....)

9 I remember I wore smart clothes but I .... (.....)

a) you .... take a written test.

b) although you .... be too old.

c) ever lose your cool. You .... to stay calm no matter what is happening.

d) fitness test and you .... remain healthy.

e) ~~*have to* train for a long time.~~ ....

f) because the examiner was only interested in my driving.

g) and do an emergency stop.

h) maths and physics.

i) any questions.

j) .... to speak foreign languages, but you do now.

Appendix 1

Irregular verbs

The verbs in blue have a different past and past participle form.

Verb	*Past*	*Past participle*	*Present participle*	*Verb*	*Past*	*Past participle*	*Present participle*
be	was / were	been	being	fall	fell	fallen	falling
beat	beat	beat	beating	**feed**	fed	fed	feeding
become	became	become	becoming	**feel**	felt	felt	feeling
begin	began	begun	beginning	**find**	found	found	finding
bend	bent	bent	bending	fly	flew	flown	flying
bet	bet	bet	betting	forbid	forbade	forbidden	forbidding
bite	bit	bitten	biting	forget	forgot	forgotten	forgetting
blow	blew	blown	blowing	forgive	forgave	forgiven	forgiving
break	broke	broken	breaking	freeze	froze	frozen	freezing
bring	brought	brought	bringing	**get**	got	got	getting
broadcast	broadcast	broadcast	broadcasting	give	gave	given	giving
build	built	built	building	go	went	gone	going
burst	burst	burst	bursting	grow	grew	grown	growing
buy	bought	bought	buying	**hang**	hung	hung	hanging
catch	caught	caught	catching	**have**	had	had	having
choose	chose	chosen	choosing	**hear**	heard	heard	hearing
come	came	come	coming	hide	hid	hidden	hiding
cost	cost	cost	costing	**hit**	hit	hit	hitting
creep	crept	crept	creeping	**hurt**	hurt	hurt	hurting
cut	cut	cut	cutting	**hold**	held	held	holding
deal	dealt	dealt	dealing	**keep**	kept	kept	keeping
dig	dug	dug	digging	**kneel**	knelt	knelt	kneeling
do	did	done	doing	know	knew	known	knowing
draw	drew	drawn	drawing	**lay**	laid	laid	laying
drink	drank	drunk	drinking	**lead**	led	led	leading
drive	drove	driven	driving	**leave**	left	left	leaving
eat	ate	eaten	eating	**lend**	lent	lent	lending

Verb	*Past*	*Past participle*	*Present participle*	*Verb*	*Past*	*Past participle*	*Present participle*
let	let	let	letting	**sleep**	slept	slept	sleeping
lie	lay	lain	lying	**slide**	slid	slid	sliding
light	lit	lit	lighting	speak	spoke	spoken	speaking
lose	lost	lost	losing	**spend**	spent	spent	spending
make	made	made	making	**split**	split	split	splitting
mean	meant	meant	meaning	**spit**	spat	spat	spitting
meet	met	met	meeting	**spread**	spread	spread	spreading
pay	paid	paid	paying	spring	sprang	sprung	springing
put	put	put	putting	**stand**	stood	stood	standing
read /riːd/	read /red/	read /red/	reading	steal	stole	stolen	stealing
ride	rode	ridden	riding	**stick**	stuck	stuck	sticking
ring	rang	rung	ringing	**sting**	stung	stung	stinging
rise	rose	risen	rising	stink	stank	stunk	stinking
run	ran	run	running	**strike**	struck	struck	striking
say	said	said	saying	swear	swore	sworn	swearing
see	saw	seen	seeing	**sweep**	swept	swept	sweeping
seek	sought	sought	seeking	swim	swam	swum	swimming
sell	sold	sold	selling	**swing**	swung	swung	swinging
send	sent	sent	sending	take	took	taken	taking
set	set	set	setting	**teach**	taught	taught	teaching
sew	sewed	sewn	sewing	tear	tore	torn	tearing
shake	shook	shook	shaking	**tell**	told	told	telling
shine	shone	shone	shining	**think**	thought	thought	thinking
shoot	shot	shot	shooting	throw	threw	thrown	throwing
show	showed	shown/showed	showing	**understand**	understood	understood	understanding
shrink	shrank	shrunk	shrinking	wake	woke	woken	waking
shut	shut	shut	shutting	wear	wore	worn	wearing
sing	sang	sung	singing	**weep**	wept	wept	weeping
sink	sank	sunk	sinking	**win**	won	won	winning
sit	sat	sat	sitting	write	wrote	written	writing

Find another verb that follows the same pattern as verbs 1–5.

Example: ring, rang, rung *sing, sang, sung*

1 creep, crept, crept ……………

2 feel, felt, felt ……………

3 lend, lent, lent ……………

4 tear, tore, torn ……………

5 sting, stung, stung ……………

Appendix 2

Phonemic symbols

In this book pronunciation is shown using the symbols below.

ɪ	pit	ʊ	put	ɑː	arm
e	wet	ə	ago	ɔː	saw
æ	cat	i	cosy	uː	too
ʌ	run	u	influence	ɜː	her
ɒ	hot	iː	see		
eɪ	day	aʊ	how	ʊə	sure
aɪ	my	ɪə	near	aɪə	fire
ɔɪ	boy	eə	hair	aʊə	sour
əʊ	low				
b	bee	k	key	t	ten
d	do	l	led	v	van
f	fat	m	map	w	wet
g	go	p	pen	z	zip
h	hat	r	red		
j	yet	s	sun		
dʒ	general	θ	thin	ʒ	measure
ŋ	hang	ʃ	ship	tʃ	chin
ð	that				

Unvoiced and voiced consonant pairs

The second consonant sound in each pair below is voiced (formed using your voice).

/p/ and /b/ /t/ and /d/ /tʃ/ and /dʒ/ /k/ and /g/ /f/ and /v/ /θ/ and /ð/
/s/ and /z/ /ʃ/ and /ʒ/

Here are some words in phonemic symbols. What are they?

1 **/græmə/** ....
4 **/sɪmbəl/** ....
2 **/wɜːd/** ....
5 **/stʌdɪ/** ....
3 **/naʊn/** ....

Glossary

active verb: used when we want to focus on the person or thing doing the action: *Susie* ***opened*** *the parcel. Three cars* ***blocked*** *the road.*
adjective: a word which describes a noun: *lovely, bad, big, exciting*
adverb: a word which describes verbs, adjectives or adverbs, and often ends with *-ly: easily, nicely*
article: *the, a, an*
auxiliary verb: (*be, do, have*) a verb which is used with a main verb to give short answers and to express negatives, questions, the passive and some tenses: ***Do*** *you like sport? Yes, I* ***do****. Jamie* ***doesn't*** *eat meat. This song* ***was*** *written ten years ago. We****'re*** *having breakfast at the moment. They****'ve*** *travelled all over the world.*
clause: a group of words which contains a subject and main verb. Sentences can have one or more clauses: *The plane took off* (clause 1) *and we were on our way* (clause 2).
comparative adjective: *bigger, easier, more comfortable: You are* ***taller*** *than me.*
conditional: a clause or sentence usually beginning with *if*: ***If*** *it's sunny tomorrow we****'ll*** *have a picnic.* ***If*** *you had more money what* ***would*** *you do?*
conjunction: a word which joins two phrases or clauses together: *and, but, when …*
contraction: the shortened form of two words put together: *I'll, I'd, I'm, we're, you're, it's* etc.
countable noun: a noun that can be singular or plural: *cat – cats*
demonstrative: *this, that, these, those*
determiner: a word which gives more information about a noun or noun phrase. These can be articles, demonstratives, possessives, quantifiers.
direct speech: repeating the exact words that somebody has said. *'I'd like to be the president one day.'*
doer: the person or thing that does / did something: *I* (doer) *gave the present to Dana. The house was built by Jack Harcourt* (doer).
ellipsis: leaving words out: *I walked up the stairs and* (I) *opened the bedroom door.*
emphasise: show the importance of something: *I* ***do*** *love you.* (stronger than *I love you*)
function: what the language is used to do: *Would you like some cake?* = an offer *Let's go to the cinema.* = a suggestion
imperative: a verb form that looks like the infinitive without *to* and is used to give orders and instructions: ***Come*** *here.* ***Take*** *the top off the bottle.*
indirect question: a way to ask a question and express thoughts without being direct: ***Can you tell me*** *the way to the station?* ***I wonder if*** *Mike has arrived yet.*
infinitive: a form of the verb; *(to) go, (to) eat, (to) write, (to) like*
intensifier: a word (usually an adverb) which makes the meaning of adjectives, adverbs and verbs stronger: *It was* ***very*** *hot. He ran* ***really*** *fast. I* ***completely*** *disagree.*
intention: an aim to do something in the future: *I'm going to be a doctor when I grow up.*
intransitive verb: a verb which does not have an object: *He* ***laughed****.*
main verb: a verb which usually shows actions and situations: *She* ***went*** *to bed early last night. I* ***live*** *in London.*

modal verb: (*will, would, can, could, may, might, must, should* etc.) a verb which is used with a main verb to add extra meaning. Modal verbs express, for example, ability, possibility and obligation: *I can speak English. They* ***might*** *have some tickets. You* ***should*** *buy your mother a present.*

narrative: a story and description: *I was walking down a dark road when suddenly a loud noise made me jump and set my heart racing …*

negatives: *I didn't like the food. It is* ***not*** *the same in my country.*

noun: this is usually the name of something: *table, student, love, bag, ability, memory, furniture*

noun phrase: a group of words with a noun (or pronoun) as the main part: ***The woman who is wearing a red coat*** *is my mother.*

object: a noun (or pronoun) affected by the action of a verb: *He watched* ***a film.***

passive verb: used when we want to focus on the person or the thing affected by the action: *The parcel* ***was sent*** *three days ago. The road* ***was blocked****. The parcel* ***was opened*** *by the girl. That book* ***was written*** *by me.*

past participle: the third form of the verb: *ask – asked –* ***asked****, go – went –* ***gone***. Past participles are used for the passive and perfect tenses and as adjectives. Past participles often end in *-ed* (*finished, waited*) but many are irregular: ***lost, found, gone*** (see Appendix 1).

phrase: a group of words together

plural noun: more than one example of a countable noun: *tables, students, bags*

prediction: a guess about the future: *I think Rosie and Alistair will get married.*

preposition: *at, in, under, to, through* etc.

present participle: the *-ing* form of the verb: *ask – asking, go –* ***going*** (see Appendix 1).

possessive: a word which shows possession: *my, your, his, her, its, their, our (house, watch, car* etc.)

pronoun: a word which can replace a noun or noun phrase: *I, you, he, we, which, mine, ours*

proper noun: names of particular places, people or things. Always spelt with a capital letter: *Paris, Peter, the Sahara*

quantifier: *some, any, many, much, few, little, a lot of* etc.

relative pronoun: a word like *who, which, where* or *that* in relative clauses: *The man* ***who*** *was speaking looked like my brother.*

reported speech: used to report what someone said but not using exactly the same words: ***He said*** *that he would like to be president one day.* ***He invited*** *me to his house.*

semi-modal: a verb which can work like a modal verb or main verb: *need, dare*

singular noun: one example of a countable noun: *table, student, bag*

stative verb: a verb describing long-lasting situations or feelings: *know, live, love* (see Unit 3)

subject: a noun (or pronoun) which normally comes before the main verb: ***Sue*** *is busy at the moment.* ***Tigers*** *live in the jungle.*

superlative adjective: an adjective used to show that someone or something has more of a particular quality than anyone or anything else: *He's* ***the nicest*** *man I know.*

tag question: a phrase added to a sentence to make a question or to add emphasis: *You're the new secretary,* ***aren't you****? You don't recognise me,* ***do you****?*

tail: a word or phrase used to emphasise who or what you've been talking about: *Matthew's nice,* ***he is****.*

topic: a word or phrase used to introduce who or what you are going to talk about: ***Matthew****, he's nice.*

transitive verb: a verb which can take an object: *I* ***ate*** *the biscuit.*

uncountable noun: a noun that has no plural form and cannot use *a / an*: *love, furniture*

verb phrase: the part of the sentence which contains the main verb and any objects or other information: *Joe* ***took Sally to the party****.*